Suk Kyoon Kim

The History of
Piracy and
Navigation

novum ◆ premium

This book is also
available as
e-book.

www.novumpublishing.com

© 2020 novum publishing

ISBN 978-1-64268-135-2
Editing: Karen Simmering
Cover photos: Digikhmer,
Alexander Babich | Dreamstime.com
Cover design, layout & typesetting:
novum publishing
Internal illustrations: Suk Kyoon Kim

www.novumpublishing.com

CONTENTS

Chapter 1

PIRATES IN THE ANCIENT WORLD

The Origin of Piracy

Piracy has existed since very ancient times. Although we don't know exactly when the first act of plundering at sea occurred, piracy is almost certainly one of the oldest professions. However, what is apparent is that piracy has always existed, ever since mankind took to the sea for fishing, shipping, and trade. As humans were actively engaged in sea-faring and navigation across the seas, piracy flourished as well. For that reason, in a sense, the maritime history corresponds with that of piracy. Supposing that the history of navigation that transports people and goods by ship goes back 4,000 to 5000 years, we can conjecture that piracy has such a long history as well.

We can also use historical records to figure out that piracy was widespread across the ancient world. In the ancient world, pirates were a thorn, threatening not only the safety of navigation but also the security of people and territory. Most historical records about ancient piracy available today are about the Mediterranean and the western world. This could lead to a misconception that piracy had been widespread only in the West. This by no means implies that ancient Asia and other regions were excepted from piracy – as we will see in a later chapter, piracy thrived in ancient Asia as well.

The history of pirates goes back to the era of mythology. Greek myths tell of an episode of the god Dionysus, who encountered pirates on his journey to conquer islands. He was held by Tyrrhenian pirates who mistook him for the son of a wealthy merchant. He turned the savage pirates into dolphins as a punishment. Given that the god Dionysus was worshipped as early as 1500–1100 B.C. by Mycenaean Greeks, the episode may be a clue as to the long history of piracy, showing its origins in the ancient world.

The center of piracy in the ancient western world was the eastern Mediterranean. To be more specific, the main hotspot of piracy spans from the Adriatic and Aegean seas to the coast of Asia Minor (modern Turkey). The presence of piracy, paradoxically, indicates how wealthy and prosperous this region was in terms of shipping and trade – pirates are always lured by abundant prey.

The Ancient Mediterranean

Before exploring ancient pirates, it's important to understand the overall political circumstances in the Mediterranean, as piracy was itself a critical aspect of those circumstances. The initial explorers of the Mediterranean were Phoenicians who had inhabited the coast of modern-day Lebanon. By the early 2000s B.C., they were engaged in shipping and trade in the southern and middle of the Mediterranean. They had built warships for the first time and held a number of colonies across the Mediterranean, which included Sardinia, Corsica and Carthage. Following the Phoenicians, ancient Greeks who had developed outstanding navigational skills took to the seas south of the Italian Peninsula and the Black Sea and finally drove the Phoenicians out of the region.

Prior to the Greeks, the people of Crete who had migrated from Asia Minor blossomed into a highly sophisticated sea-faring civilization, called the "Minoan Civilization." It prospered from about 2600 to 1100 B.C. and has been described as the cradle of the European civilization. The term 'Minoan' was derived from King Minos of Crete. A myth tells that he was the first son of the god Zeus and Europa, princess of Phoenicia. Europe was named after the region where she had traveled. Minos was associated with the legendary labyrinth and the Minotaur, a creature with the head of a bull and the body of man. King Minos, who competed with his brothers for the throne, prayed to the sea god Poseidon to send him a snow-white bull as a sign of support. After he had ascended to the throne, however, he did not keep the promise that he would send the bull back. Infuriated by his behavior, Poseidon made Pasiphaë, wife of Minos, fall in love and mate with the bull as a punishment. The offspring was the Minotaur. Astonished, King Minos ordered a labyrinth built to hold him.

Then the Athenians, under control of Crete, were forced to send seven boys and seven girls each year to serve the Minotaur. The prince of Athens, Theseus, volunteered to kill the Minotaur and save the Athenians who were held in the labyrinth. In Crete, Minos' daughter Ariadne, who fell in love with Theseus at first sight, gave him a ball of thread, allowing him to retrace his path through the maze. With her help, he was successfully able to complete his mission and sailed back to his own country. However, he neglected his promise to his father King Aegeus that he would put up a white sail if he was successful. Looking at the black sail from a vantagepoint high on a hill, Aegeus fell into such deep despair that he threw himself into the Aegean Sea, which is named after him.

The main players of sea-faring in the ancient Mediterranean were a large number of city-states scattered along the coast. They built booming economies and enjoyed political development and stability. As the city-states took to the sea, however, they fought fiercely against each other in an effort to establish control over the eastern Mediterranean. Among those, Mycenae and Rhodes were able to take advantage of their strategic locations situated in between the Mediterranean and the Aegean, and thereby first established a hegemony over the eastern Mediterranean. Afterwards, these city-states and coastal states of Asia Minor, like Phoenicia, were engaged in fierce clashes to gain control over the eastern Mediterranean. As land states also sought to take to the Mediterranean, clashes between maritime and land powers were inevitable. The first hegemonic struggle was a war in 2000 B.C. between Egypt and Cretan Minos. In 1650 B.C., Crete Minos waged a war with Mycenae to pursue the expansion of its colonies. By 500 B.C., the struggle for the hegemony of the Mediterranean escalated into a number of wars between Greek city-states and states in Asia Minor. The Persian Wars between the Persian and Greek city-states, which started in 499 B.C. and lasted until 449 B.C., and the Peloponnesian War (431–404 B.C.) between Athens and Sparta, are examples. The Punic Wars between Rome and Carthage, which lasted from 264 to 146 B.C., were the most prominent instances of these types of struggles. Triumphing in three wars during the period, Rome conquered Carthage and was able to gain full control over the Mediterranean, rising as undisputed leader in the area. As a result, the Mediterranean turned into the *Mare Internum* (the Inner Sea) of Romans.

Ancient Mediterranean Pirates

The first appearance of pirates in the historical record dates back to before the Egyptian Pyramids were built. The Egyptian inscriptions tell that the Lukkans, a group of sea raiders based in the southeastern coast of Asia Minor, first appeared in the 14th century B.C. They invaded Cyprus. A century later, they disappeared from the historical record. Presumably, their sudden disappearance was linked to the emergence of the 'Sea Peoples,' who were believed to have assimilated them.

Greek historians claimed that the Sea Peoples were migrating tribes that originated from the Aegean and Adriatic seas or from the western Mediterranean. They sailed around the eastern Mediterranean and invaded Anatolia, Syria, Canaan,

Phoenicia, Cyprus and Egypt. The Sea Peoples were blamed for the fall of the Bronze Age, bringing a dark age to ancient civilization. The Sea Peoples, widely known as the first organized pirate confederation, posed a grave threat to the Egyptian Empire. They invaded the empire in the late 13th century and early 12th century B.C. Egyptian inscriptions discovered in the tomb of Pharaoh Rameses II the Great tell that Egyptians won a decisive victory in a battle with the Sea Peoples off the Nile Delta around 1186 B.C., ultimately putting an end to them in the historical record. The Sea Peoples were not strictly pirates in a true sense, but were more like hostile migratory tribes with ships. Still, they are generally counted as pirates, given their aggression and looting.

Even after the disappearance of the Sea Peoples, piracy still flourished throughout the eastern Mediterranean. This happened because some ancient Greek city-states relied on piracy as a means of generating wealth. In response, others, such as the Athenians, formed anti-piracy fleets to keep the sea lanes safe for their own shipping. In the 10th century B.C., Crete was invaded by the Dorian Greeks, who raided the coast of the island in search of slaves. The raiders used the island as a piratical base where they were engaged in plundering throughout the Aegean Sea. The Cretan pirates continued this work until Athens rose to become the dominant naval power in the 5th century B.C. and were able to combat them. The Athenian navy destroyed pirates' bases and cleared pirates from the Aegean Sea.

In the 4th century B.C., the Aetolian League was created. It was a confederation of tribal communities and cities centered in Aetolia in central Greece. During the Hellenic period, they emerged as a dominant power in central Greece and were expanded by the voluntary annexation of several Greek city-states. However, they were regarded by other Greeks as semi-barbaric and reckless because they used piracy to supplement their income due to the meager resources in the region. Aetolian pirates extorted protection money from coastal towns and cities on both the Greek and the Asian shores of the Aegean basin. Their piracy lasted until they were defeated by the Romans in 192 B.C.

A majority of the Aetolian pirates moved to Cilicia (the southern coast of modern Turkey). Cilician pirates set up the largest pirate bases ever seen throughout the ancient world. Hiding in lairs in rugged coasts and small islands, Cilician pirates preyed on the ships that hugged the coast during their voyages. The Cilician pirates became the most notorious in the ancient world.

On the east side of the Greece, pirates from Illyria and Dalmatia (modern-day Croatia and Albania) flourished along the eastern coast of the Adriatic Sea. They looted settlements on the Greek and Italian coasts and took to the Mediterranean. The region continued to be plagued by these pirates even after Romans conquered it in 168 B.C.

Chapter 2

THE ROMAN EMPIRE AND PIRACY

Origin of the Roman Empire

Before exploring piracy problems in the Roman Empire, we will briefly take a look at the early history of the empire itself, as well as its sea-going history. The origin of the Roman Empire began with the myth of the legendary twins 'Romulus' and 'Remus.' The twins, who had been abandoned in the Tiber River when they were babies, were cared for by a she-wolf. One day, a shepherd came across the twin boys who were suckled by the she-wolf, and the man took them home and raised them. As the twins grew up, they became the leaders of shepherds in the region. As their power expanded, they conquered a kingdom that had ruled the region. The twins decided to divide their territory and rule separately, but soon were in dispute. Romulus eventually killed Remus and founded the city of Rome in 753 B.C., making himself a king and naming it Rome in his own honor. Rome, which was only a small tribal state when it was founded, engaged in conquering tribal states around it and ultimately was able to create a unified state on the Italian Peninsula in 270 B.C.

Ancient states were eager to take to the sea to build trade networks. By the 8th century B.C., various trade networks centered in the Greek Peninsula, the Peloponnese Peninsula and along the coast of Asia Minor were built in the Aegean and the Mediterranean. They were engaged in fierce competition to take control of the seas, and this eventually led to wars.

Meanwhile, Rome gained a foothold to rise as a great empire across the Mediterranean by winning the Punic Wars against the Carthaginian Empire (located on the coast of modern day Tunis). The Carthaginian Empire, which had been a Phoenician colony, dominated the western Mediterranean during the first millennium B.C. As the emerging Roman Republic eagerly sought to take to the Mediterranean, the emerging and hegemonic powers inevitably went to war over control of the Mediterranean. They fought against each other in three wars, called the Punic Wars, over 120 years. During the first Punic War, which ran between 264 and 241 B.C., Romans invaded Sicily, which had been under control of Carthaginians, and annexed the island into its territory. During the second war (218–201 B.C.), Rome faced a true crisis, as the Carthaginian troops led by Hannibal marched into the Italian Peninsula from across the Alps and stayed there for 16 years. Eventually Romans maneuvered a landing on the coast of Carthage across the Mediterranean to cut off supplies and attack the mainland of Carthage. Hannibal withdrew his troops back to Carthage to defend his homeland. At the battle of Zama in 201 B.C., the Roman troops led by Scipio Africanus won a decisive victory. The Roman Republic was able to establish full control over the western Mediterranean, in addition to a massive amount of reparations from Carthage.

A half century later, as Carthage challenged Roman rule, a young Scipio organized the Roman troops and besieged Carthage. The Carthaginians surrendered after three years (149–146 B.C.) of resistance, and the Romans totally destroyed the city and slaughtered all living things there. Then they spread salt on the ground so as to prevent any living thing from growing there again. The Carthaginian Empire ultimately disappeared. On the day of the fall of Carthage, a young Scipio went up to a mountain and shed tears while looking down the 700-year-old city, now in flames. Historian Polybius, next to him, asked him why. With a deep sigh, he replied that he had a sense that Rome would someday share that fate. Scipio was applying the iron principle of history – any thriving state is doomed to decline.

The Early Roman Empire and the Piracy Problem

The conquest of the Carthaginian Empire allowed Rome, which had been a merely city-state, to expand to a gigantic empire that stretched across the Mediterranean, turning it into a 'Roman Lake.' Before the Punic Wars, Rome had remained a land power; with a limited number of warships and sailors, it was not a proper naval power at all. However, the Romans created fleets of warships with the Greeks' assistance, and built up their naval power through the Punic Wars.

Meanwhile, the thriving Roman Republic had a major thorn in its side: pirates. During the Punic Wars in the western Mediterranean, and the decline of Mycenaean city-states after Alexander the Great's death in the eastern Mediterranean, there was a power vacuum throughout the sea. Pirates, taking advantage of this circumstance, were rampant. Pirates throughout Roman provinces were so powerful that they could not be curbed by regional resistance. Since piratical damages across the Roman Republic were tremendous, the eradication of pirates became a national priority.

Following the establishment of full control over the Mediterranean, Romans looked for legal justification for how to use the sea and establish the oceanic order. In the 2nd century B.C., Roman jurist Marcianus claimed that the sea, as part of natural law, should be shared by everyone. By the 6th century, the Romans' idea of the sea as common property was codified in Roman laws. Such views served as the foundation of marine policy in terms of the use of the sea. This open-mindedness toward the use of the sea was likely to be seen as natural, given the Romans' openness towards the many different ethnicities, cultures, languages and religions that dotted its huge, cross-continental territory. Whatever position they took, however, there would be no difference at all in terms of the Romans' control of the Mediterranean.

Pirates and Rivalry Between Pompey and Caesar

Interestingly, fateful events in the lives of Pompey Magnus (106–48 B.C.) and Julius Caesar (100–44 B.C.) were related to the Roman Republic's piracy problem. The episode was derived from Pompey's anti-pirate campaigns. Of the brilliant military successes that Pompey had achieved as a general, the eradication of pirates across the Mediterranean might be his foremost accomplishment.

First we need to get to know about his career, as well as his political rivalry with Caesar, to better understand his anti-pirate campaigns. Pompey, who formed a political alliance with Julius Caesar and Marcus Crassus, known as the First Triumvirate in the late Roman Republic, was one of the most powerful leaders. Pompey came from a noble and wealthy family, and he had engaged in many wars since he was very young. He achieved prominent success at the age of 18 during the Social War (91–88 B.C.) that the Roman Republic and several other cities in Italy had fought over Roman citizenship. His successes as a military commander helped him gain the nickname *Magnus*, ('the Great'), leading him to attain consulship three times.

As a sign of political alliance with Caesar, Pompey married his daughter Julia. After she had died in childbirth, however, there was nothing to halt the two rivals' contentious battle to become the first man in the Roman Republic. There is a maxim that even father and son may not share political power together. The two rivals, who had once been allies as well as family members, eventually engaged in fierce military campaigns against each other to see who would become the supreme leader of the Roman Republic. Apart from their political ambitions, both were supported by opposing groups of people in the Roman society. Pompey, hailing from a noble family, sided with other nobles and formed a political alliance with the conservative Senate. On the other hand, Caesar was supported by the common people.

When Caesar successfully concluded the Gallic Wars, the Senate – driven to an alliance with Pompey because it feared Caesar's military power – ordered Caesar to step down from his military command and return to Rome. Finding himself with no other option but to cross the Rubicon River, Caesar marched on Rome, saying "the die is cast." A civil war broke out between the two rivals. Faced with the swift maneuvering of Caesar's troops, Pompey and many of the Senate fled to the south of Italy. Pompey's troops retreated to Greece and were defeated at the Battle of Pharsalus in 48 B.C.

Pompey sought refuge in Egypt but was eventually assassinated there. Caesar's victory in the civil war meant the transition from the Roman Republic to the Principate, making Caesar *de facto* emperor – essentially 'dictator in perpetuity.' This transition happened four years before Caesar was assassinated in 44 B.C. by a group of senators who opposed his populist reforms. Most importantly, they wanted to safeguard the Roman Republic, which had been the political system of Rome over several hundred years. After Caesar's death, a series of civil wars broke out. Caesar's adopted heir, Octavian, finally rose to become Augustus after he had defeated his political rivals in the civil wars, opening the era of the Roman Empire.

Pompey's Anti-Pirate Campaigns

Pirates across the Mediterranean had been very problematic for the Roman Republic even before it rose to become the superpower of the region. However, the problem became more serious as the Cilician pirates engaged in the plundering of ships between Rome and Egypt, disrupting the transport of goods and communications, particularly grains from Egypt. At the time, the pirates were powerful enough to defeat the Roman naval force off Brundisium in southeast Italy in 86 B.C. Furthermore, the Cilician pirates were involved in the revolt of Spartacus (73–71 B.C.), a major slave and gladiator uprising against the Roman Republic, by supporting the rebels. As the survival of the Roman Republic itself was threatened, Romans were determined to launch a massive military campaign to root out the pirates completely.

In 67 B.C., the Senate decided to grant Pompey three years of imperium under the Anti-Piracy Law, which had been enacted in 101 B.C. He was given sweeping power to fight the pirates, which included the use of 6,000 talents, a fleet of 500 warships, 120,000 infantries and 5,000 cavalries. He was also given the power to tax and raise militias anywhere across the Roman territory within 50 miles landward from the sea. This might show how seriously Romans took the problem of pirates. Even in peacetime, Pompey was given much greater power than wartime commanders. At first, the conservative Senate strongly opposed giving imperium to the young and ambitious general. However, the Senate had no choice but to approve the bill of imperium because pirates were an urgent national issue.

Gnaeus Pompey Magnus

As the pirates disrupted shipping, low-class merchants and workers engaged in trade lost their jobs, and the common people greatly suffered from the soaring prices of their necessities. For this reason, the mere news of the Senate's counter-piracy bill was enough to send prices down. The common people greatly supported the bill, and the Senate promptly passed the revised bill the following day. The swift enactment was made possible, in part, due to the support of Julius Caesar. An episode behind it will be described shortly.

Under the powerful imperium, Pompey completely eradicated the pirates off the Italian Peninsula in less than 40 days. Within three months, the pirates across the Mediterranean were broken and scattered, too. What made him so swiftly and effectively complete his mission? Apart from imperium, his strategy employed coordinated strikes between maritime and land forces, and that proved key to his amazing successes. Pompey divided the Mediterranean into 13 districts and placed each of them under the command of deputy commanders, called legates. While commanding a back-up squadron consisting of 60 warships, Pompey instructed the deputy commanders to blockade the pirates from going to the sea and to drive them to land. Then Pompey launched attacks from the coast of Spain eastwards. The pirates were forced to flee to the southern coast of Cilicia (the coast of modern Turkey), once known as the safe haven of pirates. The Roman troops attacked these Cilician pirate strongholds and bases with overwhelming force. The simultaneous attacks on land and at sea were extremely successful. The Roman troops destroyed no fewer than 500 pirate ships and 120 pirate bases, killing more than 10,000 pirates. Only a small number of pirates were able to flee from the attacks. Pompey treated surrendered pirates leniently, not crucifying them.

In the aftermath, the Mediterranean was cleared of pirates for the first time throughout history, and shipping was prosperous again. The Roman marketplaces were full of foods and grains from various regions across the Mediterranean, and the price of goods stabilized. The Mediterranean enjoyed peace and security free from the pirate threat for another four centuries until the collapse of the West Roman Empire. When Pompey returned to Rome in triumph, Romans cheered tremendously for his brilliant campaigns. Pompey became a national hero and this led him to his second consulship.

Julius Caesar and Pirates

Young Caesar worked as a lawyer as well as a prosecutor. Caesar was engaged in the impeachment of a key aide to Sulla (138–78 B.C.), a general as well as politician who had risen to consulship twice and ruled Rome under a dictatorship. Caesar failed to impeach him and consequently he became a target of the Sulla faction. The young Caesar, at the age of 24, opted to go abroad to save himself from the threat. His choice was Rhodes, a Greek island off the Anatolian coast of Asia Minor (modern Turkey), which was an intellectual capital alongside Athens.

Rhodes at the time was the hub of trade as well. Its wealth and power might be well demonstrated by the Colossus of Rhodes, a gigantic statue erected in commemoration of victory over a battle with Macedonia in 290 B.C. The statue, whose height was up to 34 meters (equivalent of the Statue of Liberty from the feet to the crown), collapsed during the earthquake of 226 B.C. and was taken apart by Saracens who invaded the island in 653. Rhodes also held a significant position in terms of the evolution of the law of the sea. Rhodes was the center in the evolution of the law of the sea, particularly in terms of settling maritime and trade disputes. The early customary law of the sea is called the 'Rhodesian Sea Law.' The principle of freedom of navigation today was established through the Rhodesian Sea Law.

Young Caesar sought a refuge in Rhodes, in the name of studying abroad. On the way to Rhodes, the ship that he was aboard was seized by Cilician pirates in 75 B.C. Pompey's massive counter-pirate campaign was still 10 years away, so piracy was still rampant in the area. When the pirates demanded a ransom of 20 talents, the equivalent of annual salaries for 4,300 soldiers at the time, Caesar began to laugh loudly. If he could not afford to pay the ransom, he would have been sold into slavery or been killed. In this midst of this crisis, Caesar came up with a clever ruse. Hoping to buy time, he offered to pay 50 talents, implying that he was worth a much higher ransom if only the pirates could be patient.

The pirates were fascinated by his offer. They thought that there would be nothing to lose for them, except a delay in ransom payment, and besides, they could always execute him if it turned out he wasn't worth keeping alive. Caesar sent his followers to raise money while he was held hostage with his two servants. The pirates, who believed that they held a son of a wealthy Roman nobleman, were excited about the enormous ransom. During his captivity, Caesar laughingly told them he would have them all crucified once he was released – thinking this a good joke, the pirates laughed along with him.

For 40 days, until his followers came back with the ransom that he had offered, he stalled for time and lived among the pirates. As soon as he paid it and was set free, he rushed to nearby Miletus to prepare attacks on the pirates. Sailing from Miletus, he raided the pirates' base and captured nearly all of them. Entrusted by the governor of Asia Minor to deal with the pirates, he crucified all of them, as he had promised. After two years in Rhodes, Caesar came back to Roman politics. Caesar's support for granting imperium to his rival Pompey might have been derived from his bitter firsthand experience with the pirates.

Julius Caesar

Slave Trade of Pirates

One might be curious why Romans hesitated to fight the pirates for so long while the pirates were rampant across the eastern Mediterranean, disturbing trade and shipping. This might have happened because the Romans enjoyed some benefits generated by piracy. The main spoils of the pirates were slaves. Typically, pirates raided coastal settlements or towns and captured locals to sell as slaves. City-states across the Mediterranean, as well as Rome, had great demand for slaves to work on farmlands. Roman landlords ran huge farmlands, and as such the Roman Republic itself was a principal market for slaves, and the landlords were principal customers for the pirates. The main reason behind the Roman Senate's objection to the anti-piracy campaign led by Pompey was its concern over the shortage of workforce on their farmlands. Such concern was larger for Sicily, which had greater demands for slaves.

The Delos island, in the middle of the Cyclades archipelago in the south Aegean Sea, had thrived as the hub of the slave trade. Alexandria and Rhodes were also widely known as marketplaces for slaves. As many as 10,000 slaves were traded in such marketplaces. Many cities on the coast of Lycia (the southern coast of modern Turkey), such as Phasalis, even made agreements with pirates to secure a stable supply of slaves. The city of Side, for example, allowed pirates to use its harbor. With the backing of such city-states, pirates made an enormous income. Under these circumstances, pirates expanded their activities to Africa from Cyprus and eastern Turkey, as well as the Iberian Peninsula, which was under the control of Rome.

Chapter 3

MEDITERRANEAN PIRATES AFTER THE COLLAPSE OF THE ROMAN EMPIRE

Introduction

This chapter deals with Saracen pirates who dominated the Mediterranean after the collapse of the West Roman Empire, commonly referred to as the Roman Empire. But before discussing the Saracen pirates who looted the Mediterranean Sea off the Italian Peninsula while Muslims ruled the Middle and Near East and North Africa, we first need to know about the late Roman Empire and its decline. Moving straight into the era of Muslims and Saracen pirates without understating the late Roman Empire would only provide a partial understanding of what led to their rise.

Any particular historical event is a result of the interaction of numerous complicated factors throughout a long history. The appearance of Saracen pirates is also a historical event brought by a power vacuum after the collapse of the Roman Empire. The Roman Empire is often considered to be synonymous with ancient European history itself.

Saracen pirates were totally different in nature from previous Mediterranean pirates. Piracy before the collapse of the Roman Empire was an internal problem of the Roman Empire, and in many cases, these were Christian pirates attacking other Christians. However, in the Mediterranean which came under Muslim control, Muslims from North Africa attacked the Italian Peninsula and the Christians under the rule of the Byzantine Empire.

The Decline and Fall of the Roman Empire

The brilliant history of the Roman Empire over a millennium ended with the fall of the Western Roman Empire in 476. The Eastern Roman Empire, based in the capital of Constantinople, would continue to exist until the city was captured by Osman Turks in 1453. The Byzantine Empire, built on the Greek Orthodox religion and Byzantine culture, was a totally different empire from the Western Roman Empire. In this sense, the Roman Empire is widely considered to have ended with the fall of the Western Roman Empire.

The territory of the Roman Empire at its height extended to Spain in the west, Asia Minor and the Near East in the east, and North Africa in the south. Extending north into modern-day Europe, the Rhine River to the west and the Danube River to the east had served as the frontlines of the empire over several hundred years. Romans built military posts along the frontlines and stationed troops to defend them. The frontlines were not only defense lines, but also boundary lines which divided the land between what Romans considered 'civilization' and the lands inhabited by tribal peoples. The Roman Empire was a civilized society where people enjoyed economic prosperity, academics, and arts flourished, and the value of individuals under the rule of law was highly regarded. By a stark contrast, beyond the frontlines, there was a barbaric world which had remained tribal states and eked out a living from aggressive actions and sackings.

For Romans, it was vital to formulate laws and institutions which could be universally applied to various nations with different cultures, ethnicity and religions under their rule. Besides, it was also essential to build traffic networks to connect Rome with its provinces across several continents. The Roman roads, built initially for military purposes, enabled the rule of the emperor to reach every corner of its territory, and at the same time, any event that happened across the provinces could be reported swiftly to the emperor in Rome. As the saying goes: "all roads lead to Rome." The Roman roads operated like a body's nervous system, allowing troops to move swiftly in the event of rebellions in the provinces or the aggressive actions of barbarians across the frontlines.

In the period of the "five good emperors" (96–180), the Roman Empire enjoyed its most majestic days. The political situation remained stable, the economy prospered, and the empire's territorial reach was at its height. The empire's defenses were so secure that barbarians could not attempt to cross the frontlines. The values of Rome were regarded as universal. The era of *Pax Romana*, which meant peace or order established by Romans, was at hand.

Following a period of peace and expansion during the rule of the five good emperors, the Roman Empire entered its so-called 'Crisis of the Third Century.' After the death of Emperor Marcus Aurelius (120–180), a number of unqualified rulers ascended to the throne. Throughout this period, several proclaimed themselves emperor simultaneously, setting off a series of assassinations. Concurrently, rebellions in Palmyra (an ancient city in what is now Syria) and Gaul (mainly modern-day France and Belgium) broke out. The Roman Empire was challenged by the largest crisis it had faced since its foundation. Meanwhile, the spirit of noblesse oblige of the ruling class, along with their open-mindedness, gradually faded away, and the economy was on the wane. As the wealth inequality grew, social conflicts intensified. Romans were no longer able to maintain adequate military forces to defend the frontlines, while barbarian aggression was growing.

At the same time, a new civilization was born at the frontier of the empire. The barbarians who had looted and pillaged the territories of the Roman Empire grew more civilized as they integrated advanced Roman culture and technologies through wars with Romans. The barbarians increased the intensity and frequency of anti-Roman aggression, while evolving into tribal states with systemic ruling organizations and military forces.

It is not easy to pinpoint exactly when the decline of the Roman Empire started. However, what is apparent is that the

Roman Empire, after the Crisis of the Third Century, started to decline rapidly in the late fourth century. The Roman Empire in decay was incapable of financing military forces to defend its huge frontlines. The massive provinces across several continents had been a symbol of expansion of the Roman Empire, but their defense became an extremely heavy burden for the Roman Empire as it fell into decline. As a consequence, the barbaric mercenaries who had lived in the Roman territories took the place of Romans. This meant that the national defense of Rome itself was actually handed over to the tribes that had been its enemies.

The Roman Empire, which had become impossible for a single emperor to rule, was eventually divided into the Western and the Eastern empires in 395. The Western Roman Empire was totally vulnerable to the barbarians who invaded deep inside the territories. In the end, the brilliant millennium of the Roman Empire came to an end in 476 with attacks led by tribal chief Odoacer.

Advent of Muslims

Following the fall of the Western Roman Empire, German barbarians occupied the Italian Peninsula and North Africa. Justinian the Great of the Byzantine Empire, who sought to revive the empire's greatness and reconquer the lost western half of the historical Roman Empire, recovered the Italian Peninsula from the barbarians over 20 years. After he died, however, the southern territories of the historical Western Roman Empire were occupied by the Longobards. As such, the Italian Peninsula was divided into two parts – one part ruled by the Eastern Roman Empire and the other, by the Longobards.

Meanwhile in the Arabic Peninsula, which had been under the rule of the Eastern Roman Empire, one of the most seismic events in world history took place. That is, Islam was founded. The Prophet Muhammad, the founder of Islam, received the revelations of God delivered by Gabriel at the age of 40 while he prayed in a mountain cave, named *Hira*. After he started preaching in 613, Islam spread rapidly throughout neighboring regions, the religion spreading like wildfire through a dry field. Muhammad, who proclaimed "God is One" was persecuted by Meccan polytheists, and he escaped to Medina in 622 in the *Hegira* which marks the beginning of the Islamic calendar.

Mohammad conquered Mecca with his followers in 629. Islam expanded into a dominating force that ruled nearly all the Arabian Peninsula in less than 20 years since its foundation. Following Mohammad's death in 632, the Islam community led by the Caliph, a supreme religious, political and military leader, evolved towards an enormous empire as it continued to conquer the neighboring regions. At last, the Caliph completed the conquest of the entire Arabian Peninsula in 634, and in the following year, Damascus in Syria. The Byzantine Empire sent troops to recover its province but was defeated, and as a result, Damascus came under the full control of Islam. The Islamic forces advanced to Mesopotamia in the east, West Asia to the west and Egypt to the south and conquered Alexandria in 642, making Egypt an Islamic state.

The Islamic forces continued to conquer North Africa, bringing most of the region under its control by 689. The conquest of the entirety of North Africa in a short period was made possible in large part because of its flat geography, allowing Islamic forces to move swiftly on their Arabian horses. The grain belt, which had supplied one-third of the Romans' food, came under the rule of Islam.

Islamic Conquest of the Iberian Peninsula

Following the conquest of North Africa, the Islamic force crossed the Strait of Gibraltar to advance upon the Iberian Peninsula in 711. The Islamic force, which attempted to go into France through the Iberian Peninsula, was blocked by the Frankish Kingdom after the Franks won the Battle of Poitiers in the Pyrenees Mountains in 732. As a consequence, the ambitious Islamic goal of expansion into Western Europe failed. Afterwards, the Muslims stayed in the Iberian Peninsula for about 780 years, until they were forced to leave Granada, the last bastion of Muslims, in 1492 during the *Reconquista* – otherwise known as the Christians' recovery of those conquered territories from Muslim rule. Assumption is not allowed in history. However, supposing that the Franks had been defeated in the battle, Western Europe would have been under the rule of Islam, and the history of modern Europe – and by extension, the history of the world – would be greatly changed.

The tremendous wave of the Islamic forces, represented by the phrase "A sword on the right hand, Quran on the left hand," swept through Central Asia, conquering the Sassanid Persian Empire (226–651). Most of the former territories of the Roman Empire came under control of Islam, except for Western and Eastern Europe. As a consequence, Christians and Muslims confronted each other across the Mediterranean Sea. A totally different circumstance from the era of the Roman Empire, in which Christianity was the state religion, appeared. The conditions for Saracen pirates, who left a big scar in the history of Europe and the Mediterranean over several centuries, emerged.

Saracen Pirates

The term 'Saracen' is derived from 'Saraceni' that ancient Greeks and Romans had used in reference to Arabs. Initially, Europeans had called Arab Muslims 'Saracens.' Later on, they referred to all Muslims living in North Africa, including Berbers and Moors, as Saracens. Despite the fact that North Africa was a fertile region, the Arabs, Berbers and Moors who occupied North Africa had no interest in or aptitude for farming in settlements. Instead, the nomads in desserts were attracted to the plundering of Christians across the Mediterranean. At this juncture, one might be curious of how a desert people, not familiar with sea-faring, could become engaged in looting by sailing across the harsh Mediterranean Sea. The answer to the question might be found in the facts that Arabs developed the highest level of science and math as well as technology at the time, even to the extent that they used compasses. They employed Greeks who had the highest level of navigation skills, as crews. Additionally, they felt they had found a righteous cause in looting Christians, making piracy a front in a holy war against non-Muslims.

It was known that Islamic pirates first attacked a Christian community in 652. The Muslim ships that had departed from Alexandria raided and looted Siracusa, Sicily, capturing 800 locals as prizes. The pirates sold the captives at slave markets. This event was recorded as the beginning of the Saracens' lootings across the Mediterranean, which would persist for the next millennium. The Saracen pirates, based in cities on the coast of North Africa, such as Cairuan, Carthage and Tunis, continued to attack the Sicily Island. While the Islamic forces advanced to the Iberian Peninsula, their plundering ceased for a while until they resumed in 725.

During the period between the 7th and 8th centuries, the Mediterranean Sea was 'the Sea of Islam.' The Mediterranean Sea off the Italian Peninsula under the attacks of Saracen pirates turned into the 'Sea of Lawlessness' itself. Despite the constant aggression of Saracen pirates, the Byzantine Empire did not have naval power to protect its shipping from pirate attacks, and it also lacked the capability to combat the pirates. As for the Byzantine Empire, which had lost the Near East, North Africa and Asia Minor to Islamic force, even the security of Constantinople was at risk. The Byzantine Empire was also under attack from northern Slavs. Such instability was also the case for the Longobards who had controlled the southern part of the Italian Peninsula. They still remained divided and thus had no ability to deal with the pirates. Under these circumstances, the seas off the Italian Peninsula were exposed to the uncurbed lootings of Saracen pirates.

The vulnerability of navigation off coastal areas to pirate attacks resulted in the shrinking of sea-borne trade. Merchant ships that had been actively engaged in shipping valuable goods across the Mediterranean gradually disappeared. Fishing vessels operated only inshore, instead of going to distant waters. As such, the pirates were no longer able to rely on their typical method of plundering the ships traveling offshore. Thus, they opted to raid settlements or towns in coastal areas. This was quite a different method from piracy attacks in the Age of Discovery, in which pirates engaged in marauding merchant ships passing through major sea routes.

The ships that Saracen pirates used for looting were small galleys, known as the '*fusta*,' which were mainly propelled by rowing. Their speed, mobility, capability to move without wind and their ability to operate in shallow water made them ideal for piracy. They took Arabian horses aboard the *fustas* and rode them inland, looting coastal areas and returning with plunder. The *fusta* was a small size ship, but it required at least 16 to 20 rowers. The rowers were mostly Christians captured during raids. Other Christians were sold at slave markets to serve as rowers for other Muslim ships, or they were sent to the military after they were forced to convert to Islam. Otherwise, they were sent to concentration camps, called 'bathhouses.' Romans had a strong tradition of communal bathing, and had built a large number of bathhouses across their territories. The bathhouses built in North Africa changed to concentration camps after the fall of the Roman Empire.

The Saracen pirates, with a small fleet of less than 10 ships that had been concentrated in Sicily and its coastal area gradually expanded their activities towards the southern coastal areas of France and Italy. The pirates, based on islands like Sardinia and Corsica, used the seasonal summer winds to propel their ships on raiding missions to the coastal areas of Italy. They expanded their activity even further, getting closer to the pope's stronghold in Rome. Residents in these areas of the Italian Peninsula could no longer expect that the emperor in Constantinople would protect them. Thus, they sought to protect the security of themselves, their families and their towns without outside help.

Torre Saracena

Residents in coastal areas built watchtowers as a way of protecting themselves, to spot pirate ships' approach early and give themselves time to escape. Many old pirate watchtowers still exist to this day. They are called *Torre Saracena* in Italian, which means the 'Tower of Saracens,' and they dot the coastal cities in Italy and along the coasts of Sardinia and Sicily. Today they are tourist attractions that provide a scenic view of the blue Mediterranean, but their history tells of the pain that came with living in fear of Saracen pirates.

It was difficult to tell whether approaching ships were friendly or not, as the invention of the telescope was still many years off; in many cases, pirate ships were only identified when they came near to the shore. The pirates did not fly the now-famous 'Jolly Roger,' skull and swords flag – that symbol came into being several hundred years later during the Age of Discovery. Neither did they fly any flag of piracy, or even the Islamic symbol of the crescent and star.

Speaking of the symbolic flag of Islam, it was derived from historic events of Islam. On the night when the Prophet Muhammad had received revelations at the mountain cave *Hira*, a crescent and stars were twinkling in the dark sky. On the night when Muhammad escaped to Medina from Mecca to avoid persecution, there were also a crescent and stars in the dark sky. For this reason, the crescent was regarded by Islam as a symbol of truth, ushering light through darkness. Osman Turks were the first to use the flag of a crescent and stars. Following the collapse of the Byzantine Empire, the Osman Turks had built a great empire that stretched over much of Asia, Africa and Europe. Thus, for the Europeans who came under attack by Islamic pirates, the flag of a crescent and stars symbolized only terror.

Torre Saracena

Saracen pirates also sailed in disguise by flying the flag of a Christian state or the ally of the target area. Thus, it was hard to tell by only the flag of a ship if it was a pirate ship or a merchant ship traveling for trade. This historical legacy might have led to the provisions of the UN Convention on the Law of the Sea today: It affirms that ships should sail under the flag of one state, and that changing the flag during a voyage is not allowed;

a ship which sails under the flags of two or more states, using them according to convenience, may be regarded as a ship with no nationality.

The coastal residents of southern Italy frequently weren't aware of an approaching raid until the pirates came inshore, setting off a panic in which residents fled – often, too late to save themselves. Since shores were left defenseless, pirates were able to go on shore with ease. The Byzantine Empire, beleaguered from external aggression, was incapable of defending the southern coast from the sacking of Saracen pirates. Thus, the coastal residents had no choice but to flee as quickly as possible when pirate ships came inshore. Watchtowers helped the locals buy themselves at least a little more time to escape. The best option for the locals was either to flee, carrying valuables, deep inland or hide away somewhere out of reach of pirates. Otherwise, they would lose their property and even their lives at the hands of horseback-riding pirates who destroyed and set fire to villages and committed various atrocities. Those who were captured would live a hellish life either as rowers aboard ships or in labor camps for life.

The coastal residents had built multiple watchtowers along the coast. If the first watchtower onshore emitted signal fumes, the next watchtower would relay the message to those inland. At that time, the residents hid out deep inland, where the fourth or the fifth watchtower was located. When the pirates left, this method was provided the signal to confirm that it was safe to return to the sea.

The main targets of Saracen pirates were monasteries and churches. Monasteries, which owned abundant properties and lands, were located in remote areas, making them a good target for pirates. The pirates also preyed on churches that served as hideouts for locals. Pirates were able to capture a large number of residents at once and to loot their properties with ease. The houses of wealthy landlords and rich people were definitely a good target.

Borgo and Casbah

Saracen pirates gradually expanded their activities deeper inland, looting settlements and towns and capturing residents as plunder. To flee or hide away from the pirates was merely a temporary solution. Thus, the residents decided to move their settlements to remote areas, out of reach of pirates. It was a desperate effort for residents as they fought for their survival. The residents who hid away in a remote area in the mountain might build a town on the rugged and steep cliff, for example. The medieval towns built for the purpose of avoiding pirate aggression were called *borgo* in Italian. This led to a new lifestyle: Coastal residents would stay in the *borgo* in the summer, during peak raiding season, and return home in the fall. In a sense, it was natural for coastal residents to return to the sea, which was the base for their livelihood, when the risk of pirate attacks diminished.

However, on the part of city residents, it was an entirely different situation since a city of thousands could not be moved out every season. Thus, citizens had to rely on existing structures, build new defenses, or rely on geography to defend or escape from pirate attacks. One of the main defense structures was a labyrinth of a city, known as a *casbah*. These days, the legacy of the casbah is found in the northern cities of Italy, like Amalfi. When building a city, the focus of design was on defense for survival, rather than functional considerations, such as convenience and comfortableness. In this design, complicated and twisted alleys made it hard for pirates to find targets and easy for them to get lost. The divergent roads distracted the pirates, and thus allowed people time to escape or provided spaces to hide out.

Casbah

The Holy Raman Empire's Campaigns Against Pirates

The region of Gaul (*Gallia* in Latin, modern-day Western Europe), which had remained divided and ruled by several Germans, became united under Charles the Great (Charlemagne, 742–814) of the Frankish Kingdom. Western Europe had gone through the period of division over the 400 years following the fall of the Western Roman Empire. During that period, it had been ruled by numerous kingdoms. Most of Europe, except Britain, the Iberian Peninsula and the southern Italian Peninsula, became united under the rule of the Franks. Against this historical backdrop, the origin of the European Union (EU) today can trace its roots back to the unification of Western Europe by Charles the Great. Following the unification of Europe through a series of wars, he undertook a military expedition to Rome across the Alps in 800. Pope Leo III greeted and crowned him Holy Roman Emperor and 'Augustus of the Romans' in Saint Peter's Cathedral in the Vatican.

The creation of the Holy Roman Empire might be attributed to following historical conditions: conflicts between popes and the Byzantine Empire, and corresponding interests between Charles the Great and Pope Leo III. Even though Saracen pirates came to the front door of Rome – the symbol of Christianity as well as the residence of popes – the Byzantine emperors in Constantinople were helpless. Meanwhile, in 726, the Byzantine emperor instructed the pope to dismantle icons because they were believed to promote idolatry. The pope rejected the instruction and excommunicated the emperor. On this occasion, the emperor and the pope were engaged in serious conflict.

In response to excommunication, the emperor encouraged the Longobards to attack the pope. The pope, with no military force to defend himself, had no choice but to rely on the Franks for survival. This was a strategic consideration that prompted the pope to crown Charles the Great Holy Roman Emperor. For his part, Charles the Great, a leader from a barbarian tribe, desired to become the successor of the Roman Empire. In this context, he used 'Roman' and 'Holy' to express his identity as a Christian and his will as its protector as well.

Charles the Great, as the emperor of the Holy Roman Empire, was responsible for safeguarding Christianity from the aggression of Muslims. The Franks, who had lived in a state of barbarism north of the Rhine River, were not familiar with sea-faring at all. But Charles the Great created two naval fleets to carry out his responsibility. One was responsible for the coast of southern France, and the other one for the Italian Peninsula and Sicily. These two fleets were quite successful in combating Saracen pirates – so much so that Pope Leo III sent a thank you letter to Charles the Great for protecting Christians.

However, the situation totally changed after Charles the Great died in 814. The Holy Roman Empire was taken apart in less than 30 years after his death and divided by his descendants into present day Italy, France and Germany. The two fleets had disappeared, although it is unknown exactly when this happened. Western Europe went back to a time of war. People were engaged only in ongoing wars, and thus had no time to be concerned with the safety of the sea at all.

The Battle of Ostia

Taking advantage of the chaos in Europe, Saracen pirates took to the sea for piracy again. The pope, without help from guardians of Christians like Charles the Great, had to fight the pirates alone to safeguard Christianity and Rome. At that time, on the Italian Peninsula, a number of coastal city-republics, known as 'Maritime Republics,' were thriving. They included Genoa, Amalfi and Naples on the west coast and Venice on the east coast. These coastal city-states were ruled by a small number of merchants who had accumulated wealth by sea-borne trade. They were engaged in direct trade with Muslims in North Africa across the Mediterranean or transit trade with Western Europeans, trading valuable goods that they had brought from China and India through the Middle East. Although they were small city-states, they had naval fleets. For the city-states that lived on sea-borne trade, the security of navigation was vital for their survival itself. Since they had to protect themselves while being engaged in trade with Muslims in North Africa, building strong naval power was an essential issue.

Saracen pirates built a large fleet and attempted a massive invasion that went beyond small-scale looting. With the aggression of Saracen pirates on the horizon, Pope Leo IV was determined to fight the pirates firsthand, so he reinforced the fortresses around Rome. He also strung across the Tiber River to deter pirate ships from sailing inland. The pope called in the leaders of Naples and Amalfi to discuss the strategy to combat pirates and formed a league with them. He recruited volunteers and ships across Italy in the name of holy war against Muslims.

The league decided to wage a battle off the port of Ostia. In 849, the fleet of the league commanded by the Neapolitan commander confronted Saracen pirate ships face to face. Pope Leo IV addressed the fleet to boost their spirits and prayed for victory.

When the battle was about to take place – whether or not thanks to the pope's prayer – stormy southwest winds struck the Saracen fleet from the back. The fleet of the league swiftly moved back towards the safety of the port, but the Saracen fleet was directly hit by the stormy winds. As a result, the Saracen ships collided with each other and were destroyed and went adrift inshore. Many of them struck on rocks and ultimately sank. When the sea calmed down, the fleet of the league was able to seize the pirate ships and capture the pirates with ease. The battle ended with an enormous victory for the Christians.

The Muslim captives were taken to Rome and the pope put them to work building the walls around the Vatican. In preparation for possible Muslim invasions, the pope built the walls to protect Saint Peter's Cathedral. Ironically, the walls to protect one of the holiest buildings for Christians were built by Saracen pirates. The walls were named after Leo IV. The Battle of Ostia was portrayed by Raphael in the era of the Renaissance.

Following the defeat of its large-scale fleet, Saracen pirates went back to their old method of small-fleet looting. They could not afford to give up the enormous income generated from piracy.

Conquest of Sicily

Saracen pirates, who had remained inactive for quite some time in the aftermath of their defeat in the Battle of Ostia, were reengaged in piracy. The target was the island of Sicily. The pirates launched a full-scale attack on Sicily. Siracusa (the province of modern Syracuse), Sicily was a beautiful and flourishing city, called the 'Pearl of the Mediterranean.' Siracusa, which had been under the control of the Byzantine Empire since the fall of the Western Roman Empire, served as an outpost of Christianity in the midst of Muslim aggression.

Siracusa had remained unoccupied even in the midst of Islam's persistent attempts to conquer Sicily, but eventually fell into the hands of Islam in 878. With the collapse of Siracusa, Sicily came under a full control of Saracen pirates. The pirates totally devastated Siracusa in retaliation for the massive damage they sustained during the attacks. In addition to the nobles and soldiers who had resisted them to the last moment, they indiscriminately slaughtered residents, young and old, and captured them for slaves. Churches and icons were ravaged, and the destroyed buildings were rebuilt as mosques. The Muslims' rule in Sicily lasted for 200 years, until Normans occupied the island in 1072.

Following the conquest of Sicily, Saracen pirates' movements were unconstrained. Their aggression extended to the central and northern as well as southern Italian Peninsula. Through the coast of northern Italy off the Ligurian Sea, Saracen pirates advanced to the coast of southern France. Marseille was attacked twice. The coast of southern France was fully exposed to attack, and the pirates even built a base on the shore.

Popes in the Vanguard of Combating Saracen Pirates

Medieval popes in the Dark Ages, regarded as an agent of God on earth, were considered the sole and perfect guardian for Christians. Because the security of Rome was threatened, popes like Leo IV, were directly engaged in military campaigns to combat pirates in the name of safeguarding Christianity. Pope John X, for instance, commanded troops to fight Saracen pirates in southern Italy. He had first formed an alliance with Emperor Constantinus IV of the Byzantine Empire and King Berengar of Italy. Then he recruited volunteers in the name of a holy war against Islam. A large number of people volunteered at the news that the pope was directly recruiting soldiers and would command them to fight pirates. The pope believed that naval forces were likely to be a key to recovering the Garigliano River in central Italy, which was used as a base for Saracen pirate ships. As such, he called for maritime republics such as Naples, Amalfi and Gaeta to join in the holy war.

In 916, Pope John X undertook an expedition to recover the Garigliano from the rule of pirates. The pope commanded the troops during a three-month-long series of battles with the marauders. Literally, he was 'a pope with a sword in his hand.' The battles ended with the victory of the Christian forces. In a sense, this was the 'Maritime Crusades' to combat Saracen pirates. The first of the actual crusades took place in 1096, about 200 years later, under the slogan of 'God Wills It.' "It" meant the recovery of the Holy Land from Muslim rule. The campaign for the recovery of the Garigliano might be viewed as the beginning of the crusades, given that the Christians gathered in the name of a holy war to recover territory from the Muslim occupation. Pope John X made a great contribution to combating pirates, but his career was unfortunate. He was ousted by Roman nobles and sent to prison, where he was smothered.

Afterwards, Saracen pirates disappeared everywhere from the Garigliano to the Tyrrhenian Sea, ranging from central to southern Italy. However, it did not necessarily mean that the Saracen pirates completely ceased piracy. For internal reasons, they suspended it for a while. Peace was short-lived, however. Christians were under the illusion that the problem had been settled by the victory in the battle. Thus, they were not concerned with preparations for renewed attacks from pirates. They had even made an agreement that they would pay 22,000 pieces of gold annually to the pirates on the condition that they would not attack their merchant ships. Being overconfident in their victory, they relaxed their vigilance.

Maritime Republics' Efforts to Combat Pirates

Saracen pirates sailed across the Mediterranean using seasonal winds in the summer. In this way, they could easily reach Provence in southern France, the coast of Liguria in northern Italy, the coast of Tosca in central Italy and the southern coast of Italy, depending on their departure points on the coast of North Africa. Summer was a fearful season for Italians. The coastal residents had undergone enormous loss of life and damage to properties from Saracen pirate attacks between the 8th and 10th centuries.

Maritime republics such as Genoa, Pisa, Naples, Amalfi and Venice prospered after the fall of the Western Roman Empire. They were small coastal city-states, typically with populations of less than 100,000 – Genoa and Pisa had less than 50,000. They had no choice but to engage in sea-faring for livelihood because of the shortage of farmland in their territories. These republics, which lived on sea-borne trade, had naval fleets to protect their merchant fleets and homeland from attack by sea. During the period of the crusades, Genoa, Pisa and Venice had built up relatively large fleets composed of 100 to 200 warships. In fact, they were a significant driving force that had sustained the crusades. Interestingly, the more closely a republic was located to North Africa, the earlier it developed into a powerful maritime republic. This is likely because they had to build up their ocean-going capabilities to help fend off pirate attacks.

Since Venice was located far up the coast of the Adriatic Sea, it was harder for Saracen pirates to access than other republics. For that reason, the development of Venice into a maritime state came later than others. Venice was founded by Romans who had escaped from the aggression of Huns that had invaded in 452. Seeing that they had nowhere else to flee when they arrived on the northeast coast, the escapees desperately built a city in a swamp. It was Venice, nicknamed the 'City of Water.'

Maritime Republics

Venice greatly expanded Oriental trade in the wake of the crusades. Venice, whose territories extended to Greek islands and the eastern Mediterranean, was at its height in the period between the 14th century and the 15th century. Venice had built itself into a strong naval power in the Medieval Ages and the Renaissance, and rose to become a sea-borne trade hub in the Mediterranean. Venice remained independent until it was occupied by Napoleon in 1797. By the 11th century, the maritime republics, which had previously held a defensive position against Saracen pirates, joined forces with each other to go on the offensive. This might indicate that their capacities grew stronger than the pirates. The Amalfi navy defeated Saracen pirates who attacked Naples. The Venetian navy saved Bari in southern Italy, which had been ravaged by pirates. The Pisan navy defeated Saracen pirates engaged in looting Calabria in southern Italy.

The way that the maritime republics responded to Saracen pirates varied depending on their capabilities. The overriding concern for Venice was to safeguard the navigation of their ships engaged in trade with the Orient through the Adriatic Sea. Venice opted for providing escort services to their merchant ships transiting the waters vulnerable to pirate attacks. The escort services were very costly, but the expense was worth it to transport valuables. Venice did not attack pirate ships unless they were attacked first.

On the part of the maritime republics, having a stable supply of rowers for the navigation of galleys was a critical concern. Saracen pirates forced Christian captives to work as rowers. For the maritime republic, however, the supply of rowers was an extremely difficult issue. Venice was never involved in using slaves as rowers since the act of piracy was strictly prohibited. As such, the only option was to employ its nationals or foreigners after training them. The job of rowing aboard trade or warship galleys was extremely hard as well as dangerous work, since rowers were required to engage in battle if the ship suffered an attack. On the other hand, the job of rower provided a high-income job for those with no certain job skills.

The Maritime Crusades

The republics had a hostile relationship with Muslims in North Africa. Saracen pirates who constantly sailed across the Mediterranean to threaten their life and properties were their most fearful enemy. Saracen pirates under the patronage of Islamic rulers in North Africa shared their plunder with them. Despite this hostile relationship, the maritime republics were deeply engaged in trade with the Muslims in North Africa. Although Muslims in North Africa were pagans as well as enemies, they were also essential trade partners. This kind of self-contradictory behavior ran afoul of the popes' commitment to fight Muslim aggression. Popes frequently prohibited trade with Muslims on the grounds that it would benefit only the Muslims. However, there was no way to halt trade with Muslims that was done out of necessity.

For the maritime republics, their religious commitments were a totally different matter from their concerns about their livelihood. They did not care who they traded with, as long as trade was beneficial. Considering the nature of contemporary international relations, where trade often takes place even among hostile states, their behavior might not be regarded as extraordinary. To modern sensibilities, engaging in trade that generates profit is as natural as water flowing downward. The goods that the republics exported to North Africa included wood for building ships, textiles for sails, armor and other products. The goods purchased from North Africa by Italian merchants included wheat, olives, furs and date palms.

With the expansion of trade, the maritime republics opened trade offices in the major ports of North Africa to facilitate trade and stationed consuls there. Their duties included the protection of their nationals, the opening of new trade agreements, and the collection of information on trade. Through the activities of the consuls, shocking news was delivered to the Christian world. It was about Christian captives, called 'Raqiq,' who had been brought to North Africa as a consequence of piracy and held in concentration camps. The miserable reality of those Christian captives in concentration camps, known as 'bathhouses' was revealed. The captives were ordinary Christians captured across Europe, mostly on the coast of Italy and France, and brought by Saracen pirates.

The news about the Christian captives quickly spread to Christians throughout Europe. Shocked and outraged Europeans engaged in actions to recover them. On the vanguard of this movement was Pope Victor III. In 1087, he claimed the need for so-called 'maritime crusades' to recover the Christian captives and he called for the maritime republics to join. It was 10 years before the crusades were launched. Genoa, Amalfi and Pisa decided to participate in the campaign. However, Venice refused to join it. Presumably, the non-participation of Venice was due to its geography – situated deep inside the Adriatic Sea, it suffered less piratical damage than the others.

The maritime crusades, launched in 1087, were composed of 300 warships and 3,000 sailors. Given the scale of maritime republics' naval forces, it was quite a massive expedition. Seemingly, the expedition was aimed at the redemption of Christian captives. The ulterior motive, however, was the launch of a counter-attack of Christians beleaguered by Muslims. The landing target was a port off Cairuan, a principal base of Islamic force in North Africa. The Maritime Crusades had faced strong resistance from Islamic forces, but they had successfully completed the expedition. The maritime crusades made a peace agreement with the leaders of surrendered Muslims and recovered Christian captives held in labor camps.

Separately, Genoa and Pisa launched military campaigns in alliance with the lords of southern France to secure the safety of navigation in the Tyrrhenian Sea. The aim was to combat pirates in the Balearic Islands. The allied forces, composed of 300 warships and 40,000 sailors, undertook a massive counter-piracy operation. As a result, the pirates in Majorca were wiped out, and numerous Christians captives held in labor camps were rescued. However, when maritime republic surveillance eventually relaxed, the Balearic Islands once again became a pirate haven.

Rescue of Slaves

The crusades, the first of which was launched in 1096, were massive expeditions undertaken seven times in a period over 200 years. Except the first and second expeditions through land routes from Europe to the Middle East, the rest were by sea. The maritime republics played a vital role during the expeditions by shipping war supplies, such as siege artillery, weapons and food, that was not suitable for land transport.

The crusades were the best opportunity for the maritime republics to expand their Oriental trades. Pisa, Genoa and Venice had built trade centers at the major ports of the crusades' expeditions and enjoyed fulfilling the extraordinary demands of the crusaders' missions. Saracen pirates continued to commit attacks throughout the crusades. At the initial stage of the crusades, the pirates shrank from the busy movement of ships carrying war supplies. However, they resumed acts of piracy, recognizing that the crusaders were not much interested in themselves. In 1291, the crusades ended, but the piracy of Saracen pirates did not. Piracy had become a major industry in the Islamic community in North Africa, as with modern day Somali pirates. The tradition of piracy was so deeply rooted that it was hard to terminate.

Meanwhile, two charity organizations were founded for the rescue of Christian captives held in concentration camps across North Africa. One was 'The Order of the Most Holy Trinity for the Redemption of Captives' (in short, the Trinitarian Order), a Catholic religious order founded in 1198. The other was 'The Royal, Celestial and Military Order of Our Lady of Mercy and the Redemption of the Captives,' also known as the Mercedarians, a Catholic mendicant order established in 1218 for the redemption of Christian captives. The founding intention for these orders was to recover Christians captives beyond national borders. With the charities donated in their homelands, they tried to rescue as many Christian captives as possible, trading them for ransom that they negotiated with the leaders of Saracen pirates. However, the number of redemptions out of all the captives held across North African was extremely small since ransom money was limited. The number of rescued captives in a single mission ranged only from 100 to 300 captives, depending on the amount of ransom available. The redemption missions did not take place annually. It took years to prepare the ransom.

However, this hope was like a light in the darkness for the captives who otherwise would spend their whole life as slaves. Out of numerous captives, only those with good fortune were able to go home and see their families. Otherwise, they were doomed to be engaged in slave labor for life. Between 1119 and 1132 when the founder of the Trinitarian Order, John de Matha, labored to recover captives, allegedly 7,000 captives in all were brought home. Given the fact that the Trinitarian Order was constantly engaged in redemption over the next 500 years, the total number is estimated to be hundreds of thousands. Paradoxically, ransoming the captives was a contributing factor that helped Saracen piracy persist. Holding Christians captives was extremely profitable.

The higher priority for monks or knights who engaged in rescue missions was to recover sick and old captives. Such priority was very beneficial to pirates because they redeemed those who held the lowest value as slaves. Pirates could sell young captives as slaves with higher prices. Saracen pirates, recognizing the value of Christian captives, were constantly engaged in piracy.

Chapter 4

THE VIKINGS

The Emergence of Vikings

While Saracen pirates were rampant across the Mediterranean, Vikings were terrorizing England and the northern coasts of Europe. In terms of the etymology of 'Viking,' various theories have been put forward. A leading theory is that the word means 'a person from a valley river.' Presumably, this word was derived from the unique Scandinavian geography, specifically the formations known as 'fjords' – long, narrow inlets with steep sides or cliffs, created by glacial erosion. Over 800 years, the word Viking has been used to indicate the Scandinavians both at home and abroad who had lived in Sweden, Norway and Denmark throughout the era of aggression, trade and colonial activity.

Originally, the Vikings had been ordinary people actively engaged in trade. By the first century, they had traded with Romans, and by the fifth century, they invited foreign merchants to thriving Scandinavian commerce cities and were actively engaged in trade with them. While trading with foreign countries, the Vikings observed the wealth of their trading partners and dreamed of taking it by force. The Vikings first ruthlessly looted monasteries in England and on other European coasts, and they killed or enslaved monks. Afterward, the Vikings developed a reputation as brutal, bloodthirsty predators.

One might be curious about what made the Vikings turn to piracy instead of continuing normal trade. Amongst various factors, the infertile natural environment of Scandinavia is usually considered the most salient. Other than fishing and hunting, the cold weather and barren soil of Northern Europe made the

Vikings struggle for their livelihood. The population had constantly increased, and farmlands were insufficient to support it. Under these circumstances, they took to the sea. Because of the Viking tradition that the first son was to inherit the entirety of the family's wealth, younger siblings had no choice but to engage in trade or plunder at sea. Additionally, political instability served as a driving force. In the late ninth century, King Harald of Norway, who had unified small kingdoms throughout Scandinavia, intended to get rid of the rulers of provinces. These provincial lords escaped to foreign countries with their people. But above all, it is believed that the Vikings had a natural drive to explore, along with fearlessness in sea-faring, and a toughness of spirit derived from their harsh natural environment.

Vikings

Outstanding Navigational Skills

Outstanding navigational skills of the Vikings made them the masters of the sea. The Vikings sailed inshore, using geography and natural features as landmarks to guide their navigation. They relied on primitive positioning equipment, but principally located their position at sea using the position of the sun and stars, the direction of winds, the shape of waves, the color and temperature of water, and the existence of sea birds and sea mammals.

The Vikings were able to sail long distances at extraordinary speeds, with the maximum speed of 28 km per hour on open oceans. The Vikings could operate on the rivers as well. Since the Vikings believed that their outstanding navigational skills would allow them to go back home safely, they were not afraid of ocean-going beyond offshore seas. The Vikings' prominent contribution to navigation would be the development of tacking skill. Tacking is a maneuver wherein a sailing ship proceeds windward. Tacking indicates that a sailing ship has turned its bow toward the wind so that the direction from which the wind blows changes from one side to the other, allowing for a ship's progress in the desired direction. The Vikings set the sail at an angle of 45° to the wind and maneuvered their ships to proceed windward. The Vikings' tacking was possible with a set of outfitting and steering, although they were primitive. The Vikings originated the tacking techniques commonly seen on modern-day yachts.

The Vikings was the masters of latitude sailing. When they made a long and distant sea voyage, they relied on latitude sailing to find their way around. Latitude sailing involved maintaining a certain latitude that followed, as closely as possible, the latitude of their destination. If the Vikings were sailing for a known island or point on a faraway continent, they would know the latitude of the destination. Once the Vikings got to the proper latitude, it was simply a matter of keeping the ship on that latitude and traveling in the direction of their destination until they reached it. At night, they steered their ship according to the position of Polaris, or the North Star, if they intended to go northwest. They continually observed the position of Polaris and changed the course of their ship according to the relative position between themselves and the star.

The Vikings' latitude sailing was possible with two navigational aids – the sun compass and sunstone. The sun compass was a primitive inclinometer that the Vikings used to determine their latitude. The sun compass was made on the circular plate, with a peg inserted through the hole in the center of the plate. The peg was known as the gnomon. The Vikings marked the edge of the shadow cast by the gnomon and then inscribed a line connecting the points. This line is known as the gnomon line. When a Viking navigator wanted to find the same latitude later, he kept the tip of the shadow on the gnomon line. If the shadow of the gnomon extended past the gnomon line, he knew that he was too far north of his desired latitude. If the shadow fell short of the gnomon line, the navigator knew that he was too far south.

A principal navigational instrument that the Vikings used to locate their position in a cloudy sky was a sunstone, a translucent rock. The sky of Europe off the Arctic was frequently shrouded in heavy fog, rain and clouds. On such occasions, the Vikings used the sunstone. The stone turns a blue and purple color when it is turned at right angles to the sun, even on cloudy days, so Vikings could detect the direction from which polarized light was striking the sunstone and set their course accordingly.

The Vikings were not simply predators, but adventurous explorers. With outstanding navigational skills, they sailed across the oceans beyond their world. Across the North Atlantic, they sailed further to Canada, Iceland and Greenland. Since Viking ships were an open deck structure, the Vikings were fully exposed to strong waves and rain as they sailed. The Vikings wore fur and oiled leather clothes, but they usually remained wet and cold. At night when they sailed inshore, they went on shore and camped on the ground. During a long-distance voyage, they slept in leather sleeping bags on the deck. Their food on the voyage was dried and salted fish and jerked meats.

Even though the Vikings were the masters of the sea, they were simply weak human beings before Mother Nature. Numerous Vikings lost their lives on harsh voyages in in the midst of strong waves or cold and wet weather. However, the harsh condition of the sea could not discourage their will for exploration. The Vikings went anywhere there was prey to loot and did not avoid bloody battles. The phrase "the Vikings had lived on the sea," found in runic inscriptions that recorded the Vikings' lifestyles, demonstrates their inherent talent for survival at sea as well as their predatory natures.

Viking Ships

The Vikings were required to be strong master shipbuilders and to have the navigational skills to sail long distances. The Vikings had held a long tradition of sailing across the fjords on ships with no sails, traveling further to the distant sea in good weather. Over 2,000 years, the Vikings had held a tradition for building light and speedy ships. They reinforced their traditional ships with a sail to increase speed, along with a robust mast and a keel to stabilize at sea.

There were many types of Viking ship, built for various uses. The best-known type is probably the longship. A longship, designed for speed and agility, was suitable for sailing in the distant sea. The longship had a long, narrow hull and shallow draught to facilitate landings and troop deployments in shallow water. Of the various types of longship, the largest was Drekar, a dragon-headed longship, named after its dragon shaped hull. Drekar was designed for attack and for the transport of troops. The ships were the Vikings' most important instrument, allowing them to explore the unknown world and to loot by sailing across seas or rivers.

When the Vikings built a ship, a man in charge supervised the craftsmen specialized in each part of ship. They used a long and straight oak tree for the keel and other trees for the curved parts of the hull. When they completed building the hull, they installed round shields on the sides of the hull and a dragon head-shaped decoration on the bow. The sail of the Viking ships was made of squared woolen fabric, which provided extremely powerful mobility. However, the problem was that it was hard to steer the ship in strong winds or when the sail was wet with rain. The Vikings, who had great pride in these sails, used to paint slashes or diamonds on them.

The Pillage of England

In the period between 800 and 1100, the Vikings' voyages to new lands – as well as their attacks on these lands – were at their peak. The first attack on Christian sanctuaries was a monastery on Lindisfarne Island, off the northeast coast of England on 1 January 793. The Vikings had raided the monastery, destroyed and pillaged it, setting it on fire. They slaughtered the monks and held survivors as captives for selling in the slave market. The monks who resisted were thrown into the sea.

Afterwards, the Vikings kept raiding the British islands and the coastal areas of Europe. Christians viewed the Vikings as the incarnation of evil. The Vikings' pillage of Christian sanctuaries was not an act of hostility toward Christianity specifically. They were simply preying on places that were the richest targets with the fewest defenses. Monasteries and churches had a wealth of valuables, such as golden crosses and people who could be sold as slaves.

In 877, the Danish Vikings raided England and occupied the western and eastern regions, which were half of England.

The occupied regions were called the 'Danelaw,' which means the regions under the law and customs of the Danish Vikings. Even though England, prosperous and fertile, was a main target for the Vikings' pillaging, it was not the only target. Ireland – the hub of Christian arts and studies – was an attractive target for the Vikings. The monasteries and churches in Ireland were like a storehouse of riches, and Ireland itself had abundant green lands that the Vikings could lay claim to. By the middle of the 9th century, the Vikings settled on the coasts of Limerick, Waterford, Wexford and Cork. At first, the Vikings used these settlements as winter bases to expand inland and quickly sack villages and run away. However, as time passed, these settlements turned into permanent settlements as well as a base for expanding further inland. By 950, the Vikings had opted for living in settlements, instead of pillaging, and thus the aggression of the Vikings virtually ended. With the defeat in the Battle of Clontarf in 1014, the Vikings' rule in Ireland came to an end. The legacy of the Vikings is found in the cities that they built, as well as trade and place names.

Expansion to Russia

As years passed, the Vikings' raids became more daring, and they ventured deeper inland. By the early 800s, they traveled up along the rivers by ships that were navigable in shallow waters. Some traveled to the Russian continent across the Baltic Sea. The Vikings had built trade bases inland near the Baltic Sea and ventured to the Black Sea through the Dnepr River and to the Caspian Sea through the Volga River. They had to travel a long distance inland to reach the two rivers in central Russia. The ships that the Vikings used for venturing inland were much smaller in size than typical Viking ships. Known as dugouts, the ships were built by hollowing out a log. The Vikings used a small sail to increase mobility in fair winds. The most prominent feature of dugouts was their lightness. The Vikings carried them on land when they could not sail in rough in shallow waters.

The Vikings pillaged throughout Russia and captured locals for slave-taking. The Russian slaves, known as 'Slavs,' were traded in Sweden. The words 'Slave' and 'Slavery' were derived from Slav slaves. One can guess how large the number of Russian captives was from the origin of the words. The Swedish Vikings, called 'Rus' (by Slavs) who took to the Black Sea attempted to occupy Constantinople by force several times. According to the historical records of the Byzantine Empire, tens of thousands of Rus attacked Constantinople by sailing across the Black Sea. As part of peace deals, the Byzantine emperor offered the right to pay tributes and trade with them. Despite such deals, the Rus resumed the sacking of monasteries and towns again years later, including the attack on Constantinople. Allegedly, the Rus named the occupied lands 'Russia' and built a trade network with the Byzantine Empire as well as the Arab world. The Byzantine Emperors could do nothing about the Vikings' predations. Ironically, some of the Swedish Vikings were enlisted in the guard of Byzantine emperors or served as mercenaries in the service of the empire.

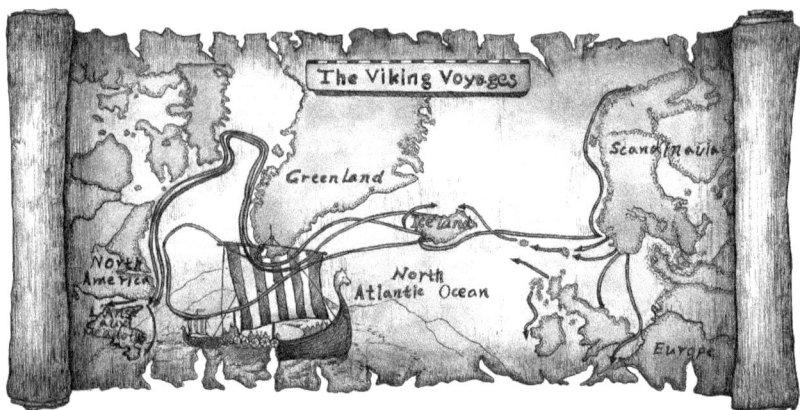

Routes of Viking Expansion

Attack on Paris

As the Vikings expanded to the European continent, they first attacked Paris, in the Frankish Kingdom. In November 885, the Norman Vikings traveled up along the Seine River, with a fleet of 700 ships and 40,000 warriors aboard. The Seine River was totally covered by the fleet, whose length extended as far as five miles downstream. The intention of the Vikings was to plunder fertile inlands through Paris. The Vikings were more attracted by fertile lands deep inland than Paris itself, which was still a small city off the Seine River. However, the Vikings' intention was blocked by two bridges in Paris. Ships were unable to pass through the bridges, which had fortified towers built on them.

The Frankish military and Paris citizens had desperately fought together against the Vikings between December to the following January. One bridge was washed away in heavy rainfall in February. Meanwhile, some Vikings quickly passed through the bridge and went further up inland. In Paris, as the siege continued for a year, Paris citizens suffered greatly from poverty and disease.

Charles III (also known as Charles the Fat) of the Holy Roman Empire came to Paris with his troops to save the Parisian citizens. However, he entered into negotiations with the Vikings without engaging in battle. They reached agreements that included permission for Vikings to travel inland and only loot during the winter – they must leave the next year. In addition, the Vikings got 700 pounds of silver.

In 911, Charles III, beleaguered by the Vikings, came up with an astonishing solution. He granted the Vikings the feudal lordship of the areas where they had occupied in exchange for their loyalty. The Vikings were satisfied with the solution because the occupied areas became their own lands. This was the foundation of the Duchy of Normandy in northern France. Since the Norman Dynasty was founded in England, the region remained a source of conflict between England and France. Hundreds of years later, it also marked the beginning of the

Hundred Years' War (1337–1453), a long-running struggle between England and France for the throne of France.

Vikings' Settlement in Europe

The Vikings terrified France as well as all of Europe with the
fear of death and destruction. In 844, the Vikings attacked Cadiz
in Spain. The Vikings expanded to the Italian Peninsula and
sailed across the Mediterranean to raid North Africa. While
engaged in aggression and pillage, some groups of the Vikings
settled in their occupied areas. They became assimilated to the
lifestyle of the occupied areas by being adapted to the local culture, religion and language. Some of the Norman Vikings who
had settled downstream of the Seine River were termed the
Normans (People of Normandy). The Vikings who had settled in Normandy – the region well known for landing operations of the Allied Forces during the World II – got married
to French women, converted to Christians, spoke French and
were adapted to local customs. Interestingly, the Danish Vikings
who had expanded to England bathed every Saturday and regularly washed their clothes to please their clean English wives.
Furthermore, some Vikings even regarded divineness as iden-
tical to cleanness.

A legacy of the Vikings in the European food culture is a
buffet. The Vikings celebrated their victories in battles or successful lootings by enjoying various cuisines set on a large plate.
The Vikings' custom spread to France and later evolved into the
buffet. By 1000, the Normans were no longer cruel and ferocious
Viking warriors. Christianity took root in Scandinavia and the
Vikings became assimilated to the European culture and lifestyle. As a result of settlement overseas and political unification,
young people in the homeland that intended to go into piracy

had gradually been reduced. The Normans settled in Normandy expanded to southern Italy under the control of the Byzantine Empire and Saracens. They engaged in expelling these rulers in alliance with the locals who desired to be out of their rule. Launched in 1017, the Normans' expansion to southern Italy ended with its conquest in over 20 years.

In 1039, the Normans attacked Siracusa under control of Saracens to recover Sicily from Muslims. The recovery of Sicily met with a strong resistance from an allied force of the Muslims in North Africa and the Saracens in Sicily. Given the circumstance of southern Italy where Saracen pirates were prevalent, the recovery of Sicily was suspended for a while. Afterward, the attempts to recover Sicily were made slowly, but steady. In 1086, the Normans eventually occupied Sicily.

Conquest of England

As the Norman rulers developed a firm control on their lands, and the boundaries were clearly drawn, there were harsh competitions between the Norman rulers. The best example would be the conquest of England in 1066 by William the Conqueror. Commanding the Norman troops, he crossed the English Channel and killed King Harald Godwinson, becoming King of England.

Here, we need to briefly take a look at the circumstances of ancient England. Since Caesar's expeditions to Britannia in 54 BC and 53 BC, it had remained Rome's province for a long time until Romans withdrew from it. In the aftermath of massive immigrations of Anglos, Saxons and Jutes from northern Germany in the period between the early 5th century to the 9th century, many kingdoms were founded in England. At that time England had been isolated from the continent, but began its own developments. The states built by Anglos, Saxons and Jutes were tribal rather than kingdoms.

Alfred the Great (rein from 872 to 899) spurted the development of ancient England, which had been made slowly. He opted for buying peace with money, rather than waging wars with the Vikings. As a consequence, the Danish Vikings bypassed Wessex under his rule and instead invaded other regions. Wessex thrived while other regions were collapsed by the Vikings. Alfred the Great sought a permanent peace with the Danishes. The outcome was the creation of Danelaw, as described earlier.

Alfred the Great secured the safety of his kingdom named 'England.' England broke the peace deal with the Vikings, which had lasted over a hundred years. In 1002, King Ethelred ordered the Danishes in the Danelaw killed. As a consequence, the incident brought about a massive aggression of Denmark next year. England was not robust enough to become a rival of Demark. In the aftermath of 10 years of war, King Knud of Demark who had conquered England rose to the throne of England and ruled for 20 years. After King Knud died, the throne was succeeded by Edward from Alfred's family. King Edward made a secret deal with William the Conquer, his cousin, to give him his throne after his death. However, following the death of King Edward, the throne was succeeded by Harald Godwin of Wessex.

William the Conqueror, who thought that his throne was stolen, landed in England with the Norman troops composed of 7,000 infantries and hundreds of archers. In the Battle of Hastings, which took place in October 1066, he killed King Harald and rose to the throne of England at Westminster Abbey on the eve of Christmas. Thus, William the Conqueror opened the Norman dynasty in England, making King Harald the last of the Anglo-Saxons. Since then, the English dynasties to date have been the decedents of William the Conqueror. That is, they are the decedents of Danish Vikings who came from the continent.

Chapter 5

THE BARBARY PIRATES

Descendants of Saracen Pirates

Four to five centuries after the Vikings ruled the seas, Barbary pirates were rampant across the Mediterranean and on the coast of North Africa. The term 'Barbary pirates' refers to the Muslim pirates engaged in predation and destruction over Europe on the coasts of modern-day Libya, Tunis, Algeria and Morocco for 300 years. The word 'Barbary' was derived from the Greeks, who had called other peoples Barbarians. Later on, this word was also used to refer to Berbers, North African nomads. Barbary pirates traced their roots to the Saracen pirates who had looted the Italian Peninsula and southern Europe since Islam ruled North Africa. While Saracen pirates had been active in the period between the 8th century and the 13th century, Barbary pirates appeared in later centuries.

The Saracen pirates had been fear itself for Europeans, but Barbary pirates bested even their ancestor Saracens in terms of the scale and evilness of their acts. In addition, Barbary pirates' activities expanded to the oceans beyond the Mediterranean. Numerous Europeans had been subject to killing or capture by Barbary pirates. Interestingly, Cervantes, the author of *Don Quixote*, had been held captive and a hundred years later, Daniel Defoe, the author of *Robison Crusoe*, underwent the same fate.

Here, we need to briefly take a look at the historic background of the advent of Barbary pirates. After the crusades, religious battles did not cease – Arabs and Barbary pirates kept fighting Christians in the sea. The Muslim ships and coasts were safe from Barbary pirates' attacks. The attacks on so-called 'faithless people' were a key motivator of Barbary pirates. They justified their piracy on 'faithless non-Muslims' by quoting from the Koran, saying that "*all the people who do not recognize the authority of the Koran are offenders, and thus it is our obligation to find the offenders and wage a war against them and hold them captives for making slaves.*" However, the infertile natural environment of the Barbary region in North Africa was a greater cause even than religious belief. For the people living on the coast of North Africa, surrounded by deserts, sea-borne trade was essential to their survival. But without strong infrastructure in place for sea-borne trade, they had no choice but to rely on piracy to get food and necessities for livelihood. They used plunder or traded and used the captives as slaves or sold them for ransom. Tributes paid to avoid plundering were also a principal income for Barbary pirates.

The historic event that had provoked Barbary pirates took place in 1492. As described earlier, Spain had completely driven the Muslims out of the Iberian Peninsula as a result of the '*Reconquista,*' when Christian Iberians fought and drove off the Muslim people who had lived and ruled there for 800 years. The Moors were expelled from their last base, Granada, to North Africa. Inflamed by thoughts of revenge, the Moors were soon engaged in a jihad against Christians and their ships.

Expansion to the Oceans

Barbary pirates, like the Vikings, expanded beyond their original base and took to the oceans. Starting in the 17th century, they were able to make long-distance voyages to the sea by sailing ships. Galleys powered by rowers were suitable only for voyages in the calm Mediterranean Sea. Although the Vikings had traveled by galleys across the oceans beyond the Strait of Gibraltar, known as 'the Pillars of Hercules,' galleys relying only on the power of rowers were not capable of sailing through the strong waves and harsh currents of the Atlantic Ocean. Since the advent of sailing ships, however, circumstances had totally changed. Sailing ships had much better seaworthiness in the harsh condition of the oceans, and their force as fighting vessels was greatly strengthened by broadside guns.

Barbary pirates were able to greatly expand their activities by using sailing ships. These days, the traces of Barbary pirates are found in the names of areas where they had attacked and the records that they captured hundreds of thousands of people as captives. Nearly all the coasts of Europe were subject to the attacks of Barbary pirates, called 'Razzias.' Barbary pirates attacked not only the coasts of Spain, Portugal, Italy, Greece, France and England but also the coasts of Iceland and Denmark, capturing residents and selling them into slavery. Thousands of ships from France, England and Spain became good prey for Barbary pirates. The residents of coastal areas moved inland, where they were safer from the threat of pirate attack. Only in the 19th century did these abandoned coastal areas begin to be repopulated – a fact that demonstrates the seriousness of the Barbary threat.

Alliance with Barbary Pirates

The Islamic states on the coast of North Africa had supported Barbary pirates since the 15th century. While Barbary pirates, loyal to the Ottoman Empire, were committing acts of piracy, they also fought for Muslim rulers during wars. In 1511, Spain occupied Algiers, capital of modern-day Algeria. Barbary pirates, expelled from their bases by Spanish forces, asked the sultan of the empire for an alliance. Sultan Selim Kan I, who regarded the offer as a good opportunity to gain control on the coast of North Africa, sent his troops and drove the Spanish forces out of Algeria.

In 1533, the sultan of the Ottoman Empire appointed Barbary pirate Barbarossa to be his admiral in chief and put him in charge of a large fleet in order to fight the mighty Spanish fleet. The next year, he conquered the whole of Tunisia for the Turks, Tunis itself becoming the base of piracy on the North African coast. The Holy Roman emperor Charles V led a crusade that captured Tunis and Goletta in 1535, but Barbarossa defeated Charles V's fleet at the Battle of Preveza in 1538. As a consequence, the eastern Mediterranean fell under the control of the Ottoman Empire for the next 33 years, until its defeat at the Battle of Lepanto in 1571. The sultan, in commemoration of Barbarossa's accomplishments for the Turks, accorded him the title of *Beylerbey* – the commander of commanders – and appointed him chief of the Mediterranean navy of Turks.

Barbary pirates had built very close ties with the lords of coastal cities on the coast of the southern Mediterranean, including Algiers, Tunis and Tripoli. The lords offered refuge and markets for trading slaves and prizes. In return, they shared the profits of pirates. The lords requested 10 percent of prizes and also fees for the use of their ports. The deals with pirates were quite a profitable business for the lords.

Despite enormous damage by Barbary pirates, European countries, however, had continued to pursue an appeasement policy. This might have happened because of the circumstances of Europe at the time. Between the 16th and 18th century, Europe had suffered civil wars, religious wars and wars with other regions, and thus could not concentrate on anti-piracy operations. Europeans decided that securing the safety of their people held captive by paying bribes or providing aid to Islamic states would be more pragmatic than spending tremendous costs for a massive expedition to wage a war against Barbary pirates.

As such, ships from small regions, such as Tuscany, Sardinia, Sicily and Venice, lacked the economic capability to negotiate with Barbary pirates and continued to fall prey to them.

On the other hand, some European powers instigated Barbary pirate attacks on the ships of their trade competitors or enemies. France, for example, actively used Barbary pirates to attack the regions of its traditional rival, Spain. England and the Netherlands also used Barbary pirates as diplomatic leverage against France. European countries sent their fleets to combat the pirates, but it was only for show. They never seriously intended to prevent piracy, and as a consequence, they never engaged in preemptive strikes during expeditions.

Slave Hunting

Barbary pirates were engaged in indiscriminate slave hunting, which was their most profitable business. The most preferred captives were white women that they could sell to the red-light district. Principally, Barbary pirates reserved their harshest treatment for non-Muslims, but Muslim women were also not safe from this profitable business. They did not care about the religion of captives, so long as they were profitable.

The Barbarossa brothers had held 4,000 people captive for slave-taking when they attacked Naples. The captives were sold at the slave market, together with 9,000 captives captured in Lipari Island, situated in the Tyrrhenian Sea. There was a notorious slave hunter, named Turkut, a friend of the Barbarossa brothers. He had held all 6,000 residents of Gozo Island, which belonged to Malta, and sold them out at the slave market. He also sold 4,000 captives that he had held in the coast of Spain. Other Barbary pirates were committed to slave hunting. In 1544, they attacked Vieste in southern Italy and held 7,000 residents captive. In 1558, Barbary pirates attacked Ciutadella of the Menorca Island, which belonged to the Balearic Islands, and totally destroyed the town and slaughtered nearly all the residents. The 3,000 survivors were taken to Istanbul. The Balearic Islands had been a hotspot for piracy. Under these circumstances, all the islanders of the Formentera (another Balearic island), beleaguered by pirates, ultimately abandoned their homes and escaped inland.

In 1627, Barbary pirates raided Iceland and ravaged its capital of Reykjavik. In the aftermath of the pirate attack, called the 'Raid of Turks,' 30 people were killed, and 400 people were held captive. The raid left a deep scar on the city. Shortly after the pirate attack, a law requiring that one should kill Turks when one encountered them was enacted in Iceland. In fact, although no one had been subject to the law, it continued to be in force for 350 years afterwards.

Barbary pirates did not discriminate in their slave-hunting targets. They recklessly captured people, irrespective of their social status or wealth. The people of rank or the wealthy were good for ransom, and others were good for the slave trade. The vast majority of captives were sold as rowers of pirate ships. Once they were sold as galley slaves, they were doomed to work as rowers until the end of their lives. If lucky, some were sold for gardener slaves. Women were picked as maids for the sultan or mistresses for nobles and were doomed to spend their lives in harems – domestic spaces that were reserved for the women of the house in a Muslim family and were inaccessible to adult males except for close relations. The number of captives held in slave hunting and brought to Morocco and Algeria was up to 1.5 million people. In the 16th century, the slave market in Algeria was the largest. The captives were first held in a prison in Algeria. A historic record tells that the prison had continuous custody of 20,000 captives. That number demonstrates how enormous the scale of slave-taking was at the time.

Barbary Pirates and Creation of the U.S. Navy

In the late 18th century, the United States of America had paid protection money to the lords of Islamic states in North Africa to prevent its nationals from being captured for slave-taking and to protect its emerging sea-borne trade. Most Americans appear not to have knowledge about this. This may be because the U.S. did not want to widely publicize this somewhat shameful fact. As a growing number of its merchant ships were subject to Barbary pirate attacks, the U.S. had to choose whether it should send an expedition fleet to combat the pirates or take a compromise policy. Since the U.S. at the initial stage of nation-building did not have the naval power to undertake an expedition, it had no choice but to opt for the latter.

In 1784, a year after the U.S. concluded its war of independence from Great Britain, Moroccan pirates seized a U.S. merchant ship. In the same year, two merchant ships were seized by Algerian pirates. The crew was taken inland and forced to build a fortress. Initially, the U.S. had taken a defensive stance toward pirates by either directing its merchant ships to follow the merchant ships of states that had paid tributes, or by paying tributes itself. However, U.S. merchant ships kept becoming the victims of piracy and the crews held captive were sold as slaves. By losing valuable goods, the U.S. suffered enormous damage from Barbary pirate attacks.

In the wake of the seizure of 12 U.S. merchant ships, the U.S. Congress concluded that it needed to demonstrate its determined resolve by deploying armed forces to troubled waters, including the Mediterranean Sea. On 27 March 1794, U.S. President George Washington signed a bill to create the U.S. Navy and to commission the building of six escort ships. The U.S. Navy had its roots in 1775 as the Continental Navy. But since the U.S. sold all its warships two years after it had won the American Revolutionary War, the U.S. Navy was virtually non-existent at the time.

In the midst of troubling pirate attacks, President Thomas Jefferson took more determined measures against pirates. He waged the Tripolitan War in the period between 1801 and 1805, while refusing to continue the payment of tribute to the rulers of North African Barbary states. Despite his opposition to the expenses of maintaining a navy, Jefferson dispatched an American naval squadron to Tripolitan waters. During the following years, American warships fought in the waters around Tripoli, blockading the Barbary coast. U.S. troops landed on the coast and attacked the cities of Barbary states. In 1804, a U.S. frigate on patrol was seized in the Tripoli harbor. In four months, the U.S. special squadron raided and set the captured frigate on fire to inflict financial damage on the pirates. The combination of a strong American naval blockade and an overland expedition from Egypt finally brought the war to a close, with a treaty of peace in 1805 that was favorable to the United States. The other Barbary rulers, though considerably chastened, continued to receive some tributes until 1816.

The war against pirates enabled the U.S. Navy to gain experience in the sea battle, leading to the U.S.'s victory in the Battle of New Orleans in 1815 as part of the War of 1812 between the U.S. and the Great Britain and their respective allies. Suspended because of the war with Great Britain, the war with Barbary pirates resumed when the U.S. fleet, composed of 10 warships, reappeared in the Mediterranean. In the second campaign, the U.S. defeated the pirates by swift maneuvering. The surrendered leader of the pirates signed a treaty recognizing the U.S. right of navigation and pledging no tribute-taking in return.

European states were encouraged by the U.S. resolute actions against pirates. U.S. success indicated that their compromising behaviors were not a right solution, although their enormous tribute sums had been justified at the time as necessary in the desperate effort to protect their ships.

In later years, Great Britain and France were determined to colonize Africa, and in 1830, France dispatched its troops to Algeria. A series of military campaigns terrified Barbary pirates and as a consequence, the pirates immediately surrendered upon the launch of military maneuvering. France ruled Algeria for 132 years and had annexed the Barbary coast itself in 1865. As European powers expanded to the Barbary coast, at last the long-dominant Barbary pirates came to an end in history.

Chapter 6

THE AGE OF DISCOVERY

Dawn of the Modern Age

The era between the fall of the Western Roman Empire in 476 and Christopher Columbus's voyage to the Americas in 1492 is commonly referred to as the Middle Ages. This thousand-year period is also widely described as the Dark Ages, and it can be thought of as a preparatory period to bring forth the flower of brilliant modern civilizations.

The branches of the Middle Ages flowered into three blossoms. First, it ushered in the Age of Discovery. The Iberian Peninsula first opened up the Age of Discovery, a move which turned it from a peripheral part of Europe into a powerful hub. Second, the Renaissance. The Renaissance, which originated in northern Italy, opened up Europe to more humanistic ways of thinking and pulled it away from Medieval conceptions of religion. Third, the Protestant Reformation. A combination of factors, including the upheavals brought on by the more humanistic thinking of the Renaissance, triggered the reformation. As a consequence, the religious unity of Medieval Europe collapsed, and thus modern Europe sought a new social order.

In the Age of Discovery, the paradigm of pirates shifted in accordance with the global trend. The salient change was that the hotspots of piracy shifted to the Atlantic and Indian oceans and the Caribbean Sea, following trade ships traveling to the New World. The traditional methods of piracy – attacking coastal areas for plunder and taking residents as slaves – shifted to attacks on merchant ships as they sailed across oceans, where they could be robbed of valuables and goods aboard.

The trade ships, fully loaded with treasures and goods extracted from the colonies, were good prey for pirates. Pirates in the Age of Discovery were, in some respects, the result of competition among European maritime powers to take to the sea. European maritime powers officially recognized that looting the ships of rival states was a way of overcoming the shortage of their own naval power. Under this entirely new set of circumstances, pirates needed to have large ships, experienced navigators and crewmen, and weapons and navigational aids to commit piracy on oceans. They also needed to amass enormous amounts of capital to acquire ships, crewmen and a wide array of navigational supplies. For this reason, pirates had to have very close ties with capitalists, and the scale of piracy grew into its own industry.

Pirates in the Age of Discovery are often depicted romantically, full of machismo and daring, in literature, dramas and movies. However, even though the Age of Discovery brought on new types of pirates and methods of piracy, the essential nature of the profession had not changed. The plundering of goods and use of brutal violence and slaughter were still constant. Pirates were the most dreaded enemy for mariners, as well as the largest common enemies for maritime powers that disturbed seaborne trade and challenged state power.

It is sometimes hard to make a clear-cut distinction among global historic trends in terms of time, space, cause and effect. This is because historic phenomena are a result of complicated interactions among various factors generated from different times and spaces. In the Middle Ages, when Ptolemy's earth-centric view of the universe had dominated, the advent of the Age of Discovery could not simply develop in a day. It was the result of multiple interactions of various factors that triggered the outbreak of the new era.

Before getting into pirates in the Age of Discovery, this chapter explores major global historic events and trends that greatly affected maritime history and the circumstances in which pirates appeared.

Fall of the Byzantine Empire

The Byzantine Empire was the longest-lived empire in history, existing for 1,123 years – from 330 when Constantine the Great built a new imperial capital in Constantinople to 1453 when the Eastern Roman Empire collapsed. On 29 May 1453, at last, the Eastern Roman Empire was forced to close its brilliant history when Constantinople was occupied by Mehmed II of the Ottoman Empire. The fall of the Byzantine Empire was a key event in the late Middle Ages, significantly influencing the history of Europe as well as the Age of Discovery and the history of pirates. With the conquest of Constantinople, the Turkish Empire began to strongly influence the Mediterranean Sea. Ottoman Turks threatened sea-borne trade, which had been under the control of Venice and Genoa. As these two cities declined, the hub of sea-borne trade shifted to the Iberian Peninsula.

While the rise of the Renaissance was dominating Western Europe, the conflicts between Christianity and Islam, the West and the East, had remained unchanged in Eastern Europe. However, these long-held conflicts were nearing an end. The Byzantine Empire had held a position of safeguarding Western Europe against the aggressions of the Islamic forces and Mongolian invaders. By the middle of the 15th century, the Byzantine Empire, whose territory had spanned from North Africa to the Balkan Peninsula to Turkey, shrank to only Constantinople and nearby regions. The gigantic empire had fallen to a tiny state, like a small Greek city-state.

In exploring the fall of Constantinople, the aggression of the Mongols is considered a distant cause. Following the conquest of China, Genghis Khan rapidly advanced to Central Asia and occupied Baghdad in 1206. Thereafter, he continued to expand to the West. The Ottoman Empire, threatened by the expansion of Mongols, moved its capital to Bursa, situated at the edge of Asia Minor. Bursa was opposite Constantinople over the Bosporus Strait and the Sea of Marmara.

fall of Constantinople

Constantine the Great had built Constantinople as the imperial capital of the Eastern Roman Empire. For this reason, Constantinople, which literally means "the city built by Constantine the Great," was named after him. Constantinople had kept its name for 1,600 years until the Turkish Republic moved the capital city to Ankara and changed it to Istanbul. Constantinople at its height was a metropolitan city with a population of one million, where trade was bustling and more than 70 different languages were spoken. Constantinople, situated at the crossroads of West and East, produced the brilliant Byzantine culture that intermingled Christianity, Islam, the West and the East throughout the rule of Greece, Rome and the Ottoman Turks.

In 1402, the Turks were utterly defeated by the Mongols, but they rebounded in 20 years. Ottoman Turks did not attempt to occupy the Byzantine Empire, whose territories were diminished to contain only Constantinople and the region around the imperial city. In the midst of precarious peace, the Byzantine Empire had lasted for more 30 years. However, the circumstances had totally changed as Mehmed II ascended to sultan of the Ottoman Empire at the age of 19. For a young and ambitious sultan, Constantinople was too great a prize to ignore. In April 1453, a year after his enthronement, he launched attacks on Constantinople.

Constantinople, situated on a triangle-shaped peninsula, was a natural fortress. On the east side, it was on the sea, called the Golden Horn. The Byzantines slung chains across the entrance to prevent invasions from the sea. On the landward side, it was protected by ramparts whose length was up to 22.5 kms. The ramparts, named the Walls of Constantine, were initially built by Constantine the Great, and the double lines of walls, known as the Theodosian Walls, were built by Emperor Theodosius II in the 5th century. Under these fortified defensive systems, it was extremely difficult for Turks to conquer Constantinople.

At the outset of the Turks' attack, before the siege of Constantinople began, the Turks had cast cannons to destroy the ramparts, but they did not work as intended. Then Mehmed II ordered construction of a road made of greased logs across Galata on the north side of the Golden Horn to bypass the chain barrier. The Ottoman troops dragged 72 ships over the hill directly into the Golden Horn. This seriously threatened the flow of supplies coming from the allies of the Byzantines. However, this extraordinary operation was not conclusive either, because the Byzantines had desperately resisted the attacks. Alternatively, the Ottomans sought to break through the walls by constructing underground tunnels. However, this attempt also failed, as the Byzantines had counter-attacked on the basis of prior intelligence. Following these inconclusive offensives, Mehmed II was determined to directly attack the walls, with a massive force of 80,000 troops. The Byzantine troops, including volunteers from throughout Europe, desperately resisted the offense of Turks. Ultimately, Constantinople fell because of the sheer dominating force of the Ottomans, 58 days after the launch of the battle.

Constantinople, which had been a beautiful and sacred place, described in the phrase 'God would have intended to live in the city,' turned into a living hell. Looting, arson, rape and slaughter were prevalent throughout the city. Terrified citizens came to the Hagia Sophia to pray for a last miracle that could save them. However, they were slaughtered by Ottoman soldiers that raided the cathedral. At last, the Byzantine Empire, with its brilliant, thousand-year history, came to an end.

Why did the city fall? Above all, the Byzantines indulged in abundance and comfort much as the late Roman Empire had done, and had been idle about issues of national defense. Since the early days of the empire, they had employed mercenaries to go to war for them. Even when their territory had shrunk to Constantinople and nearby regions and they had been besieged by enemies, their easygoing spirit remained unchanged. Of the 7,000 soldiers who had fought to the last battle, only 3,000 soldiers were themselves Byzantine, and the rest were merchants, volunteers and mercenaries from throughout Europe. The citizens remained divided even during Turks' invasion. They had been hostile to each other over integration with the Vatican. The religious sects in conflict had held separate services and only held an integrated service on the day before Christian Constantinople met its doom.

The Turkish Empire, which had risen to become the superpower of East Europe, occupied Egypt in the early 16th century, dreaming of the revival of the old Islamic Empire. Ottoman Turks occupied Hungary and threatened Vienna. In 1538, they defeated the allied fleets of Spain, Venice and the Vatican. The year 1453, when the war ended, was a watershed in the history of the world. The history of Europe shifted toward a more modern age through a long dark tunnel and shortly after, the Renaissance blossomed. With the rise of the Ottoman Empire, the geography of the world expanded and diversified. The trade routes that connected the Arabian Peninsula to other continents through the central Mediterranean were blocked. As such, Western Europe was engaged in the exploration of new trade routes outside the Mediterranean, leading to the era of geographic discoveries.

Mongol Invasions and Conquests

Following the unification of the nomadic tribes of Northeast Asia in 1206, Genghis Khan conquered all of China and further advanced to Eastern Europe. Mongols had conquered a vaster territory in the shortest period of any other conquerors throughout history. During the 36 years after unifying the Mongol tribes, Genghis Khan and his descendants conquered more territories than those that the Roman Empire had occupied for 400 years. This resulted in the vast Mongol Empire, which by 1300 covered much of Asia and Eastern Europe. The territories that the Mongols conquered were equivalent to modern Africa, encompassing 30 states and 3 billion people on the modern world map. The Mongol troops were no more than 100,000, drafted from Mongol tribes.

There are various views about which forces drove a nomadic tribe to build a vast empire. Among them, the outstanding leadership of Genghis Khan was likely to be most highlighted. He unified nomadic tribes into a kingdom and constructed a unified command chain by organizing people into separate units of ten, a hundred, a thousand and ten thousand. However, his capability alone appears to fall short of explaining the foundation of the vast Mongol Empire. This is because even though Genghis Khan had laid the foundation of the Mongol Empire, the vast territories were mostly achieved by his descendants after his death.

The Mongols took advantage of their swift mobility to the greatest extent. They built stations, called 'Jam' in Mongol, along occupied regions. The stations enabled Mongol troops to communicate swiftly with the homeland. The stations were built on the major roads every 40 to 50 km, with 400 horses at each station.

Mongol troops were composed of only cavalries. The enemies' troops, mostly infantries, were not able to compete with the Mongol troops' rapid mobility. Mongol troops moved at a maximum speed of 130 km a day – speed was their strongest weapon. They largely relied on surprise attacks to overcome the disadvantage of inferior troop numbers. Their swift mobility was possible because they did not carry a lengthy supply line with them. While they were moving, they lived off the milk and the meat of stolen livestock. The records of Marco Palo, an Italian merchant born in Venice who had traveled throughout China, tell that Mongol soldiers were able to move without making food for 10 days. They drank the blood of horses and had a lump of dried milk for meals. They carried dried meats on horseback, and they had raw meats fermented under the saddle.

In addition, Mongol troops were equipped with light armor, which weighed 7 to 8 kilograms and made them much more agile in horseback battles than European knights' 70-kilogram armor. European horses, weaker in endurance, were easily exhausted from carrying heavy knights on their backs. However, the foremost distinction might be that the battles were between nomads who had nothing to lose and people under the opposite circumstance. The outcome of the battles would have been decided at the outset.

The Mongol Empire and the Amalgamation of Civilizations

The most prominent legacy of Mongol conquests might be that they connected and amalgamated civilizations which had remained isolated over centuries. As a result, they had created a new civilization and global order. This is the reason why Mongol conquests deserve exploration to provide context for the Age of Discovery.

Around the year 1162, when Genghis Khan was born, the world was composed of numerous regional civilizations. They had no the knowledge of other civilizations, only direct neighbors. China did not know about Europe, and Europe did not know about China. Only Muslim merchants between China and Europe had been engaged in trade with them. The trade network connecting these three civilizations to each other had yet to be built.

Europe at the time was left much behind China and the Islamic states in terms of civilization, science and technology. In Christian Europe, science and technology which explore the relationship between cause and effect, and elevate analytical thinking, could not develop. The massive destruction and brutality that Mongol troops committed during invasions and conquests were sufficient to provoke the fear of Asians among

Europeans. With the spread of advanced science and technology developed in Islamic regions – including printing, the compass, firearms and the abacus – by Mongols to Europe through the stations, trade had totally expanded. The barrier between China, Islam and Europe naturally collapsed by virtue of the Mongols' activities. The new science and technology, knowledge and commercial wealth had awakened a sleeping Europe, and served as a driving force for the Renaissance. The Renaissance changed every aspect of European life.

History, in a sense, is the result of ironies. Paradoxically, the destroyer of civilizations often laid a foundation among the ashes for the emergence of a new civilization. It can be said that in the modern European civilization that blossomed afterward, capitalism was the result of invasions and destructions of Mongols.

The Maritime Silk Road

The emergence of the Mongol Empire was credited with booming trade through the maritime silk road, and, in a large part, the opening of the Age of Discovery. Mongols, who had been nomads, paid attention to the benefits of the sea. Following the conquest of the Nan-Song Dynasty, they had become deeply interested in sea-borne trade since they witnessed vast incomes that merchants earned from maritime trading. Mongols, who had difficulty in transporting goods throughout the vast empire, came to recognize that shipping is much more efficient than land transport in many respects.

Mongols learned ship-building skills from the invasions of Japan and Java. Shortly after the failure of these expeditions, they began to use the knowledge they learned from these invasions to bolster their commercial activities. Above all, the diversification of trade goods and trade expansion served as the essential factors that attracted Mongols to the sea. A camel was able to carry no more than 300 kilograms of goods, and thus the amount of goods that a caravan was able to transport was very limited, even with numerous camels.

Kublai Khan, a founder of the Yuan Dynasty, encouraged the building of large ships suitable for carrying massive amounts of goods, as well as ports to accommodate those ships. Mongols were committed to developing essential navigational aids, such as the compass and more accurate hydrographical charts. Mongols employed Arabs, also known as 'color-eyed people,' who had the highest level of navigational skills, to address the shortage of their own navigational skills. The color-eyed people generally referred to the blue-eyed Arab merchants that had migrated to China since the Tang Dynasty and had been engaged in trade.

By virtue of Mongols' efforts, sea trade routes were explored that spanned from Quanzhou in southern China to Java, Ceylon and Malacca in Southeast Asia, and via Indian ports, to Hormuz in the Persian Gulf. It was the maritime silk road that connected the Far East with the Middle East. While traveling along the maritime silk road, Mongols could bring sugar, ivory, pepper and cotton – products that were not attainable in their territories – from ports in Vietnam, Java, Ceylon and India. They were regularly involved in trading more diverse goods with Arabia, Egypt and Somalia. Mongols encouraged vassals in southern China to migrate to foreign ports and build trade networks in an effort to expand trade to the regions in which their rule was out of reach. During the reign of the Mongols, tens of thousands of Chinese migrated to the coasts of Vietnam, Cambodia, the Malaysian Peninsula, Borneo, Java and Sumatra and built and settled in regional communities.

Mongols also highly regarded domestic trade. Most Chinese dynasties had traditionally discouraged the activities of commerce. Confucian bureaucrats regarded offering goods to foreign countries for trade as paying a tribute. Contrary to the Chinese, who considered merchants to be of low social status, only a step higher than gangs, Mongols treated them as second only to the highest class, bureaucrats. On the other hand, they treated Confucians as the ninth highest class – a social class higher than beggars, but lower than prostitutes.

Goods from the Orient arrived at the coastal areas of the Black Sea or the Mediterranean by the land silk road or in Alexandria by the maritime silk road. Oriental goods, such as ceramics and peppers were collected by merchants from Venice and Genoa. They were sold to Western Europe through either the Alps or the Strait of Gibraltar of the Iberian Peninsula. Commercial cities in Western Europe were created along the trade routes, and the coastal cities that served as trade hubs vastly prospered.

Oriental Goods

Since the middle of the 14th century, Italian coastal cities like Venice and Genoa, which had prospered by the trade of Oriental goods to Europe, had undergone many challenges. The goods brought from the Orient were greatly reduced due to the Ming Dynasty's ban on sea-going and the collapse of trade bases throughout the East China Sea and the Indian Ocean, in the aftermath of the fall of the Yuan Dynasty. Another reason was a trade blockade by the Timor Empire, which established control on Central Asia, and the Ottoman Empire which ruled Eastern Europe.

As a consequence, the prices of Oriental goods in Europe soared. This was because the most important trade goods – spices – were transported by Arabic merchants to Mediterranean cities like Alexandria, and directly traded to merchants in Venice or Genoa. Spices traded through these routes were sold to European consumers at 30 times or at a maximum 80 times higher than original prices. Europeans, who had grown accustomed to the taste of Oriental goods, were desperate to have them. Spices such as pepper, ginger, cinnamon, clove and nutmeg enabled Europeans, to store meats longer, remove the smell of fats in stored meats, and add to the flavor. The most popular spice was surely pepper. Pepper was used not only for seasoning but also as a digestive aid and pain-killer. In Medieval Europe, dowry, tax and rent were occasionally paid by pepper. Due to great demand for pepper, it was said that if only one ship out of six ships carrying spices came back safely, it was profitable. Europeans' exploration of new trade routes were said to be a result of the zeal for spices and adventure.

The European goods to trade in exchange for spices were simply wooden stuff and hemp cloth. Thereafter, silver became a means of payment for costly goods from the Orient, and the exchange of silver for spices between Venetian and Genoese merchants and Arabian merchants took root. Such an exchange system led to the prosperity of southern Germany, which had massive mining fields. The silver and spices exchange system triggered Europeans to open up an era of Atlantic voyaging. Initially, Oriental goods had been largely luxuries for nobles. As Oriental goods became necessities for commoners, demand for them soared. Accordingly, the need for the exploration of new trade routes with the Orient grew to meet the demands, so Oriental goods could be more cheaply and safely supplied.

Chapter 7

THE RISE OF THE IBERIAN PENINSULA

Iberians: Main Initiators of the Age of Discovery

The Iberians, who had been in the outer edge of Europe, by no means missed an opportunity to explore new trade routes to the Orient. Geographically, the Iberian Peninsula has open access to the Atlantic. Situated on the boundary of the Atlantic and the Mediterranean, the Iberian Peninsula could take geographical and commercial advantage of transit trade between the Orient and Europe.

The Iberians boldly rode the back of fate – when fate approached, they grabbed it by the bridle and held on, rushing forward. That is, they created their new destiny of becoming the main player of the Age of Discovery. As a result, the Iberians could emerge as the main players of the new Oriental trade, taking the place of Venice and Genoa, which had dominated Oriental trade through the Mediterranean. Indeed, the pioneers in creating the new destiny were the Portuguese. A new era often gives birth to new heroes. But, sometimes it's the pioneers who have special insight into the trends of an era that are the ones who are best able to create a new era.

Prince Henry the Navigator (1394–1460) of Portugal was the right figure at the right time. He was full of passion for new knowledge and the exploration of the unknown world. While serving as governor of Ceuta, which had been conquered by his father, Prince Henry sponsored Portuguese explorations. At the age of 25, he returned to Portugal and opened a school of navigators, ship builders, astronomers, cartographers, craftsmen and explorers in Sagres, situated in the southwestern part of Portugal. He collected a variety of travel books, maps and navigation materials. The international community for information, knowledge and creation was founded in Sagres. The Sagres school would play a pivotal role in the expansion of Portugal, along with Lisbon.

The navigation school was made possible because the Portuguese had developed a spirit of tolerance toward different religions, cultures and races during the rule of Arabs over previous centuries. Their open-mindedness allowed them to learn about the knowledge and technology of Arabs and to employ Arab scholars without hesitation. They made use of the wealth and knowledge of Jews as well, and on the basis of this openness, the Portuguese were successful at creating a cocktail of civilizations that mingled Christianity with Islam and Judaism.

At the age of 26, Prince Henry was appointed Grand Master of the Military Order of Christ. This had a significant implication in the history of Portuguese expansions. He became a key figure for the explorations of the Atlantic because he was able to use the human and material resources of the Military Order of Christ, sponsored by the pope. The Military Order of Christ, as with other religious organizations, established a well-organized chain of command. As he deftly exercised his power, he was able to mobilize the resources necessary for the exploration of the Atlantic, while fighting opposition voices that claimed the voyages were reckless and unprofitable.

The pope promised that he would regard the expeditions of the Portuguese Military Order of Christ as crusades and grant an indulgence to those partaking in the expeditions. With the support of the pope, who held the ultimate authority in Christendom, Prince Henry justified the expeditions by saying that they were businesses to convert pagans to Christianity.

Sagres School

Jewel of Iberia: Caravel

In order for the Iberians to take to the Atlantic, new ships suitable for ocean-going navigation, durable enough to withstand strong waves and harsh sea conditions, were required. The traditional galleons with masts with a triangular sail, primarily powered by rowers, could not sail across oceans. As such, ocean-going sailing required sailing ships which could use the winds. In early expeditions sponsored by Prince Henry, small sailing ships, referred to as barques, with three or more square-rigged masts, were commonly used. However, the barque had a decisive drawback: It was not suitable for sailing windward. The new type of ship, the caravel, also known as the 'Jewel of Iberia,' was developed by the ship builders in Sagres to address the drawback. The caravel was the product of efforts made by Prince Henry that combined the rigging of Viking ships with Muslims' ships. The early caravels, which had two square-rigged masts, were highly maneuverable in sailing windward. As voyages grew longer, caravels with three masts became common. The salient feature of the caravel was its central steering gear, which allowed crewmen to steer in a pilot house and greatly improved maneuverability. The attachment of central steering gear was somewhat like the fins of fish.

With ocean-going sailing increasing, caravels, originally developed for sailing inshore, demonstrated their limitations in voyages across oceans. Thus the square-rigged caravel, known as *caravela redonda*, was newly created by the Portuguese in the second half of the 15th century. The *caravela redonda* was larger in size than the caravel. To improve its ability to withstand ocean-going voyages, its foremast was square-rigged, and the main and stern masts were lateen-rigged (triangular sail). A triangular sail allowed a ship to tack against the wind. The lateen evolved out of the dominant square rig by setting the sails more fore-and-aft – along the line of the keel, while tailoring the luff and leech. Indeed, the evolution of the *caravela redonda* was a great revolution in shipbuilding history in that it connected the Atlantic world together and made the Age of Discovery possible.

Caravela Redonda

Guns had been mounted on the decks of ships since the 14th century. However, the improvements of the guns starting in the mid-14th century considerably increased their weight, forcing ships to mount them low on the hull for stability. A gun port – an opening in the side of the hull of a ship – above the water-line, allowed the muzzle of artillery pieces mounted on the gun deck to fire outside. Ships featuring gun ports were said to be pierced, since the ports were cut through the hull after the construction. Piercing gun ports had grown into a common practice by 1501. As a result, a heavier armament for large ships was possible. Even with more cannons in the hull, the stability and maneuverability of a ship were better than if cannons had been mounted on the deck. A musket, which was a muzzle-loaded, smoothbore long gun, capable of penetrating heavy armor, was developed in Sagres. Caravels, cannons mounted in the hull and muskets were new forces that ushered in the Age of Discovery.

Searching for the Golden State

For ocean-going sailing, navigational aids such as the compass and quadrant were essential. Prince Henry instructed the leading engineers, invited from Italy, to devise navigational aids. He also employed experienced Italian sailors. While Prince Henry had ruled Ceuta, he learned of an interesting story about Africa. It was about the legendary Christian empire that the priest king Prester John had built as well as the Golden State that was presumed to be situated somewhere south of the empire. Prince Henry, motivated by religious passion and economic gains as well, sent expeditions to the coast of West Africa, upon the completion of preparations for voyages.

Allegedly, he was greatly influenced by *The Travels of Marco Polo*, a book that recorded Marco Polo's travel to China and other Asian countries. As described previously, Marco Polo, an Italian merchant born in Venice, traveled to China with his father and met Kublai Khan for the first time in 1269. A year later, he embarked on another journey to Asia. He returned after 17 years in Asia to find Venice at war with Genoa. Marco Polo was imprisoned in Genoa and dictated his stories to a cellmate. Coincidentally, Marco Polo's book described Prester John and a small island country in Asia, covered with gold and also known as 'Zipangu' (Japan) or 'the Land of Gold.' This might indicate that the zeal for searching for gold was a principal motivation that spurred Prince Henry to engage in voyages across the Atlantic.

Prince Henry the Navigator and Sinbad the Sailor

We run across an interesting story about the Arab scholars who worked for Prince Henry. We can find that the Portuguese explorations of new trade routes were closely related to the tales of Sinbad. The tales of Sinbad are a late addition to the compilation of Arabic folk tales called 'One Thousand and One Nights.' After Sinbad misspent his inheritance, he went to the sea to rebuild his fortune. During his seven voyages throughout the seas east of Africa and south of Asia, Sinbad had fantastic adventures in magical places, meeting monsters and encountering supernatural phenomena. Sinbad ventured out to the Gulf of Persia, the Gulf of Bengal and the South China Sea. On his seven voyages, he visited many cities along the Malabar Coast and traded in Sri Lanka, traveling to ports in Sumatra, the Malacca Peninsula and Singapore. Sinbad advanced further to Guangdong, China, using seasonal winds called 'southwesters.'

The tales of Sinbad formed a kind of logbook that went beyond simple legendary tales. They were a record of marine observations. The tales included lessons about people in the unknown world, the implications of winds and weather in various waters, warnings of pirates and dangerous waters, navigational skills and information, statements on navigation route selection, advice on the practices of ports. The vivid information contained in the tales would be analyzed by scholars in Sagres and were extremely useful to Prince Henry, who intended to travel to the same regions.

The tales explain that Sinbad was from Baghdad, but he was possibly from Suhar, Oman. I have had a chance to read an interview article by the vice minister of the Ministry of Tourism of Oman, made during her visit to the 2013 *Yeousu Expo*, held in Korea. While stressing that Oman and its capital city of Muscat were chosen as one of the ultimate bucket-list items by *National Geographic*, she also claimed that the tales of Sinbad were about a sailor as well as explorer who had existed in Oman.

Oman is situated on the southwest coast of the Arabian Peninsula, with ports of Muscat, Sur and Suhar, along the lengthy coast, which had been open to the world since ancient times. Ships traveling from the Persian Gulf, Egypt and Africa to India and Asia, called in those ports. Given that Suhar was called the 'Gateway to China' and 'the Asian Department Store,' I assume that it is highly possible that the tales of Sinbad originated in Oman.

Voyages beyond Cape Bojador

Cape Bojador was considered by Europeans to be the frontier of the world over a thousand years. Cape Bojador is a headland on the northern coast of West Sahara. The cliff is 20 meters high and was formed by several tall sand dunes projected into the sea. A rocky shoal and patch widely extend into the sea to the north and west of the cape. Arabs called the cape 'Abu Khatar,' meaning the 'father of danger,' due to the risk of sailing over the rocky spots under the sea.

Beyond the cape, Europeans believed that there was boiling water and the Green Sea of Darkness. Mariners were fearful of taking to the coast of West Africa south of the Iberian Peninsula because they believed that nobody would return home around Cape Bojador. Indeed, no sailor had survived sailing beyond the cape since the navigation of Phoenician galleons. Ultimately, the myth was broken by the Portuguese mariner Gil Eanes, who first discovered a passable route around Cape Bojador in 1434. His expedition beyond the cape was considered a major breakthrough for European explorers and traders en route to Africa and later to India. Today, Christopher Columbus is commonly referred to as an initiator of the Age of Discovery. However, it seems that people do not much know about Eanes's expedition, which was a prelude to the Age of Discovery. In the 15th century, Eanes and Cape Bojador were more highly regarded than Columbus and India because at the time sailing beyond the cape was recognized to be a bolder and more valuable deed for mariners than navigating across the Atlantic. Following Eanes's exploration of Cape Bojador, Portuguese expeditions ensued. They sailed along the coast of West Africa and went further to the Cape of Good Hope and ultimately they took to India after sailing around it.

Prince Henry planned and arranged the expeditions in Sagres. The expeditions required vast expenses. He spent his personal assets at first for the expeditions and later was financed by the Military Order of Christ as he became its Grand Master. In the period from 1419 through 1433, he had sent more than 40 expeditions. He firmly believed that he could find enormous treasures by sailing south. The barrier to his expeditions was definitely Cape Bojador. Despite persistent attempts, no sailors were successful in taking to the south after sailing around Cape Bojador. Some captains who led his expeditions feared to sail southward and thus took to the west. They ran across many islands in the Atlantic, such as Madeira and the Azores. The discovery of those islands was considered a poor accomplishment at the time. Thereafter, they were used for midway bases of voyages across the Atlantic.

In 1433, when Prince Henry almost ran out of patience in the midst of continued failures, he picked Eanes as a captain of his new expedition. Among all captains, Eanes had a reputation for being the most capable and loyal. He was ordered to advance a few miles beyond Cape Bojador. He failed in his first attempt, as many previous captains had. He tried again under the orders of Prince Henry, with the same ships used in the first attempt, that had to sail south beyond Cape Bojador. In late May 1434, Eanes embarked on a voyage toward the south of West Africa again.

The type of ship that Eanes sailed was a barque, a prototype of a caravel. The ship had a gross tonnage of 55, with two masts. It was greater than 18 meters in length and no greater than 6 meters in width. The freeboard, which means the distance from the waterline to the upper deck level, was no fewer than 1.5 meters. The ship was suitable for inshore sailing. Ten days after departure from Sagres, the Fuerteventura Island, situated east of the Canary Islands, appeared. The sailors were dismayed to believe that they would shortly get to the frontier of the world. The sailors feared that there would be a sea monster preying on ships, and that the sun was hot enough to boil the ocean, and people would be burned to death. When they arrived in the shallow water where the water appeared to be boiling, the ship began to roll. The extremely terrified sailors gathered at the bow and began to make the sign of the cross. They witnessed water boiling under the keel, like white milk. They begged that they should return. Instead of sailing back, however, Eanes ordered the sailors to put down an empty wine barrel into the water and fill the barrel with water and pick it up. Then, he put his hands into the water and ordered the sailors to do the same. Eanes shouted that "Just like the sea on the coast of Algarve, water here is not boiling. It is simply the white bubbles made when the waves break after crashing into the cliff on the coast." Eventually, the sailors were soothed.

However, the sailors' calm did not last long. A sailor responsible for measuring the depth of the sea reported that it was fewer than three meters. At this juncture, Eanes made a historic decision which led to the Age of Discovery. He changed the navigation course to the west, rather than continuing to sail inshore. Then, he sailed all day long until the coast was not visible. Around the daybreak, after sailing to the west all night, he sailed toward the south again. He slowly proceeded at the angle of 60 degrees, sailing windward. The sight of a new coast appeared. The sailors gathered at the bow, looking fearfully at an unfamiliar coast. The land stretched southward, far away. The coastal area had sands that were flat and shining in the sunshine. There was no headland on the coast. The sailors finally realized that they had passed through the frontier that they believed they would never cross. At last, they had sailed beyond Cape Bojador.

The Opening of African Trade Routes

In the summer of 1434, the myth had crumbled. For the Europeans who believed that the world ended at the underwater reef of Cape Bojador, it took more than a thousand years for them to travel merely 1.6 kilometers farther from the coast of West Africa. Eanes's expedition laid a foundation for Portuguese voyages to the south of West Africa.

Thereafter, Prince Henry sent several more expeditions. In 1444, a sailing ship that Prince Henry had sent came back with gold dust and Africans aboard from 480 kilometers past Cape Bojador. This addressed to a certain degree Prince Henry's lack of financial gains from his many sailing expeditions, but it marked the beginning of slave trade, which remains a disgrace in the history of the Atlantic. The slave trade, prior to spice trade, was a lucrative business generated from the exploration of African trade routes. In 1445, a caravel of Prince Henry arrived at the Cape Verde Islands, situated in the westernmost end of Africa. Active trades took place on the coast of Guinea there. Portuguese merchants traded their firearms, dyed linens and cottons, clothes, necklaces, mirrors and steel goods with slaves brought by the regional leaders. In 1450, 25 of Prince Henry's ships came back fully loaded with slaves and goods. At last, Prince Henry's long-held investments were rewarded. With the discovery of the Cape Verde Islands, Prince Henry made hydrographical charts based on his findings. The discovery of Madeira and the Azores, and their subsequent use as a midway supply base were an unexpected gain for Prince Henry.

After Prince Henry died in 1460, King Alfonso granted Ferdinando Gomez the right to explore 100 leagues (equivalent to 550 km) each year. However, the king decided to directly take control of the explorations to realize vast incomes generated from the business. John II, who succeeded King Alfonso, was no less an explorer than Prince Henry himself. As Prince Henry had done, John II sent expeditions out several times around the south of Africa. Thereafter, the discovery of the Cape of Good Hope by Bartolomeu Dias in 1488 made it much easier for the Portuguese to take to the Indian Ocean.

Competition of Iberians for Ocean-Going

The Iberians took to the Atlantic Ocean while France and England were engaged in the Hundred Years War (1337–1453) over control of Western Europe. After the death of Prince Henry, the Portuguese accelerated their efforts to get to the Atlantic. John II, following his grandfather Prince Henry, continued to support exploration of the Atlantic. In 1488, Bartolomeu Dias, instructed by John II, discovered the Cape of Good Hope in southernmost

Africa. In the stormy weather, which had lasted 13 days, they passed around the southernmost part of Africa, while not knowing their whereabouts. Dias named it *Cabo das Tormentas,* meaning 'Cape of Storms.' However, John II was reluctant to use the name because of its sinister meaning and thus ordered it changed to the Cape of Good Hope, signifying that the discovery marked a new starting point to explore trade routes to India.

In 1498, Vasco da Gama arrived at Calicut (modern Kozhikode), southwest of India, sailing around the Cape of Good Hope. The Portuguese exploration of the trade route to India was in the aftermath of Columbus's Spanish-sponsored voyage to the New World a few years prior. Vasco da Gama sailed safely across the Indian Ocean, with assistance from the Muslim navigator Ahmad Bin Madjid off Malindi, Kenya, and arrived in Calicut in May 1498. Vasco da Gama visited many ports on the west coast of India, gained spices by barter and retuned to Lisbon the following September after departing from India in October.

Out of his expedition, composed of four ships and 170 sailors, only two ships and 55 sailors came back home due to diseases such as cholera and fever. Despite a large loss of life and harsh voyages, the Oriental trade would certainly bring tremendous economic wealth. The spices brought to Lisbon turned out to be 60 times more profitable than the expense of the voyages. Apart from the profits gained from the voyages, Vasco da Gama and his sailors were acclaimed by the Portuguese for their efforts to explore the trade route to India. The information on the trade route that Vasco da Gama had explored had been classified highly confidential.

As the Portuguese fleet continued to sail toward India, seaborne trade expanded, and as a consequence, disputes with Muslim merchants over commercial rights also intensified. When Vasco da Gama went to India with the fleet of 15 ships in 1502, he was attacked by a combined fleet of Muslims and Hindus. The Portuguese forces that defeated them established trade bases in Goa, Cochin and Cannanore, and dominated trade with India. Thereafter, the Portuguese, centered in Goa, exclusively controlled sea-borne trade for 150 years.

The exploration of the trade route to India by Vasco da Gama had an enormous impact on Europeans' expansion to the East. His exploration allowed the West and the East, engaged in indirect trade by land, to trade directly with each other by ship. The prices of European goods plunged as Oriental goods flowed in enormous volume. This greatly changed the daily and economic life of Europeans, becoming a trigger of the commercial revolution to come. Europeans, who began to learn about the weak military power of the East, began to conquer many regions by using their dominant forces armed with cannons and firearms. In the early 16th century, the Portuguese occupied the regions of Hormuz, Goa, Malacca and Timor.

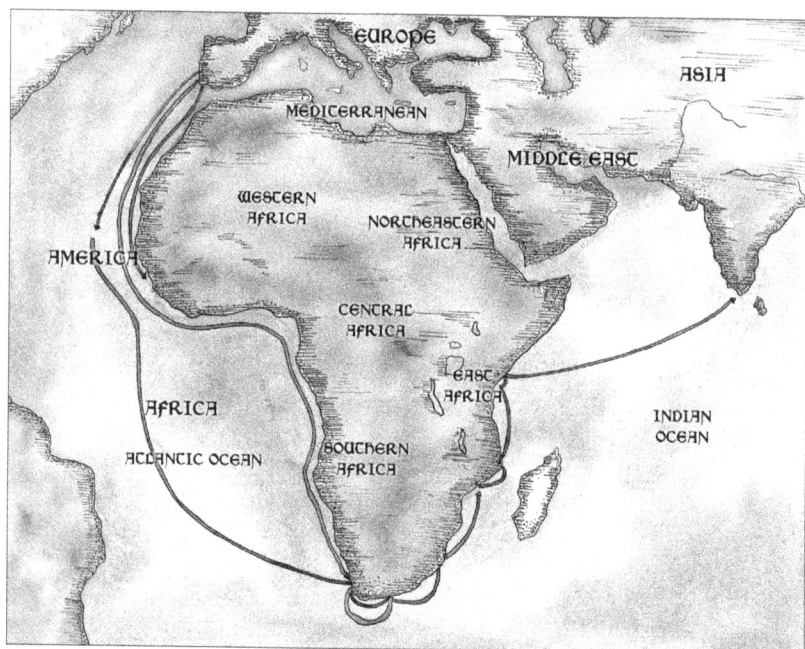

New Trade Routes Explored by Iberians

Portuguese Expansion to Asia

The Portuguese, armed with Christianity, cannons and muskets, advanced to the Far East, following back the expedition routes that Zheng He had explored during the early Ming Dynasty. After a captain named Pinto led a Portuguese expedition to Macao, China for the first time in 1513, the Portuguese landed in Tanegashima (種子島), an island belonging to Kagoshima Prefecture, Japan, in 1543. The Portuguese there handed over two muskets to the Japanese. For this historical background, the early type of Japanese musket was called *tanegashima* or *hinawaju* (火繩銃). The Japanese produced more than 600 muskets less than six months after the acquisition of these muskets from the Portuguese. None would expect that the two muskets would bring about a revolutionary change to armed forces throughout Asia. Tanegashima was used by the samurai class and their foot soldiers (*ashigaru*) and within a few years the introduction of the *tanegashima* in battle changed the way that war was fought in Japan forever. Among powerful *daimyos* (大名), a feudal ruler subordinate to the shogun (將軍), in the Senkoku period(戰國時代, 1467–1603), during which powerful feudal lords fought against each other over control of Japan, Oda Nobunaga was the initiator of the use of muskets in battle. He devised a way of consecutive firing where after soldiers in the front row fired, soldiers in the back row fired while the front row soldiers reloaded. In the Battle of Nagashino in May 1575, he saw success by using his firing method. Under the direction of Oda Nobunaga, the shooters stood up in 23 rows and began to fire row by row, allowing the soldiers to fire a thousand bullets every 20 seconds. The battle was regarded as a historic turning point that changed warfare during the Senkoku period. When Japan invaded the Chosun Dynasty (on what is now the Korean Peninsula) in 1592, the muskets were used as the main firearms of Japanese soldiers.

Oriental trade became the core of the Portuguese economy in the 16th century. The Portuguese court, which enjoyed enormous income generated by the Oriental trade through the trade route to India, justified it as 'God's Business.'

Spanish Ocean-Going

Spurred by the Portuguese exploration of trade routes to India and the wealth they gained by the exclusive control of Oriental trade, the Spanish joined the rush for the exploration of new trade routes. This coincided with the period when Spain completely drove Muslims out of the Iberian Peninsula in the name of '*Reconquista*.' The Spanish were afraid that if Spain, a latecomer in the explorations, followed the Portuguese trade route to India, it would remain behind Portugal. Spain, which did not intend to provoke Portugal either, opted to explore the Atlantic – a tactic that Portugal had not attempted.

It was Christopher Columbus, an Italian explorer and navigator born in Genoa, that made it possible. Thanks to Columbus, Spain was able to catch up with the front-runner Portugal in terms of the exploration of new trade routes. On the basis of the information on African expeditions and his belief that the Earth is round, Columbus concluded during his stay in Portugal that sailing west would be a quicker way to reach the Indies. In the years of 1484 and 1488, he presented his plan to John II of Portugal to request his sponsorship for the Atlantic expedition. John II, inflated by Dias's discovery of the Cape of Good Hope, rejected the Columbus's proposal because Portugal was only interested in an eastern trade route around the Cape of Good Hope.

Columbus turned his eyes to the Spanish crown. After continued lobbying at the Spanish court and two years of negotiations, Columbus was finally successful in January 1492 in having financial support from the Spanish crown. King Ferdinand and Queen Isabella had just conquered Granada, the last Muslim stronghold on the Iberian Peninsula. On the evening of 3 August 1492, Columbus departed from Palos de la Frontera with three ships: a larger carrack, the *Santa María,* and two smaller caravels, the *Pinta* and the *Nina.*

The voyage went smoothly. Columbus arrived at an island 69 days after departure. Columbus called the island (in what is now the Bahamas) *San Salvador,* meaning *Holy Savior,* to express gratitude for safe arrival. Following the first voyage, he made three more voyages and built a base on modern-day Haiti and explored the West Indies and the coasts of Jamaica, Puerto Rico, Panama and Honduras. Columbus always insisted, in the face of mounting counter-evidence, that the lands where he visited were part of the Asian continent, as previously described by Marco Polo and other European travelers. Columbus refused to accept that the lands he had visited and claimed for Spain were not part of Asia.

Why did he firmly believe that the lands he had visited were the Indies? The most convincing answer might be found in his wrong nautical count. He vastly underestimated the distance to East Asia from Europe. He estimated that the western route to India from Europe would be 8,000 kilometers shorter than the route around Africa and the distance from the Canary Islands to Japan would be 2,400 nautical miles. He also needed to believe that his voyages, sponsored by the Spanish crown, were successful. Whatever the reason, he firmly believed until he died that the lands he had visited were the Indies. The Italian explorer Amerigo Vespucci found later that the lands Columbus had visited were not the Indies, but an entirely new continent. The American continent was named after him.

Geographical Re-Discovery

Encountering claims contrary to commonly known historical facts can be an embarrassing thing. However, our understanding of history extends by rediscovering evidence and records. There are convincing claims that the lands that great explorers such as Columbus, Dias, and da Gama had reached were actually a 'rediscovery,' and that others had in fact reached these lands hundreds of years before. German author Bernhard Kay in his book *Navigation History* tells some amazing stories of navigation and exploration of the unknown world. Two thousand years prior to Bartolomeu Dias' voyage, the Phoenicians sailed around the Cape of Good Hope from the east to the west. The Irish priest Saint Brendan was the first European who had visited the American continent around 570. His exploration was first described in the book *Voyage of Saint Brendan the Abbot*. His journey was said to be inspired by religious passion to search for the Garden of Eden. He set out on the Atlantic Ocean with 16 monks. From the descriptions of geography of their arrival, they are presumed to have arrived somewhere around the Chesapeake Bay and visited the Ohio River over the Appalachian Mountains. It was alleged that the Vikings who arrived in the new continent somewhere between the 10th and the 11th century discovered traces of the Irish. The exploration of the trade route to India by Vasco da Gama is said to be not the first venture. Around the 1st century B.C., 1,400 years prior to his exploration, the route to India was said to be explored by unknown sailors. It is alleged that there existed a regular voyage shuttling between the Mediterranean and the Orient. It is hard to imagine, but it is alleged that 120 ships had shuttled the route annually.

In the absence of hydrographical charts, the logbooks that previous navigators recorded were essential for the safety of navigation. The Eritrean logbook served as an accurate and detailed navigational guidebook for navigation from the Red Sea to the Indian Ocean. By 60, the logbook was recorded by the Berenice (modern Benghazi) merchants. The logbook tells that merchants in the 1st century traveled in August to India from

Africa. They sailed aboard ship of 750 tonnage, which could load a large amount of goods. They sailed toward India using the southwest monsoon in the late summer. In India, the merchants traded goods along the coasts. If all these things are true, our perception of navigational history should be greatly enhanced.

Treaty of Tordesillas: Division of Control over the Southern Hemisphere

As Spain was actively engaged in the exploration of trade routes to Asia, competition between Spain and Portugal over the ownership of the lands that they found had intensified. With the late-comer Spain reaching a previously unknown continent, Portugal's discontent ran high. As a consequence, the threat of war overshadowed the two countries. In the midst of the higher threat of war, Pope Alexander VI was involved in meditating the two sides.

Under the mediation of the pope, the two countries agreed to divide the Atlantic and the Pacific in the Southern Hemisphere. In May 1493, Pope Alexander VI decreed in a papal bull that all lands west of a pole-to-pole line 100 leagues west of any of the islands of the Azores or the Cape Verde Islands should belong to Spain. The bull did not mention Portugal or its lands, so Portugal could not claim newly discovered lands even if they were east of the line. Another bull in September1493 gave all mainlands and islands, "at one time or even still belonging to India" to Spain, even if east of the line. Indeed, the pope's mediation favorably reflected Spain's position. Requested from Queen Isabel to consolidate the Spanish title of the lands that Columbus had reached, the Vatican, which had been under Spanish influence, took sides with Spain. The Portuguese King John II strongly protested that arrangement, arguing that Portugal was prevented from controlling events on the newly found continent.

In 1494, the representatives from Spain and Portugal met in Tordesillas, a small town in the northwest of Spain, and reached an agreement that the initial demarcation line should move 270 leagues (equivalent to approximately 1,296 kilometers) west. Under that arrangement, the new continent America came under the full control of Spain. The adjusted demarcation line stretches to the tip of the eastern part of Brazil. Accordingly, Portugal was able to advance and establish control over Brazil. This is why modern-day Brazil remains the single Portuguese-speaking country in all of Latin America.

Spain and Portugal, which divided the oceans of the Southern Hemisphere in half, enjoyed the status of maritime hegemons. Ships from the two countries were allowed to sail freely, but ships from other countries were prohibited from sailing without permission. In fact, sailing these oceans without permission was regarded as piracy. Portugal made an enormous income by selling passage licenses in Asia, on the grounds that the pope had granted the exclusive right of control. The Vatican officially approved the Treaty of Tordesillas in 1506. The treaty served as a precedent for the linear demarcation of boundaries in the 19th century, regardless of nations, natural environment and culture, in the lands that European powers had conquered.

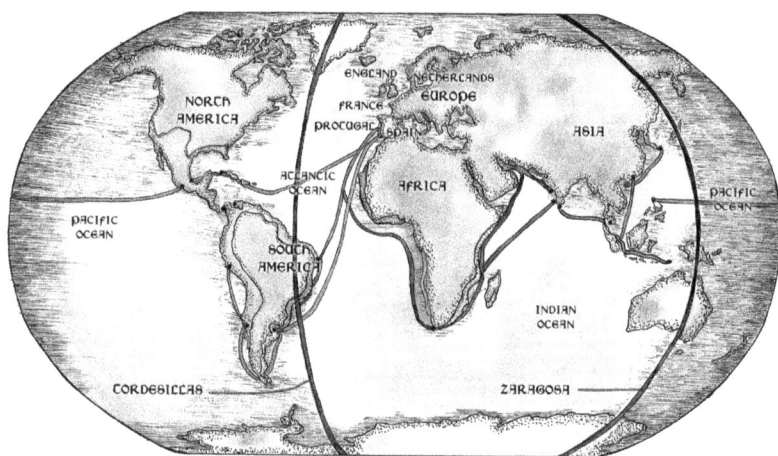

Treaties of Tordesillas (1494) and Saragossa (1529)

One might be curious of how this was possible. The answer might be found from the historic background that papal power was superior to royal power, signified by the Humiliation of Canossa in 1077, in the Middle Ages. The Humiliation of Canossa refers to the event that Holy Roman Emperor Henry IV went to Canossa Castle, Italy where Pope Gregory VII was staying and was forced to get on his knees and wait for three days and three nights before the entrance gate of the castle, to seek the absolution of the pope and a reversal of his excommunication. In the Middle Ages, the pope was considered the apostle of God, mandated to relay and enforce God's messages. Popes did not have their own military forces, but had a very powerful weapon – excommunication. In Christendom, the stigma of being non-Christian was considered the heaviest penalty. There was no obligation to obey the rule of an excommunicated king because he was no longer Christian. For this reason, excommunication was the most powerful weapon for popes and at the same time, it was the most fearful punishment for kings. With the leverage of excommunication, popes could force other countries to comply with the Treaty of Tordesillas.

Another factor might be attributed to the circumstance that many European countries, such as the Netherlands, England and France, were not capable of ocean-going yet. Meanwhile, Italian city-states like Venice still concentrated on Mediterranean trade. As such, Spain and Portugal were able to enjoy exclusive rights within the oceans under their control.

In the 16th century, the Protestant Reformation, triggered by Martin Luther, was widespread throughout Europe. As papal power weakened, England, France and the Netherlands were actively involved in sea-borne trade and the Treaty of Tordesillas gradually became nominal and was largely disregarded. However, it was apparent that on the basis of the demarcation line, Portugal advanced to the Indian Ocean around Africa, and Spain proceeded to the Pacific around the southern part of America.

Treaty of Saragossa: Division of the Pacific

The earth is round. Mindful of this fact, it would be natural to see the two rival countries clash on the other side of the earth. The location of this encounter was the Moluccas, which was a gateway connecting the Indian Ocean to the Pacific Ocean. The Moluccas, called the 'Spice Islands,' were the main producers of cloves and nutmeg. Indeed, cloves were produced only in the Moluccas. This spice was most notably used by subjects in the Han Dynasty to freshen their breath before they saw the emperor.

In 1511, the Portuguese forcefully occupied the Moluccas, which had been under the exclusive trade control of Arabs. Spain, a late arriver to the Pacific spice trade, soon clashed with its Portuguese rival. In the midst of the intensifying threat of war, Spain and Portugal signed the Treaty of Saragossa in 1529 that divided the Pacific with a base line of 17° east of the Moluccas. Under the treaty, Portugal gained control of all lands and seas west of the line, including all of South Asia and its neighboring islands, leaving Spain with most of the Pacific Ocean, including the Philippines. With Portugal in decline, ultimately the Netherlands gained control on the Moluccas, following the control by the allied forces of England and the Netherlands.

Decline of the Maritime Empire of Portugal

Portugal, which had explored Oriental trade routes prior to Spain and advanced to India, South Asia and China, made enormous profits from spice trades. When Portugal was at its height in terms of trade, approximately 100,000 Portuguese out of the entire population of 1 million were estimated to be working overseas. This accounted for 35 percent of its entire male population. With the Oriental trade booming and wealth concentrating in Lisbon, the capital city of Portugal had grown to a flourishing metropolitan city with a population of 100,000. By 1570, more than 40 Portuguese trade bases were established across vast regions, which spanned from Sofala in Africa to Hormuz, Goa, Ceylon, Malacca, Macao and Nagasaki, Japan. Goa, India served as a hub of the Asian trade network. Pepper and other spices were the most important goods for the Asian trade. The Portuguese merchants traded copper brought from India with pepper. Pepper shipped to Portugal made earnings of as much as 150 percent.

The booming Oriental trade began to decline in the middle of the 16th century. Among a variety of causes, some critical points are presented here. First and foremost, a small country on the Iberian Peninsula might have hunted prey that in the end was too big to swallow. It was extremely challenging for Portugal to manage trade bases across the huge regions and maintain an exclusive trade status with only small fleets and troops. By 1540, the Portuguese residing in Asia were no more than 7,000, and merely dozens of ships were present there. It was impossible to expeditiously communicate between the homeland and the colonies due to the long distances between them, which required at least four to five months of navigation. Second, the fragile financial status of the Portuguese court was a principal cause. All overseas trade had been under the exclusive control of the Portuguese court. Trade goods were carried only by the ships owned by the court, and all the profits generated from trade were returned to the king of Portugal. The Portuguese court borrowed money from German and Italian merchants, with interest rates of 25 percent, excluding the Portuguese capital to maintain exclusive trade status. With the financial status worsening, it became harder to finance the enormous expenses required for expeditions, such as shipbuilding. This resulted in the circumstance that they could not afford to arrange the merchant fleets with their own financing. With the revival of the Levant trade through the Red Sea starting in 1540, Portugal was forced to compete with Mediterranean commerce cities, including Venice, ultimately leading it to lose its exclusive status in the Oriental trade.

Third, the high rate of shipwrecks in the merchant fleets was also a cause. The rate of shipwrecks caused by overloading and piracy was up to 40 percent in the 16th century. The high rate of shipwrecks might be attributed to overloading and substandard equipment due to the pursuit of excessive profits. Exclusive sea control was threatened starting in the late 16th century by emerging maritime powers such as the Netherlands and England. On the other hand, the doctrine of *Mare Clausum* (closed sea), which upheld the exclusive sea control of Portugal and Spain, was challenged by the doctrine of *Mare Liberum* (free sea), which upheld the free use of the sea. In the 17th century, Hugo Grotius, a Dutch jurist, claimed in his work, *Mare Liberum,* that the sea should be open to all states for exploration and trade, and his claim has become a dominant doctrine that governs the use of the sea.

In 1578, Portugal was completely defeated in an African expedition, and ultimately was annexed by Felipe II of Spain. Portugal, which had lost its independence, was incapable of protecting Oriental trade routes and its colonies, and as a consequence, were exposed to attacks from natives and pirates. The empire built overseas quickly collapsed thanks to attacks from England, the Netherlands and France. Portugal lacked troops to station overseas, and so it could barely protect the colonies by building a coalition with Arab-Indians, blacks, slaves and mixed-blood Christians. In 1640, Portugal regained its independence. However, it could not afford to send troops overseas because it needed to be ready for possible Spanish attacks. England and the Netherlands, taking advantage of this, intensified their attacks on Portuguese colonies. In 1641, Malacca was taken by the Netherlands, and subsequently trade bases such as Colombo and Cochin were taken by the Netherlands and England. As a result, the mighty eastern empire of Portugal shrank to a number of small coastal fortresses in India and part of Macao and Timor. Ultimately, Portugal, exposed as a paper tiger, was forced to retreat from Asia.

The Spanish Maritime Empire

Spain at its height built a vast maritime empire which spanned from Madrid to Manila including lands on the American continent. Spain invested enormous resources in voyages across the Atlantic in the wake of Columbus's first journey. The Spanish were spurred by the discovery of Columbus to explore colonies west of the demarcation line under the Treaty of Tordesillas. Spanish troops subsequently occupied Hispaniola (1496; modern-day Haiti and the Dominican Republic), Puerto Rico (1508), Jamaica (1509) and Cuba (1511).

Afterwards, Spain turned its eyes to the business of ocean exploration. Spain hired Ferdinand Magellan, a Portuguese explorer, to carry out the grand project. He commanded a fleet of five ships to explore the route to India around the American continent. On 10 August 1519, the expedition fleet left Seville and descended the Guadalquivir River to Sanlúcar de Barrameda, at the mouth of the river. They stayed there more than five weeks. Finally they set sail on 20 September 1519 and left Spain. When Magellan's fleet arrived off the coast of Patagonia, they were hit by harsh storms. Food almost ran out, and the crew had to catch rats aboard. In the meantime, a mutiny broke out involving three of the five ship captains. Magellan took quick and decisive action to conquer the mutiny, and the fleet was recovered. On 21 October 1520, Magellan discovered a strait, known as the Strait of Magellan today, connecting the Atlantic to the Pacific. Despite a great deal of difficulty, the fleet was successful in sailing toward the unknown ocean through the Strait of Magellan.

After the sailing through the strait, which was narrow and stormy, the ocean was so calm and peaceful that they called it the Pacific Ocean. Magellan called the discovered islands in the Pacific the Philippines, named after Felipe II of Spain who sponsored his expedition. But Magellan himself was not to survive the voyage; he was killed in a battle with the native tribes. In September 1522, the remaining crewmen sailed back to Spain under the command of Magellan's colleague. The expedition, which had departed Spain with a fleet of five ships and 240 crewmen onboard, came back with only 18 sailors alive largely due to food shortages, diseases and bad weather. The long, harsh voyage was the first circumnavigation of the earth. It was also historic in that the circumnavigation confirmed that the earth is round.

Portugal could quickly take advantage of the fruits of this exploration by the discovery of the origin of spices. As Portugal was preoccupied by the eastern route to India, however, Spain intended to capitalize on a western route toward the spices' place of origin – and in the meantime, it could harvest even more valuable fruits in the form of the new continent.

Spain at its height during the reign of Felipe II ruled most of the southern part of Italy, the lowlands on the coast of the North Atlantic, the Bourgogne region of France, the coast of Africa, the Golden Belt from India to China and Japan, the Philippines, the Mariana Islands and the Caroline Islands as well as the new continent. Although the phrase "the empire on which the sun never sets" became famously associated with England in later years, it originally came from Charles V of Spain, who ruled colonies throughout the planet. Less than 50 years since the discovery of the New World, Spain became the wealthiest country in existence.

Spanish control over the sea across the world was possible because of the country's powerful naval capabilities. The Spanish navy earned the nickname of '*Spanish Armada*,' meaning great and most fortunate navy, in the wake of winning the Battle of Lepanto, in which a fleet of the Holy League composed of Spain, Venice and Rome fought against the fleet of the Ottoman Empire in 1571. In the aftermath of the victory, Spain was able to deter Islamic forces from establishing dominance in the western part of the Mediterranean. The gains of Spain, however, were not as large as those of Venice, which recovered its exclusive control over trade routes in the eastern Mediterranean. Felipe II and the Spanish were full of confidence in the aftermath of victory in the Battle of Lepanto. However, this confidence spurred excessive territorial expansions overseas.

Chapter 8

NAVIGATION IN THE AGE OF DISCOVERY

Navigation in the Age of Discovery

Even in the Age of Discovery, navigational knowledge and skill still remained rudimentary. Navigation totally relied on dead reckoning. When engaged in navigation toward the new continent in the early modern times, navigators had no prior knowledge of the geography marking the boundaries of the oceans or a hydrographical chart on new oceans, either. Instead, navigators fully relied on the sky. They used Polaris to find the north at night and know geographical longitude. It was not until the end of the Middle Ages that Europeans were able to actively use celestial navigation, also known as astronavigation. Celestial navigation is the practice of position fixing that enables a navigator to know their position without relying on estimated calculations or dead reckoning. It enables one to locate a position by the use of angular measurements (sights) between celestial bodies and the visible horizon at sea.

Before this, Europe had been in a deep sleep for more than 1,000 years. Much earlier, the Greeks believed that the earth is round by witnessing that mountains rose from the sea as a ship neared the shore, and that the roofs of houses appeared to set into the sea as a ship sailed away from shore. By 200 B.C., Eratosthenes, a Greek mathematician and geographer, calculated the circumference of the earth for the first time. He did it by comparing the altitudes of the mid-day sun at two places that were a known north-south distance apart. However, in the Middle Ages, Ptolemy's geocentric model of the universe (that the earth was the center of not only the solar system, but the entire universe) was a dominant doctrine of Christianity.

Ptolemy, a Greco-Roman mathematician, astronomer and geographer, argued that the earth is a stationary sphere at the center of a vastly larger celestial sphere that revolves at a perfectly uniform rate around the earth, carrying with it the stars, planets, the sun and the moon.

Whosoever doubted or denied the doctrine throughout the Middle Ages was referred to the Inquisition and doomed to be killed. In the Middle Ages, during which time religion had dominated other values and authorities, Christian values had driven out prior scientific knowledge and development. The Medieval belief was that the earth was like a flat disk floating on a sea of darkness. Such belief was derived from Ptolemy's misjudgment, wherein he attempted to reflect the earth's spherical surface onto the flat surface. Ptolemy mistakenly calculated the circumference of the earth to be 29,000 kilometers, 28 percent shorter than the actual circumference. On his world map, the coast of eastern Africa extends to the east and is linked to the Asian continent. As a result, the Indian Ocean was drawn as a vast enclosed sea.

On Ptolemy's map, the longitudinal and latitudinal lines were first used to specify terrestrial locations. On his map, eastern Asia and Europe appear to be very close to each other. This served as a critical cause that led to Columbus's misjudgment. Columbus attempted to discover India in the west, assuming it was nearly adjacent to Europe.

The advances in celestial navigation relied on the development of sea surveying. Sea surveying allowed sailors to specify their position with numbers. It enabled sailors to specify any location with a grid of longitudinal and latitudinal coordinates. A ship could reach its destination by trial and adjustment, based on a grid of longitudinal and latitudinal coordinates. The development of navigational skills was dependent on the development of surveying, and in doing so in a way that made it easily applicable.

So, how was surveying developed and made applicable? A quadrant and an astronomical observation device were used to measure the altitude of stars. Since 1472, a goniometer, a device to measure angle measurements, was used. One might have doubts about how accurately a moving ship could make measurements, but the measurements were amazingly accurate. Sailors frequently had to land on shores or islands to enhance the accuracy of measurements. The list of latitudes measured in 1509 showed that any latitudinal error was less than one degree, and the gap from the actual location was less than 25 minutes.

In the early 17th century, as scientific knowledge further advanced, the goniometer and astronomical observation device were replaced by an octant, which was more accurate. The introduction of algebra made the complicated calculation of star angles much easier, and the invention of the watch and telescope laid a foundation for safer celestial navigation. Another essential factor to specify the location of a ship was the measurement of ship speed. Since the invention of the compass enabled sailors to set a certain course, the measurement of a ship's speed became a critical concern. Without knowing the ship speed, sailors could not calculate how far they sailed and their present position.

Columbus and his contemporaries used a sandglass to measure time. The invention of sandglass allowed navigators to fully measure time. Because a 30-minute sandglass was for the measurement of time on a daily basis, it was not adequate to measure a long time and distance. However, it enabled navigators to roughly measure the ship's speed. Navigators could specify the estimated position of a ship by taking into account the current and wind, and by marking their course, speed and time on the hydrographical chart.

It is interesting to note the way that an hourglass was used to calculate the speed of ship. A sandglass was used for multiple purposes, depending on the time limit. There were a variety of different types of sandglass: a four-hour sandglass for watch; a 30-minute sandglass; 15-second, 28-second, and 30-second sandglasses to measure the ship's speed. The 28-second sandglass in particular was like a kind of speed gun. Sailors threw a string, which had knots every 14.4 meters, into the water, and could figure out the ship's speed by calculating the number of knots which had passed for 28 seconds. In order to measure the ship's speed with a 30-minute sandglass, the most commonly used sandglass – also known as '*ampolleta*' – sailors had to turn it upside down 48 times for 24 hours. Against this background, a day on the calendar is marked as 48 *ampolletas*. The logbook of Columbus tells that the ship sailed 12 kilometers during five *ampolletas*, which was equivalent to 3.2 knots per hour (5.9 kilometers per hour).

Since watch rotated every fourth hour, a sailor on watch had to turn the sandglass upside down eight times during his watch. This was supervised by the deck officer. If the sailor on watch made the glass sphere of the sandglass warm with candlelight or his clothes, he was subject to a heavy punishment. This was because the swell of warmed glass allowed for the faster flow of sands, shortening watch hours as a result. Most importantly, the erroneous calculation of time could endanger navigation. Since the invention of the watch, the ringing of a bell on a regular basis let the captain and sailors know the status of watch. Watch started with ringing a bell, with eight bells rung over the course of a watch – one every 30 minutes. This began a long sailing tradition of making each watch last for eight bells.

Ships in the Early Age of Discovery

One might be curious as to the size of ships that sailed across the oceans in the Age of Discovery. How big were they? One might imagine that the ships at the time would be fairly large, given the size of modern merchant and cargo ships engaged in international navigation, most of which are tens of thousands of tons. To the contrary, indeed, they were unbelievably small vessels.

To begin with, we need to take a look at the types of vessels that explorers in the period of the Age of Discovery used. As described in the previous chapter, the caravel was the principal type of vessel used for ocean-going throughout the period. The caravel was a ship that combined a European hull, Oriental rigging and a Northern European key. First and foremost, the caravel was excellent in maneuverability due to its robust structure as well as in seaworthiness due to a deep draft (the vertical distance between the waterline and the bottom of the hull). In addition, the caravel was capable of having a large number of sailors aboard ship. It also had an outstanding speed. It had a jib – a triangular staysail set forward of the foremast, as with the Arabian traditional sailing vessel, the dhow. The caravel could sail as quickly as a 19th century clipper – a remarkably fast ship – in a fair wind. The ship records found in Venice described the caravel as the best ship. "There is not any reason that this ship cannot reach any port of the world. This is because this ship is the best ship of ships sailing across the seas." For these reasons, it would become a key player in geographical discovery. The caravel was the product of advances in European shipbuilding in the 15th century. The fundamental part of hull remained unchanged, because sailors tend to distrust ships that they are not familiar with. However, shipbuilding at the time had flexibility in which various experimental factors were applied as well, depending on the hull of ships.

Ships engaged in ocean navigation were much smaller than one might expect. Being small in size was itself a feature of ships at the time. Expeditions overseas were very risky projects, and thus a heavy investment from the beginning was not possible. Due to the enormous expenses involved, the expeditions could not afford to build large ships. On top of that, the merit of small ships – good maneuverability in shallow water – was a critical consideration. Ships at the time mostly sailed inshore, and as such, large ships had greater risk of getting stranded in shallow water or going ashore on a strange coast.

Table 1 – Vessels in the Age of Discovery

	Prior to Cape Bojador		Prior to Cape Good Hope	Age of Discovery
Period	Before 1434		Before 1488	After 1492
Tonnage	30 tons	50 tons	40 to 50 tons	80 to 100 tons
Type	Barque	Barinel	Caravel	Caravel
Number of Sailors	30		35	50
Number of Masts	1	2	3 to 4	4
Type of Sail	Square-rigged	Lateen plus two square-rigged	Two lateens plus two square-rigged	
Scope of Activity	10 to 15 days	6 to 10 months	1 year	1 year and 6 months
Cargo	Almost none		Almost none	5 tons

Source: Jou, Kyung Chul, *The Age of Maritime Expansion* (Seoul National University Press, 2008)

As Table 1 indicates, the ships operated in the Age of Discovery were rather small from the perspective of contemporary standards. This might demonstrate that the size of ships is not necessarily the most essential factor for ocean-going. The fact that these small ships could traverse the open ocean was classified as a national secret that should not be revealed to other countries. There are some episodes concerned with this issue. For example, John II of Portugal ordered a gag to be put on a navigator who had worked for Vasco da Gama and had spoken in public that they could reach the coast of Guinea with even a small vessel. In 1535, when Diago Botellu returned from the Indies aboard a small galleon, John II ordered that it be burned. In 1610, sailors sailed with a small *junk* ship from Japan to Acapulco, Mexico, across the Pacific. The fact that they managed this crossing should demonstrate that size is far from the only determinant in whether a ship is able to cross the ocean.

Ships in the Era of Conquest and Trade

Following the era of exploration and discovery, circumstances totally changed as the era of conquest and trade began. Although small ships were suitable for the exploration of unknown seas and lands, large vessels were advantageous for trade. However, all ships did not necessarily become equally bigger in size.

The size of ships tended to be specific to trade routes and cargo. For Northern European trade, which largely shipped corn, sugar, salt and wine, small vessels, which were speedy and sailed on schedule, were preferred. On the contrary, for trade with the Mediterranean, American colonies or the West Indies, which mostly traded in food, sugar and tobacco, large ships were required. Generally, 11 to 14 sailors aboard a ship of 150 to 200 tons were involved in ocean navigation, which took six to nine months.

Slave ships had the largest number of sailors. Roughly 20 to 25 sailors were aboard a slave ship of 200 tonnage class. This was a safety measure against the possible mutiny of slaves, as well as the high rate of mortality on a voyage. Navigation for the slave trade took 10 to 11 months. The largest slave ships belonged to the East India Company. These ships were as large as warships of 300 to 500 tons because they had to load a large number of personnel and goods, enough to last for voyages that could take more than two years.

The size of vessels differed according to their types of trade as well as their trade regions, and different regions also required different numbers of sailors aboard. There was a notable distinction in size between the ships engaged in trade with Asia and the ships engaged in American trade, for example. Portuguese ships engaged in trade with India were fairly large – an average of 400 tons in the first half of the 16th century. They grew larger, to 750 tons in the late century, with 100 crewmen aboard. On the other hand, Spanish vessels engaged in voyages to America were on average 150 to 250 tons.

Table 2 – Size of Spanish Vessels Engaged in Voyages to America

Period	Number of Ships	Total Tonnage	Average Tonnage
1506–1566	2,500	380,000	150
1555–1600	3,800	780,000	205
1600–1650	3,800	950,000	250

Source: Jou, Kyung Chul, *The Age of Maritime Expansion* (Seoul National University Press, 2008)

The explorers in the Age of Discovery ventured out on ocean journeys aboard incredibly small vessels. The fact that the explorers navigated across the oceans aboard small ships, relying on celestial observation, wind and currents, might prove that their indomitable courage and initiative spirit of adventure were not merely rhetoric, bur real.

Risks of Ocean Navigation

Portuguese ships that departed for India set sail in March to April and arrived in September to October. The return journey from India usually started in December or January, bringing them back home anytime between June and September. It took approximately 20 months for a round trip. In the period between 1600 and 1635, out of 912 Portuguese ships that departed from Lisbon, 60 ships (6.5 percent) returned home without completing their voyages; 84 ships (9.2 percent) went missing; and 768 ships (84.2 percent) arrived safely at their destinations. The statistics show that other than the ships that immediately returned, 10 percent of 825 ships were involved in accidents on a voyage.

Of those ships that arrived at their destinations, a total of 510 ships, excluding the ships that needed repairs or were used for patrol, embarked on a return voyage to Europe. Seventy-five ships sank and the rest of the 435 ships safely returned home. The rate of accidents on the way back home was 14.7 percent, higher than that of voyages to India. In generic terms, the rate of accidents was up to 20 percent, given that 159 ships out of 852 ships that set sail from Lisbon were subject to maritime casualties. In 1662, when a ship from the Dutch East India Company was sinking, it was said that the captain, without hesitation, had thrown 40 sailors into the water to prevent the rescue boat from being overloaded. Subsequently, he threw another 13 sailors into the water. Eventually, he threw five more sailors out so that the rest of the crew could come back home safely.

Sailors

Sailors were one of the largest and most significant wageworker groups in the 18th century international market economy. Overseas trade in the 18th century, called the Era of Trade, required enormous capital investments. Capital was invested by individuals (often two to ten merchants who banded together to form a joint investment). Joint investment not only helped defray the risks of the investment – it made investing possible in the first place, because often a single investor could not afford to sponsor a ship alone. Most of the Atlantic trade, which concentrated on sugar, tobacco and the slave trade, were capital intensive. A voyage required 2,000 to 10,000 pounds in expenses. In addition, an essential factor in international trade was maritime labor forces. The century of trade was an era during which the maritime labor class inevitably expanded. As capital became concentrated on shipping, anywhere from 20,000 to 50,000 sailors were involved in maritime jobs in the period between 1700 and 1750.

This period was an era in which sea-borne trade with America remarkably expanded and the British shipping industry matured. It was in this period that the British established control over the sea, and their dominance over the sea remained stable and persistent. In the meantime, sailors grew to become one of the first and largest wageworker groups in the British and American economies.

What was life like for these sailors, who explored the unknown world and fueled maritime trade? Sailors were often depicted as romantic, free-living figures, puffing a pipe in the sunset. However, the romantic image of navigation hides the real life of sailors. Sailors were not those who sought adventure in a vagabond lifestyle. They were merely a maritime labor class who struggled for their survival in the closed and self-contained space – the ship – that battled against the harsh nature of the sea.

Ocean navigation was a life of constant stress. Sailors were fully exposed to harsh labor and brutal violence. They lived always with the threat of death. Such life was well described by historian Marcus Rediker, who defined the sailors as being caught between evil and the dark blue sea. On one side, there were captains, who wielded tyrannical power and violence with the support of merchants and bureaucrats. On the other side, there was dangerous and harsh Mother Nature. In between, sailors existed.

Generally, sailors went to sea in their late teens or early twenties. In the early 18th century, the average age of sailors was 27. The low-ranking sailors were mostly in their late 20s, and the captains and navigators were largely their early 30s. Most of them were the sons of poor farmers or small landlords who had come to cities to find jobs; those who were forcibly recruited by the navy and later became seamen on merchant ships; those who were attracted by high wages in wartime; or those who were deceived by brokers. The majority of them had to go to the sea for economic reasons against their will.

The sailors who lived the harsh life at sea had their own features in appearance, lifestyle, language, behavior and clothing. They lived together in a certain area of the city. Their appearances was menacing and tough. They had their own way of talking, with expressions and sounds that were often a mix of curses and crude language. Their walk was also unique – they swayed like pendulums as they walked, a habit which helped them stay stable on the decks of ships. Their clothes, too, were distinctive. They wore loose pants made of heavy, coarse and red-colored fabrics. Pants were water-proofed with tar to prevent their legs from being paralyzed by cold water. Their shirts were blue and white checked linen with, blue or grey woolen jackets, grey socks and a flat and round cap, called the Monmouth Cap.

The sailors generally lived a wanton and dissipated life. It was common that the sailors who returned to port quickly spent the small wages that they had risked their lives to earn. During their stay on land, they squandered the wages by drinking and visiting prostitutes. One anecdote is particularly telling: A sailor rented three carriages – one for his cap, one for his pipe and the last for his cigarette case – and went scuttling around downtown Amsterdam. When they ran out of money, the sailors continued the vicious cycle and returned to sea.

Recruitment of Sailors

As shipping developed, the number of sailors required to operate a ship tended to diminish. Changes in the technology of shipbuilding between 1700 and 1750 had a significant impact on sailors' labor. By 1700, ships were designed to need a smaller number of sailors aboard. Since merchants preferred the Dutch-type hull, which had a wider bottom, to load more goods with fewer sailors, the number of sailors became fewer relative to the weight of ships. The number of sailors who worked on a typical trade ship at the time, *Virginia*, for example, was 20 to 21 in 1700, but this was reduced to 16 in 1756 and 13 in 1770. As a result, the amount of goods and various tasks that a sailor was in charge of gradually increased. This meant that merchants could benefit from hiring fewer sailors, but the sailors themselves would have to work harder.

Sailors were disgruntled with the smaller numbers taken aboard a ship. In 1722, a group of sailors refused to embark on a voyage from London to northern Europe because the captain did not take aboard 11 sailors that he had promised to. In 1732, sailors sued a captain in the Admiralty Court on the charge of having an insufficient number of sailors aboard.

As life aboard ship grew tougher, people avoided becoming sailors and thus the recruitment of sailors became a significant social problem. As a consequence, the recruitment of sailors itself turned violent. It was carried out largely by innkeepers in ports, or brokers. They were called 'Soulless Dealers,' 'Dogs' or 'Pigs.' They often steered youngsters hanging around ports or other job-seekers aboard ships, often by deceiving them. When they signed a contract with shipowners, they brought robust sailors and registered them. However, they frequently fraudulently also brought weak sailors to the ships. As a consequence, the quality of sailors diminished, and captains had a hard time controlling them.

Those who made a deal with innkeepers or brokers to become sailors could not embark immediately. They had to wait until recruiters visited. In the meantime, they waited for long periods in damp basements or freezing attics, with minimal food and poor conditions. When the recruitment squad, playing trumpet, flute and drum, visited, applicants signed a contract. Shipowners paid them a certain amount of advance payment. Then, sailors paid for food and drinking during their stay and bought the necessities for life aboard ship such as cap, pillow, blanket and knife. The innkeepers received from shipowners a certificate that stated the information about the sailors that they had recruited, certifying that the innkeepers earn a certain amount of income from the sailors' earnings. The innkeepers could not be paid until the ship and the sailors safely retuned. If the ship sank or the sailors died, they would not earn a cent. Since ocean navigation took several months at a minimum or several years at a maximum, those involved in the brokerage of sailors were paid considerably later. If they needed money faster, they could sell certificates in advance at a discount. Those who bought the certificates were merchants, and thus, merchants ultimately made big money after the voyages completed.

In 1651, the Navigation Act of England prescribed that three out of four sailors should be British, but the provision was often not enforced. This was especially the case during wartime or during worker shortages. In certain cases, half the crew was foreign-born – a circumstance the British government allowed during worker shortages. Sailors were from various ethnic groups.

A ship was full of a variety of regional, national and ethnic identities, including sailors from England, America, the Caribbean, the Netherlands, France and Spain as well as others from Asia and Africa.

Compared to merchant ships, warships had a more serious problem in recruiting sailors. Beyond the risks of dying in a battle on the sea, navy ships were home to widespread epidemics such as typhoid. In the 17th and 18th centuries, almost the half of those drafted to the navy died at sea. Those who were fortunate enough to return home safely were often not paid. Some commanders delayed payment three to four years or six and a half years to prevent the sailors from attempting to leave their posts prematurely.

Recruitment became a national issue. For this reason, a 'compulsory recruitment squad' that recruited navy sailors out of the merchant sailor ranks was established. The compulsory recruitment squad got onboard a ship, wielding sailor's knife, known as cutlass, and forcibly took the sailors when the ship called in a port. Sailors' resistance against compulsory recruitment brought about a kind of small-scale civil war, with sailors inciting revolts or overthrowing the ship's command. Some sailors hurt themselves, making wounds that imitated the effects of scurvy by burning themselves with sulfuric acid; others pretended to be paralyzed or acted as though they suffered from seizures or were feeble-minded.

Painful Life Aboard Ship

Work aboard ship was just like imprisonment, with constraints everywhere. All the things necessary for life aboard ship, such as space, liberty, movement and food, were constrained. Space, for example, was very tight. Sailors lived in the meager space, packed like bean sprouts in a jar, while the captain and senior sailors had their own rooms. Sailors often left home unsure whether they would survive their journeys, as casualties were very common. One of the most favored songs among the sailors was 'Loath to Depart,' reflecting this painful awareness that a goodbye could be forever.'

The first stage of a voyage was to load cargo. Sailors, wharf men and other handymen carried boxes, barrels, goods, ballast, food and ship's stores to the deck. Many types of equipment were employed to lift cargo. Loading required a consideration of weight, shape and type of cargo as well as its overall balance. Ballast had to be loaded in order to keep the ship balanced on its journey. A water pump was installed to survive any water leakages. For aged vessels or vessels damaged by storms, sailors had to spend much time pumping, which was a hard job.

Once loading was completed, the work of sailors shifted from handling cargo to operating the ship, which included steering, controlling the mast, and operating sails. The skillful handling of these works led to shorter journeys, and therefore greater profits. Steering was an essential part of work aboard ship, along with observation and the measurement of water depth. The steersman adopted a ship's course according to the instruction of a senior officer on duty, watching the compass and the position of the sun and the moon. Sailors steered in rotation. On a voyage, they climbed up the top of the mast to control the sails. For merchant ships, masts were 18 to 23 meters high; sailors climbed to the top to make sails wider or narrower, depending on the winds.

As described earlier, sailors were assigned watch duty as well. Half of them were for right watch and the rest were for left watch. The captain was in charge of supervising one side, and the navigation officer was in charge of the other side. Watchmen were on duty for four hours and off duty for four hours over a period of 24 hours. The shift from 4 p.m. to 8 p.m. was called 'Dog Watch,' during which time sailors rotated every two hours. Sailors were assigned to a 10-hour duty and a 14-hour duty on rotation. They were not free even during off duty. They could not sleep over four hours at night. On a windy day, they had to close the topsails by climbing up the top of main mast or the foremost mast.

Sailors slept in their clothes while on standby. In the event of a ship's rolling or pitching in a storm, they had to tie up themselves with ropes to prevent themselves from falling out of the ship. At night, they could not see each other. On windy days, they could not even hear each other at close distances. There were a great deal of chores aboard ship that seemed minor but could mean the difference between life and death. Work aboard ship was relentless, with constant tasks such as checking rigging, rewinding ropes, maintaining gears, oiling, repairing sails, painting tar on ropes, cleaning cannons and painting the deck.

When they called in a port, the work of unloading began. At the first stage of the work, the same equipment and workforce as had been used for loading did all the work in reverse. Following the lifting of cargo from a ship's stores, they transferred it to small boats, like a barge. In the case of a small port, sailors transported goods to shore by rowboat.

Dangerous Work Aboard Ship

Work aboard ship was always dangerous. Many sailors were killed either by falling down from the mast, drowning in waves or getting hit by ship gears. Above all, the shortage of supplies was the most painful possibility. Fresh food ran out less than a few weeks after departure, and afterwards, sailors had to live on salted meat, fish and beans. The largest problem was the shortage of drinking water. Water loaded aboard ship was easily spoiled. Drinking foul, spoiled water, with moss floating in it, was painful. They found later that wood barrels caused the problem, but metal barrels did not come into common use until much later.

Some sailors chewed lead bullets to quench their thirst and as a consequence, they became addicted to lead.

The fundamental cause of food and water shortages was the limited space aboard ship. Every extra bit of space went to load cargo, which was more profitable for shipowners than supplying sailors. According to the records in the 16th century, sailors were daily allocated 1.5 to 2 pounds of biscuits, 0.5 to 1 pound of salted meat, 0.25 pounds of rice or dried vegetables, 1 liter of drinking water, 0.75 liter of wine and 0.25 liter of oil. Calculating the amount of drinking water and food required for a month, 500 kilograms of supplies per person should be loaded.

In the event of a long voyage or an uncertain schedule, more supplies were necessary, just in case. Christopher Columbus loaded the amount of food needed for 15 months and drinking water needed for six months. This meant a supply of 1,300 kilograms per person. Vasco da Gama, for a voyage to India, loaded supplies of 2,600 kilograms per person, necessary for three and a half years. Sailors also shared their space with rats, cockroaches, maggots and moths. Dogs, cats and parrots and pet penguins were also aboard. Cows, sheep, goats, pigs were raised aboard ship to supply milk and meat.

Violent Discipline Aboard Ship

Along with the shortage of supplies and dangerous life aboard ship, sailors had to endure the horrible discipline and brutal violence of the captain or senior sailors. Details of this oppression against sailors can be found in the files of lawsuits referred to the Court of Admiralty. Today, sailing boats are viewed as a symbol of beauty and proud history, but at the time, the ship itself was a torture chamber.

Things that could be used as torture devices, such as hooks, poles and iron sticks, were everywhere aboard ship. There were also axes, hammers, knives and the ropes which could be used to tie around a neck and pull a body and hands and legs. Ropes for sails and rigging were at an ideal height for hanging up uncontrollable sailors for several hours. There was a salty water box that could be showered over an injury after a whipping, and a great amount of salt that could be used to add to suffering.

The captain and senior sailors had exclusive control over the ship and wielded violence in the name of keeping order, using such instruments. The most common punishment was flogging. For this, the captain often used the Cat-O-Nine Tails, made of nine slim strings, which signified the authority of captain and was the main symbol of violence. In the name of establishing discipline aboard ship, the captain nominated Sunday as the day of flogging and drubbed the sailors. Violence was committed as a punishment against the violation of discipline aboard ship. However, occasionally, brutal violence was committed for unknown reasons.

Lashing was rather better than other brutal violence. Some cases of violence aboard ship referred to the Court of Admiralty are presented here. "They held my hair and put my head beneath the second cannon on the left side and drubbed me. I was beaten so long and brutally that I could not lift my hands and arms over my head." "For coming back late, I was beaten by the captain with an oak stick so that I could not eat food for a while," "I was beaten with fists, ropes, sticks, canes and sail strings, and lost an eye," "Four teeth were broken by a beating with stone mugs," "I was beaten until my face swelled and eyes were almost pulled out," "He poked my left eye with his thumb and beat the thumb with his right hand three times," "I was beaten with a sharp iron stick, and the captain had me climb up the top of mast in a very cold day in rain. The captain said that he would kill whoever helped me. I became handicapped by the beating," "They stuck my finger in the hole of timber and put a wedge into the hole and crushed my finger," "I was kicked

Sailors being flogged with a cat-o-nine tails

and had a bloody head and poked with a knife over several parts of my body, and I had teeth pulled and was beaten with a mop, leaving bruises all over my body."

Verbal assault was also a means of establishing discipline aboard ship. "I will cut your head or cut your liver with knife and eat it," "I want to peel off your skin." Such intimidation was commonly committed. Another means was to illegally disembark sailors before their contract ended. Many captains disembarked sailors on a remote or uninhabited island or transferred them to a warship or imprisoned them in a port. This method was often used when the unemployment rate was high, and a replacement was easily available.

The right of captains to allocate foods was a powerful means to exercise their absolute authority. Even when there was enough food aboard ship, they often left sailors starved by allocating insufficient food as a means of discipline. Since most captains at the time were stakeholders of merchant ships, there were many disputes over the quality and quantity of foods allocated.

Part of the discipline included being placed in custody aboard ship. "After being beaten, I was held in custody for 24 hours without any means of survival," "After being beaten, I was held in custody for 8 days in the iron cage. I was totally exposed to the wind, rain, moisture with no blanket." A related punishment was to hang a sailor to a mast or mast rope after a beating. This was imposed on drunken sailors or sailors suspected of committing a revolt.

These *modus operandi* were violent and private, and the most commonly used means for discipline under the authoritarian captain. Sometimes, this violence simply stemmed from the private rancor of captains or senior sailors, where the pressure and stress caused by long voyages aboard ship were released in the form of sadism. Obviously, the brutal acts of captains led to some sailors' becoming pirates. In many respects, living as sailors in the 17th and 18th centuries was as harsh and raging as life in the Middle Ages.

Poor Health Condition of Sailors

The shortage of food, water, and the eating of spoiled foods seriously threatened sailors' health. Dangerous work aboard ship always brought with it the fear of becoming handicapped. Sailors suffered a variety of diseases caused by work aboard ship, such as scurvy, rheumatism, rash, yellow fever, ulcers and dermatosis. Becoming handicapped was very common. Sailors often suffered from hernias when they lifted or pulled cargo. In many cases, hands were cut by rolling barrels or legs or arms were broken or cut by shaking cargo or getting caught in the ropes. It was common to encounter handicapped sailors walking on crutches in a port.

Among many diseases, scurvy was the most problematic. The initial symptom of scurvy was lethargy and paleness so that patients looked like people in need of blood transfusions. Then, blue spots erupted and limbs swelled and were paralyzed. The typical symptoms were a swollen palate, tooth loss, bleeding sores, high fever, and spasms. They ultimately led to death. The navigators who desperately tried to find the cause of the disease came to a vague understanding that lacking certain foods was the source of the problem. They came to know that orange or lemon juices were useful to treat the disease, based on their experiences. However, it was hard to store them fresh and they became easily spoiled, even when carrying juices aboard ship. Thus, they were found to be not a perfect measure. Instead, sailors preferred alcohol as a preventive medicine. They believed strong alcohol had a better effect. Since sailors believed that drinking before eating was the best effect, they used to have a drink first thing in the morning.

Since drinking aboard ship was the easiest way to get relief from the distressful life and loneliness, it was a main part of sailing culture. Drinking was just like taking drugs, which quickly relieved the pain of brutal labor and tension. For this reason, it was common for sailors to drink to the point of unconsciousness. Sailors' drinking played an important function in the labor culture aboard ship, despite many abuses. It helped settle conflicts among sailors and bring them together with the sense of unity and solidarity.

It was common that the half of sailors initially aboard ship died on a voyage, and even a 75 percent mortality rate was not unusual. Ships engaged in long voyages in a poor environment were just like 'floating tombs.' As previously described, the Magellan fleet departed with 240 sailors aboard, but only 18 sailors came back alive.

The treatment for scurvy was developed in the era of Captain James Cook (1728–1779). Sailors cleaned inside the ship once a week and smoked it out with disinfectant, and bedding and clothes were exposed to the wind. They had to take a shower with cold water during daytime. They were encouraged to have foods made with flour instead of meat, and to have salted cabbage which had abundant Vitamin C. When they landed on shore, they were provided with fresh vegetables and fish, while reducing the amount of meat they consumed. As a result, sailors were free from scurvy.

Resistance of Sailors

The resistance of sailors who suffered from harsh labor aboard ship was carried out in the form of disturbances and protests. The word 'strike' was derived from the collective action of sailors in London in 1768 who intended to disturb trade and capital accumulation by tearing up the sails of the ship that they were aboard. It was common that sailors took to the street to protest. Massive protests of sailors began in the 1620s. They often created disturbances over wages and working conditions. In 1653 and 1654, sailors lodged a large scale of protest, provoked by rage over their transfer to other ships before being paid wages, delayed wage payment, payment in check not cash, and compulsory recruitment.

The most powerful form of resistance over the absolute power and brutal violence of the captain was a mutiny aboard ship. The mutiny aboard ship was the intentional and organized collective action to constrain the power of the captain or ultimately to take control of the ship. In the period between 1715 and 1737, there were 48 mutinies aboard ship. This may demonstrate the higher degree of conflicts in particular between the sailors and the captain and senior sailors. More specifically, 21 mutinies aboard ship occurred in the period between 1718 and 1723. Most of them broke out on voyages to Africa or the West Indies and a few occurred on voyages to America or Mediterranean ports. The rest were on privateers.

Mutinies aboard ship were violent. They were desperate attempts, because the leaders of the mutinies would be killed if they failed. More than one senior sailor was killed in one of five mutinies aboard ship. Roughly half of the mutiny attempts were successful. The sailors involved in the mutiny took control of the ship, one-third of whom became pirates. When sailors planned to mutiny, they shared a round-robin as a mark of willingness and solidarity. A round-robin was a means of organizing resistance clandestinely. The most important thing was to maintain solidarity among like-minded sailors and to keep secret as to who the initiator and leader was. "They drew two circles on a paper. The two circles were fairly away from each other. They put down what to do inside the circles. In between the circles, the names of like-minded sailors were put down inside and outside the circles. This was for the purpose of not revealing the leaders. Thus, all are responsible." This was purported to prevent betrayal and from making excuses that they were forced to participate in cases where the plan was revealed.

Another means of resistance was to provoke a mutiny or kill sailors under the guise of accidents. They let the senior sailors get hit by falling cargo or fall into water in stormy weather. Refusing to follow instructions intentionally was a way of resistance. According to the admiralty law, sailors were not allowed to intervene in the punishments over the disturbance of order, but they ignored this because the captains did not comply with the admiralty law. This was particularly the case when a sailor was made to suffer a brutal or physically risky punishment.

Chapter 9

LEGACY OF THE AGE OF DISCOVERY: LIGHT AND SHADOW OF THE ATLANTIC WORLD

Historical Significance of the Atlantic World

Despite Christopher Columbus' erroneous belief that he had visited India – a belief he persisted in until his death – his voyages were an extremely significant global event in history. The era of ocean navigation, widely known as the Age of Discovery, was a critical turning point throughout the world history, not to mention for Europeans.

With the exploration of trade routes to Asia, Europe opened a new era, ending the chaos of the Middle Ages. The eyes of Europeans turned towards the world beyond Europe. As Europe accepted the advanced culture and technology of Asia and explored trade routes, it was able to regain the status it lost with the fall of the Roman Empire. With Europe's rise to global dominance, it was able to create a European-centric modern history of the world.

On the other hand, Asian states, such as China, which had been passive in taking to the sea and had a closed off, self-centered view of the world, saw the beginning of a long history of colonization and submission under dominant European military and maritime powers. The new continent that Columbus had discovered was subject to a harsher destiny. Its civilizations were conquered by Europeans armed with Christianity, canons, firearms and swords. The European civilization became the global standard. The standards of 'civilized' Europeans in religion, languages, institutions, clothing, and way of life became a benchmark of legitimacy and created a justification to conquer the lands of people who were regarded as living a barbaric life and to force their culture upon them.

The two sides of light and dark always exist together in history. The more critical the historical event, the more apparent this contrast becomes. On the part of European-centric history, the Age of Discovery was the 'brilliant light of the Atlantic.' On the contrary, it was the beginning of painful history for the new continent or colonial people that persists even today. An episode that happened at the 1992 World Expo held in Seville, Spain where the Columbus museum is located might symbolize the light and dark of the Age of Discovery. Right next to the poster of 'The 500th Commemoration of the Discovery of the New Continent,' the poster of "500 Years of Shame" was hanging. In the European-centric view, the discovery of the new continent by Columbus in 1492 was the great event that rediscovered a barbarian world and civilized it. By contrast, those who paid attention on the humiliating aspects of the discovery of the new continent claimed that the West should be ashamed of the barbarian acts it committed in the name of civilization over 500 years.

Apparently, the Age of Discovery was the era that handed down many legacies of light and dark on both sides of the Atlantic. The light and dark still densely overshadow contemporary history. One might wonder what the light and shadow consist of? Before exploring the answers, it's obvious that the historical facts reviewed here are colored by contemporary standards as well as the views of the conquerors.

The Leap of the European Economy and the New Crops

The European economy, which had long lagged behind Asia's, leapt ahead through the Age of Discovery, with Iberia at the forefront. Iberians were able to directly import precious spices from Asia through their new trade routes, without relying on Muslims merchants. To the west, treasures such as gold and silver, and new crops such as corn, potatoes, beans, pumpkin, cotton and tomatoes, flowed in from the new continent. These new plants made a significant contribution to the relief of starvation which were prevalent throughout Europe.

The Vicious Hunt for Gold and Silver

Europeans who first arrived in America looked to exploit the availability of gold and silver. Indeed, gold had been a motivator for exploring trade routes in the first place. Upon arrival in America, Europeans were engaged in harsh exploitation of the resources found there, gold and silver first among them. A study tells that the entire supply of gold that the natives of America had amassed for a thousand years was completely looted by conquers within two to three years of their arrival. The natives were forced to pan for gold after their gold was depleted. Since female natives were forced to produce additional gold, agricultural production became paralyzed and the birth rate significantly dropped, and as a consequence, population rapidly diminished. Afterwards, the outflow of silvers became more serious. Europeans, who had depleted gold in the West Indies, turned their eyes toward silver in America.

In 1545, the massive scale of silver mines was explored in modern Bolivia and Mexico. In Potosi, Bolivia, an unprecedentedly enormous amount of silver was mined. Potosi, built in 1546 to support the mining operation there, grew to the largest city in America with a population of 200,000, as enormous riches were generated from mining. According to a study, the amount of silver produced in the mines in Spanish America was 25,000 to 30,000 tons between 1560 and 1685. In the period between 1685 and 1810, the amount doubled. Potosi was the largest producer of those riches. The amount of pure silver and gold mined in Potosi, nicknamed Cerro Rico ('rich mountain') was up to 45,000 tons. The silver shipped from the coast of Spanish America was mostly produced from the mines in Potosi.

The gold exploited from the Aztecs and the silver from Potosi were shipped to Spain in the form of lumps. Spanish colonial rulers established mints across their colonies to mint gold and silver into coins. In 1536, the first mint was established in Mexico City, and subsequently the second in Lima in 1565 and the third in Potosi in 1573. The mining of the massive amount of gold and silver was possible with the harsh exploitation of natives' labor. European conquerors took advantage of the native population's traditional compulsory labor system, called *Mitta*, to draft the workforce required for mining. This was the compulsory method that every village was required to send a certain number of people into compulsory labor.

The labor of the indigenous people forcefully brought into mining was extremely harsh. They were allowed to come out after crawling in dark, narrow mines for six to seven days. They had to climb up 250-meter-high ladders, carrying ore mined deep underground. In this way, they had to transport to the surface 25 bags of 50 kilograms each for 12 hours a day. If they failed to achieve the goal, their payments were cut. It was said that the population of Chucuito, Bolivia was reduced to one-third during the period between 1628 and 1754.

On top of harsh labor exploitation, mercury addiction was a principal cause of indigenous deaths. As strip mines were depleted, conquerors developed a technology to extract silver out of low-silver-content minerals using mercury. When they smelted, they milled rough stones with water-powered machines and mixed the flour with mercury at a normal temperature and had the native people step on the mixture to grind it. Then they heated the mixture and extracted mercury out of it. At this moment, the deadly moisture came out, and laborers were fully exposed to it. For this reason, going to Potosi for compulsory labor was regarded as a death sentence. Indigenous people held a memorial service in advance when they sent their sons to the Potosi mines.

As labor forces diminished, the shortage of labor was filled with African slaves. According to a research result, conquerors made a petition to the king in Madrid to allow the import of 1,500 to 2,000 African slaves annually. It is estimated that a total of 30,000 African slaves were brought to Potosi throughout the colonial period. African slaves, treated like 'human mules,' were forced to do harsh labor. Since mules to spin the machine to mill rough stones died within a few months, they were replaced by African slaves, with the ratio of four to 20. Indeed, gold and silver distributed across the world in modern times was produced by the heartbreaking sacrifice of indigenous and African slaves.

America overwhelmed the rest of the world in terms of gold and silver production, accounting for 85 percent and 71 percent for each. American silver was distributed worldwide. A massive amount of silver flowed into Europe, of which a fairly large amount went on into Asia to purchase ceramics and silks from China and spices from South Asia. Although the silver spread across Europe caused inflation, it created good circumstance for commerce and industry, as the prices of industrial goods went up faster than the prices of grains or wages. As a result, the massive flow of silver prompted capitalism in Europe. By contrast, silver that flowed into Asia invigorated its commerce, but undermined the growth of Asia by leading to an outflow of wealth.

Influx of Epidemics and Collapse of Traditional Society

The most fundamental change during the Europeans' colonial rule of America was a massive reduction of the Native American population.

Out of various studies of the population reduction in America, an astonishing finding was that the indigenous population of 80 million at the time when Europeans had explored the new continent was reduced to 10 million by the mid-1500s – in other words, within 50 years. In another 50 years, by 1600, the population was ultimately reduced to one-tenth of the population of the mid-1500s. David Brion Davis, professor at Yale, called the unprecedentedly rapid reduction of the indigenous population 'the largest ethnic massacre in history.'

How can this phenomenon be explained? To begin with, many were killed in battles with Europeans and some even opted to commit group suicides as Europeans expanded their conquests. For Europeans armed with Christianity, indigenous practices were seen as unholy and war against these peoples could be justified.

However, on the new continent, rampant epidemics was a more critical cause of population reduction even than war. The introduction of new germs to a population with zero immunity to them caused incredible damage. A wide array of epidemics and parasites spread to America from across the Atlantic, including smallpox, measles, diphtheria, trachoma, malaria, cholera, influenza, mump, pertussis, tuberculosis and yellow fever.

Not only did Europeans spread the diseases, but the livestock that Europeans brought with them also played host to germs. Europeans had been experiencing these diseases for centuries, but not so for the native populations in the Americas. Indigenous people were felled by the strange diseases like dried leaves. When Columbus arrived in Santo Domingo in December 1492, the entire native population was 200,000. However, in 20 years, the population was reduced to 14,000 and in 30 years to 200.

Devastated by the epidemics, the native society fell totally into chaos. On the part of Europeans, the epidemics served as a critical contributing factor to establishing control on the new continent. The local upper classes of native people died of the diseases, and thus the ruling structure collapsed. This made the military resistance impossible. These circumstances were well described in the book of Jared Diamond, *Guns, Germs, and Steel*. The principal force that allowed Cortes to conquer the Aztec Empire with only 600 soldiers was smallpox. The disease was brought in 1520 to Mexico by a slave infected in Spanish Cuba. Since then, smallpox killed the half of the population of the Aztec, including the emperor.

In the face of the horrible disease which killed their people in such large numbers and did not create nearly the same amount of devastation among Spanish soldiers, many indigenous people lost their will to resist the invaders. The population of Mexico, which had been up to approximately 20 million, plunged to 1.6 million by 1618. The same case occurred when Francisco Pizarro landed the coast of Peru with 168 Spanish soldiers in 1531 to conquer the Inca Empire. By 1526, the smallpox brought through land routes killed most of the population of the Inca, including the emperor and the royal family. While the sons of the emperor were engaged in a civil war over the emperorship after the death of the emperor, Pizarro was easily able to conquer the Inca. Since the arrival of Columbus, 95 percent of the entire population of the New World diminished over one to two centuries.

Such phenomena had an enormous impact on the mentality of both native people and European conquerors. European conquerors had a sense of superiority. On the other hand, the indigenous people suffered a sense of inferiority and defeat. European conquerors used the widespread epidemics for a justification of their conquests. A Spanish governor in America said that "God cleansed these lands for us."

Harsh Exploiter of the New Continent: Spain

This was the brutal violence and destruction of the native American society committed by the conquistadors, led by Portuguese and Spanish. To spread Christianity and trade, their conquests began with the destruction of native Americans' religion and culture, as well as oppression of them. Notably, whereas the Portuguese established trade bases in their conquered regions and were engaged in business, the Spanish totally concentrated on destructive conquests.

The Spanish who landed on the Caribbean islands were extremely destructive from the outset. Las Casas, a 16th-century Spanish historian as well as Dominican friar, wrote in his book about the brutalities and massacres committed by the Spanish colonizers against the indigenous people. "Christians began massacres by using horses, swords and spears, and when they attacked a village, they did not allow anyone alive, regardless of children, elderly, pregnant women and women giving birth. Beyond stabbing and cutting limbs with swords, they tore them up. The Spanish soldiers made bets as to whether they could cut off heads with a single blow. They snatched children out of their mothers' arms and threw them into the rivers, laughing. Commemorating Jesus Christ and his 12 disciples, they hung up 13 Native Americans and burned them alive."

Las Casas recorded that the death toll of Native Americans slaughtered by conquistadors was up to 15 million. The atrocities and cruelties committed by the Spanish conquers was believed to be real enough – these acts have been referenced as a 'Black Legend,' while there is also a 'White Legend' that counters the narrative and describes the Spanish conquerors in a more favorable light. The Spanish built fortified villages in the conquered regions and distributed lands to conquistadors. The conquistadors enslaved Native Americans and forced them to engage in labor for them. The forced labor resulted in diseases, abuses, a high rate of suicides, and thus a high rate of mortality and rapid reduction of the birth rate, ultimately leading to the collapse of the indigenous society. In return, the Spanish brought home 19 tons of gold in the period between 1503 and 1510.

Native American Genocide

Conquest of Aztec and Inca Empires and Exploitations

The economic benefits gained from the exploitation of the West Indies were used to fund additional conquests elsewhere. The Spanish conquerors rushed to the mainland of America, following the conquests of the West Indies. Accompanied by about 11 ships, 500 men (including slaves), 13 horses, and a small number of cannon, Hernan Cortés landed on the Yucatan Peninsula in the Mayan territory in 1519. He took over Veracruz, and conquered nearby native tribes.

In the face of the invasion of the Spanish soldiers armed with horses and cannons that they had never encountered, Native Americans were extremely terrified and readily surrendered. Exploring deep into the continent, the Spanish troops marched on to Tenochtitlan (now Mexico City), the capital city of the Aztec Empire. The emperor of the Aztec greeted the white soldiers on horseback, regarding them as gods descended from the heaven. Cortés raided the defenseless palace and occupied it, ending the Aztec Empire. The Aztec Empire, with a population of 5 million, was totally destroyed by the 500 Spanish troops armed with horses and guns, without any resistance.

In a few years, following the fall of the Aztec, the Inca Empire, which blossomed into a brilliant civilization among the highlands of the Andes, was faced with the same fate as the Aztec Empire. The key actor was Francisco Pizarro. Born out of wedlock, he raised swine during his childhood. He led an expedition composed of merchants to Hispaniola Island (now Haiti and the Dominican Republic). While in Panama, he served as a mayor. In 1523, when he was 48, he attempted to explore the coast of South America, but the governor of Panama refused to grant him permission. Pizarro returned to Spain to appeal directly to King Charles I. His plea was successful and he received not only a license for the proposed expedition, but also authority over any lands conquered during the venture. He was joined by his family and friends and the expedition left Panama in 1530, with a ship carrying 180 soldiers and 37 horses aboard.

Encountering the delegation of the Incan emperor at the gateway to the Inca Empire, Atahualpa, Pizarro demanded that the empire accept Christianity and pay tribute to King Charles I. Atahualpa's refusal led Pizarro and his army to attack the Incan army. Armed with stone spears and bronze weapons, the 7,000 Inca troops were totally defeated by Pizarro's troops. Emperor Atahualpa was held captive. For ransom, he vowed that he would fill the room with gold. Allegedly, the amount of gold that he paid was up to 11 tons.

However, Pizarro, afraid of counter-attacks of Incans, sent him to trial and sentenced him to be burned to death on the charges of idolatry, incest and the killing of his brother. The Incan believed that persons who burned to death were not allowed to the world of the dead, so Atahualpa converted to Christianity to avoid this fate and instead was hung with the baptismal name of Juan Santos. Pizarro's troops were able to occupy the capital city of Cuzco in 1533 without engaging in battle. As a result, the Inca

Empire, whose territory stretched from modern Ecuador, Peru, Bolivia, Argentina and part of Chile, ended. The Incan Empire, which had a population of 14 million and 100,000 troops, helplessly collapsed in the face of a small group of Pizarro's troops, composed of only 180 soldiers and 37 horses.

Harsh exploitation of the native people after the collapse of the Inca Empire followed. The Spanish exploitations were built on the systems of *repartimiento* and the *encomienda*. *Repartimiento* was a colonial forced labor system imposed upon the indigenous population of Spanish America. It was similar to other tribute-labor systems, such as the *mita* of the Inca Empire. The natives were forced to do low-paid or unpaid labor for a certain number of weeks or months each year on Spanish-owned farms, mines, workshops, and public projects.

In the fear of depleting native labor forces under the *repartimiento*, the Spanish court introduced the *encomienda*. In the *encomienda* system, the Spanish court granted a person a certain number of natives from a certain community. Indigenous leaders were charged with mobilizing the assessed tribute and labor. In turn, *encomenderos* were to ensure that the native people were given instruction in the Christian faith and Spanish language, and protect them from warring tribes or pirates; they had to suppress rebellion against Spaniards, and maintain infrastructure. In return, the natives would provide tributes in the form of metals, maize, wheat, pork or other agricultural products. The *encomienda* was intended to prevent the depletion of native labor forces and address the malpractices of *repartimiento*, but actually it served as an institution that permanently enslaved the native people.

Tragedy of the Atlantic World: The Slave Trade

As described earlier, the conquerors addressed their labor shortages in the mines by importing slaves from Africa. With the large increase in sugarcane plantations in the West Indies, African slaves were imported on a large scale. Previously, the Spanish court had dispatched colonial governors to rule the colonies, and they had initially enslaved indigenous people for labor.

However, as the management of colonies with only native people became harder, they turned their eyes to new labor forces. In the intermediate stage of replacing indigenous slaves with African slaves, lower-class Europeans were brought to the new continent on a large scale. These were indentured servants, who were awarded money and land after a certain period of labor for landlords. European farmers were not much interested in going to the new continent. Instead, all kinds of vagabonds, including prisoners and criminals at large, embarked on the ships sailing to the new continent.

The landlords, who had spent much money to import these servants to the new continent, forced them to do harsh work to gain the greatest profits possible. The indentured workers, living in terrible conditions, frequently went on strike or committed sabotage. Consequently, the landlords turned their eyes to African slaves to replace indentured workers who had cost much money and were hard to control. Apart from this, the newly booming sugarcane industry in the West Indies required a large scale of new labor forces. The coast of the Atlantic, including Barbados, was the most suitable for the cultivation of sugarcane. Sugar production required more than three times the workforce of cotton or corn cultivation, so labor needs were vast. The African slave trade boomed, becoming one of the worst tragedies in human history.

However, to the main players of the Age of Discovery, the slave trade was no more than a means of generating enormous profits. The number of African slaves shipped to America is estimated to be 20 million over 300 years. Of those, 5 million were brought to the Caribbean region and 3.5 million to north-eastern Brazil and 0.4 million to the southern part of the U.S. The frontrunner of the slave trade was Portugal. As Portugal fell behind its competitors, like Spain, in the exploration of colonies, it concentrated on the slave trade. Portugal transferred its efforts to the slave trade in an effort to avoid competition with England or France and exercised the exclusive right of slave trade, which was *Asiento.*

However, in the late 17th century, England rose to become the leading country in the slave trade. England became a dominant power in Europe, while Portugal was pushed to the sidelines. Beginning in 1670, England remained a leading country in the slave trade for 240 years until it was banned by parliament in 1807. England, led by the Royal African Company of England, was engaged in a triangular trade connecting England, Africa and the West Indies. In the wake of the 1713 Treaty of Utrecht, signed by the belligerents in the War of the Spanish Succession, England gained the right of *asiento* to export slaves to Spanish colonies.

Triangular Slave Trade and Slave Hunting

The triangular slave trade describes the slave trade that operated from the late 16th to the early 19th centuries, carrying slaves, cash crops and manufactured goods between West Africa, Caribbean or American colonies and the European colonial powers. European traders shipped cotton, rum, guns, gun powder and steel products to countries on the west coast of Africa, such as modern Angola, Nigeria and Senegal. They traded these items with regional chieftains for African slaves. Then, they sailed to America to sell off the slaves. After selling the slaves,

European traders bought regional products and shipped them their home countries.

Bristol and Liverpool were hubs of the British slave trade. The reason that Liverpool could become the center of slave trade was that it was adjacent to industrial cities, like Manchester, Birmingham and Sheffield, and it was a good location as a port. These cities produced merchandise with which to purchase African slaves.

The most popular merchandise in Africa was colored cotton fabrics. Africans were eager to have them, and European traders exchanged these goods when they purchased slaves, called 'black diamonds.' Since 1750, however, they had shifted to slave hunting.

The total number of slave ships engaged in the slave trade in 1771 was up to 190, which shipped 47,000 slaves annually, making 30 to 100 percent in profit. The slave trade generated enormous income if even one of three slave ships came back safely. At first, African slaves were captured on the coast of Africa. But as demand for slaves constantly grew, slave hunters gradually expanded deep into the interior. The captured slaves had to walk dozens of kilometers a day to be brought to the coast. According to one record, 40 percent of the captured slaves died from the harsh treatment of traders, as well as malnutrition and disease while on the move.

Concentration camps where slaves were held before being loaded onto slave ships were like hell. Hundreds of naked slaves, curled in an extremely narrow underground dungeon, awaited export alongside animals for weeks. The shipment of the captured slaves from the coast of Africa to America across the Atlantic was called the 'Middle Passage.' The middle passage, which took one to six months, was like a living hell for the slaves who became extremely weakened while being brought to and held in the camp. As many as 500 slaves were packed into the steerage of a small ship of 100 to 300 tons. Slave traders loaded as many as possible onto the slave ships to make greater profits.

Slaves chained together were packed between the bottom and the ceiling of steerage. They could not afford to move at all because numerous slaves were laid on top of one another. Chained together, they often lay together in their own excrement. The air quality was so bad, candles often could not stay lit due to a lack of oxygen. Due to these unsanitary conditions, allegedly one-sixth of slaves aboard a ship died on a voyage.

The Cape Coast Castle built on the Gold Coast of West Africa (now Ghana) by European traders was the hub for exporting slaves to America across the Atlantic in the 18th century. When the slave trade was at its height, as many as 1,500 African slaves awaiting export were held in the underground dungeons there. They are now a tourist attraction that shows the miserable reality of the slave trade. The scribbles that slaves wrote on the wall of their underground dungeons are carefully preserved. As one writer put it, "Screams resound from the scribbles on the wall over several centuries."

Cape Coast Castle

The 1781 *Zong* massacre might well demonstrate how brutally African slaves were treated on voyages across the Atlantic. On the voyage to Jamaica, as the British slave ship *Zong* ran low on potable water due to navigational errors, the crew threw 133 sick slaves overboard into the sea to drown. Allegedly, the massacre was committed in part to ensure the survival of the rest of the passengers and in part to cash in on the insurance on the slaves – this way, the ship owner did not have to lose money on slaves who would otherwise have died from thirst.

The *Zong*'s owners made a claim to their insurers for the loss of the slaves. When the insurers refused to pay, they filed a lawsuit against the insurers. The court ruled that the act of throwing the slaves overboard into the sea was legal, holding that "the act was like throwing horses overboard into the sea." The insurers were not required to pay for the loss of the slaves, however, because the court concluded that the captain and crew were at fault for the shortage of drinking water on the voyage. Abolitionists would reference the *Zong* massacre as a primary example of slavery's evils.

Slave transactions occurred in ports. They were often sold at auction, either purchased in cash, credit, or in-kind exchanges. The best value at the slave market was robust men between 15 and 25 years of age. The humanity of slaves was totally ignored from the beginning. Having a family was not allowed for slaves. The owners of slaves did not want slaves to have children, and tried to sell them off once they had. For example, one common reason for selling a female slave was that she gave birth too often. When a landlord in Boston went to sell a 19-year-old female slave and her son, the advertisement included the phrase, "Together or Apart."

With the persistent urging of abolitionists to abolish slavery and prevent businesses from generating profits off the trade, England and the U.S. made the slave trade illegal in 1807. In 1919, England built a fleet to surveil the slave trade. Ironically, England had enjoyed a booming economy from the slave trade, but now was the nation that spearheaded its abolition. Even after England and the U.S. banned the slave trade, slave exports to Cuba, Puerto Rico and Brazil persisted for a fairly long time.

The slave trade was the tragic stain that the Age of Discovery made in history. Today, global society commemorates the 23th of August to remember the shameful history of the slave trade and the historical significance of slavery abolition. The memorial day was derived from the slave revolt in French Saint-Dominque (now Haiti) on 23 August 1791, which was an uprising by self-liberated slaves against French colonial rule in Saint-Domingue. It ended in 1804 with the former colony's independence. The uprising served as a critical moment, leading to the first independent state founded by free slaves.

The slaves sold through the slave trade were leading actors in the history of the Atlantic. The current prosperity of America was built on the tears and pain of black slaves.

Birth of a New Race: Mestizo

The conquerors who came to colonize America were mostly single men, who paired off with indigenous women – often through rape or sexual exploitation. As a result, a new race, called 'Mestizo,' was born, indicating a mix of white Portuguese or Spanish and Native Americans. Today, mestizos constitute the largest population group throughout Latin America.

Emergence of Modern Financial Systems and Development of Capitalism

Ocean navigation in the Age of Discovery helped give birth to the principal modern financial systems, such as stocks, insurance and banking. The Oriental trade of European maritime powers was a business that generated enormous wealth, but at the same time, the risk associated with these investments was very high. A long voyage by a large-scale fleet, which took more than six months of ocean navigation, was very vulnerable to shipwrecks. As piracy risks increased, traders had to deploy an escort fleet to protect merchant ships from pirate attacks. This required additional costs.

The building of fleets was a long-term, risky investment. Traders raised funds from investors to form a fleet, which had enormous expenses. At first, they began with small capital, but those were joined by big capital and governments, which got involved in the industry as profitability was proved over time. The expenses were so enormous that they could not be funded by a single or couple of investors, but required a large number of investors. A long period was required for a trade fleet to carry Oriental goods and sell them in the European markets. The investors needed to have a certificate to certify their investments during that period. This was the origin of modern stocks and bonds.

As described earlier, the rate of shipwrecks was up to 20 percent. In case of shipwreck, investors lost their investments. Given the high risk involved in ocean navigation, investors sought to protect their investments – this was the beginning of maritime insurance, from which modern insurance developed. Although ancient Phoenicians and Greeks had maritime insurance, it only became fully developed through the Age of Discovery.

Since the end of the 17th century, London has become the hub of maritime insurance. Lloyd's of London, well-known for maritime insurance, was a coffee house in London that shipowners, captains and underwriters visited. The underwriters were also called Lloyd's. With the growing importance of maritime insurance, it evolved into a corporation participated in by shipowners, ship builders and underwriters. The British Parliament enacted the Lloyd's Act 1871, under which Llyod's was changed to a non-profit corporation. Today, Lloyd's has become a principal agency of maritime insurance, which is tasked with collecting and distributing information on ship specification and registration. Additionally, the banking system developed out of a need for organizations to manage the capital investments of a large number of investors.

With early navigational risks diminishing and the size of ships growing, the scale of fleets became larger. While the high risk of Oriental trade remained, bases for safer business activities expanded, as financial institutions to manage the risk of long-term voyages were created. As financial institutions evolved, and large capital and nations joined together, capitalism was in development on a grand scale.

Chapter 10

THE GOLDEN AGE OF PIRATES

Era of Pirates in the Age of Discovery

Most of the episodes of pirates that we know today are associated with the so-called 'Golden Age of Pirates' in the period between the 1650s and the 1730s. There is no doubt that pirates existed since ancient times. As described earlier, piracy began as soon as human beings took to the sea. Piracy is one of the oldest professions that human beings have devised. Pirates have been rampant anywhere there is available prey to plunder, regardless of the age and the region.

The world became connected through the sea during the Age of Discovery. Pirates were also capable of navigating across oceans, and thus their activities expanded to the oceans across the world. Most importantly, the opening of the Age of Discovery shifted the activities of pirates from the Mediterranean to the Atlantic. The principal locus of pirates was America and the Caribbean Sea, which were the focus of exploitation of European maritime powers.

Pirates were by nature maritime syndicates who committed atrocities at sea, such as looting, kidnapping and murder, for their own purposes. From a historical view, however, the context of their existence becomes more apparent. The emergence of the Caribbean Sea as the home of pirates was a result of European states' reactions against the exclusive Spanish exploitation of America and the Caribbean Sea. Pirates rampaged in between the Spanish exploitation and the reactions of other European states. The rampage of pirates also stemmed from the outraged voices and revenge of sailors, who had undergone harsh treatment under miserable labor conditions aboard ship, against the authority of states and capitalist classes.

Pirates were primarily outlaws who wielded violence to satisfy their greed. However, they occasionally worked for their homelands. The privateers who appeared in the 15th century were the best example. During the period between 1571 and 1572, the Dutch pirates, known as Sea Beggars or *Watergeuzen*, fought for the independence of the Netherlands from Spain by joining the army of national independence led by William of Orange during the Dutch War of Independence (1568-1648). The Mediterranean pirates participated in a holy war between Muslims and Christians.

Pirates at their height were present everywhere across the world. Most Caribbean pirates were based in French ports. The pirates who looted in the English Channel were based in the Dunkirk port in northeast France. Asia at the time was no exception to piracy. Larger pirate groups than those found in the Atlantic were rampant across Asia. The Red Sea and the Gulf of Persia were notorious for piracy. The Malabar Coast was home of Mahratta pirates, who looted the ships from the East India Company in the early 18th century. The Ilanoon pirates of the Philippines sailed across the seas off Borneo and New Guinea with a large galleon with 40 to 60 pirates aboard. They brutally plundered coastal areas and ships until they were completely destroyed by the U.S Navy's expedition in 1862. The most horrible in Asia were the South China Sea pirates. They were an enormous pirate group, composed of 40 junk ships and 40,000 pirates, who were engaged in looting settlements in coastal areas and merchant ships. Their heyday ended when they were expelled from their hideouts and their leaders were hanged.

The pirates during the golden age of pirates have often provided inspiration for novels, dramas and movies. These days, this has contributed to the image of romantic pirates. The golden age of pirates began with the emergence of the Caribbean pirates. It was the era that legendary pirates, like Henry Morgan and Captain Kidd, were active. By the 1720s, piracy was at its peak. At the time, up to 2,000 pirates were engaged in looting on the both sides of the Atlantic. The pirates were the largest threat to Spanish exploiters, with large fleets and trade with colonies.

The Spanish Main

Since the discovery of the new continent by Christopher Columbus in 1492, Spain had expanded its colonies and had much of South America and the Caribbean Sea under its control. The New World was the Spanish overseas empire that the Spanish and their relentless troops explored, following its discovery by Spanish fleets. They slaughtered and enslaved indigenous people and exploited their wealth through forced labor of indigenous people and shipped the exploited wealth back to their homes in the old world.

As described in the previous chapter, Spain and Portugal divided the seas in the Southern Hemisphere and the new continent under the Treaty of Tordesillas, and they had an exclusive control on trade across the Atlantic. As a result, Spain could afford to exclusively exploit wealth in the Caribbean Sea, known as the Spanish Main. 'The Spanish Main' refers to a region that was once under Spanish control and spanned roughly between the isthmus of Panama and the delta of the Orinoco River. The term can also refer to the Caribbean Sea and adjacent waters, especially when referring to the period when the region was troubled by pirates. The territories under the Spanish Main included modern Florida, Texas, Mexico, Central America and the northern coast of South America.

The Spanish Main between the 16th and early 19th centuries was the departure point of merchant ships that carried home the treasures and goods exploited from the New World. The gold and silver mined in the coastal areas of the Pacific was brought by llamas and mules to the Spanish Main via Potosi. Goods from the Far East brought to Acapulco in southern Mexico were transported to the Spanish Main by land. The treasures and goods gathered in the Spanish Main from the Far East and America were shipped to Spain by the treasure fleets. Since the Spanish Main was the place where various treasures were loaded and shipped, it quickly became the favorite hunting ground

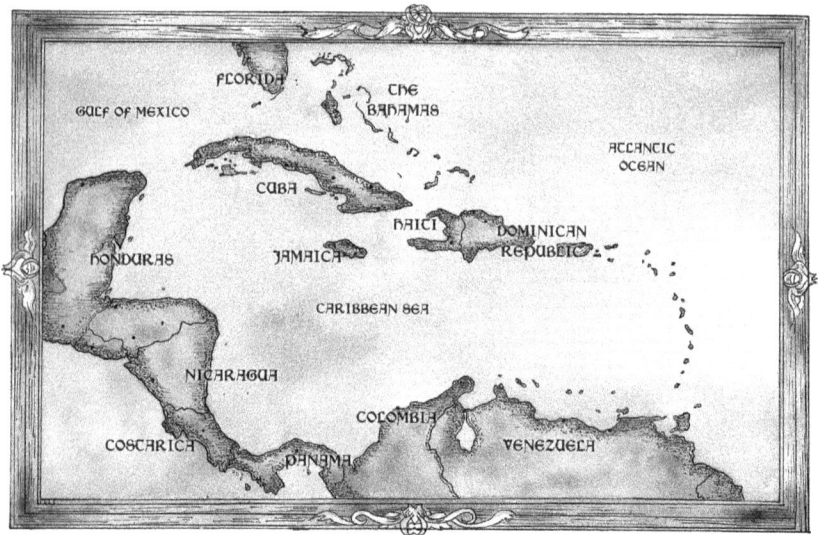

The Spanish Main

of pirates. Against this backdrop, the Spanish Main has become the background setting of pirate novels today, as well as a term used frequently to evoke the Caribbean pirates.

Spain had built a large number of fortresses in ports across the Spanish Main and reinforced its defenses to ensure the safety of merchant ships sailing to and from the Spanish Main. The main ports included modern Cartagena, Veracruz and Panama. The second-level cities, such as Portobello, Santo Domingo and Campeche, served as local administration and trade centers. These ports were regarded as a symbol of the wealth of the Spanish empire and thus subject to attacks by European invaders and pirates between the 16th and 17th centuries.

Voyages of Spanish Treasure Fleets

Spanish merchant fleets shipped European merchandise and explorers to the Spanish Main and brought back treasures exploited from the New World. In the 16th century, the treasure fleet was the best prey for pirates. Spain had been constantly plagued by pirates from neighbor countries while engaged in reckless overseas expansion. Due to the rampage of pirates, the Spanish merchant fleets operated under the convoy system in which merchant fleets were accompanied by convoy ships.

The Spanish merchant fleets were divided into three groups according to their routes once they reached the Spanish Main. The Tierra Firme Fleet sailed to Cartagena to load South American products, especially silver from Potosí. Some ships went to Portobello on the Caribbean coast of Panama to load Peruvian silver that had been shipped from the Pacific coast port of Callao. The New Spain Fleet sailed to Veracruz in Mexico to load not only silver and the valuable red dye cochineal, but also porcelain and silk shipped from China on the Manila galleons. The Asian goods were brought overland from Acapulco to Veracruz by mule train. The Honduras Fleet sailed to Trujillo and loaded dyes and spices from Central America.

The New Spain Fleet that sailed to Mexico departed from Cadiz on 1 July, reached the Caribbean Sea in August and arrived at Veracruz in September. This voyage schedule was intended to avoid the stormy summer weather in the Gulf of Mexico. While spending the winter time in the region, they engaged in trade. Then they sailed to Havana in May to June and sailed back to Spain in the late summer.

The Tierra Firme Fleet departed from Spain in March through May, reached Cartagena around June, and arrived in Panama in two months. The New Spain and *Tierra Firme* Fleets accounted for 85 percent of trade between Spain and its colonies. According to research, approximately 100 ships on average sailed across the Atlantic annually in the 1520s and carried 9,000 *toneladas* (*toneladas* is equivalent to approximately 920kg) on average annually.

By the end of the 16th century, the volume shipped by 150 to 200 ships on average increased to 30,000 to 40,000 *toneladas*. The rapid increase in trade volume might demonstrate that trade with colonies had surged.

Spain made a great effort to protect its territories and wealth in the New World from the invasions of England and France. For their part, England and France attempted to get involved in the Caribbean trade in order to generate the kind of wealth they saw Spain bringing in from its colonies. France built settlements off the Spanish Main and used them as footholds to attack Spanish merchant fleets and coastal settlements. As the Spanish settlements were occupied, the French occupants became known as *buccaneers* who attacked the Spanish empire. France and the Netherlands both plundered the Spanish Main. However, it was England that plundered the Spanish Main for a strategic purpose. Spain had expelled early English traders out of the Caribbean Sea, but the captains of privateer ships, like Francis Drake, came back and engaged in revenge attacks.

Under these circumstances, the Spanish fleets gathered in Havana, Cuba and prepared to return home under the heavy convoy system. The goods that the fleets shipped were a tremendous amount of treasures, like gold and silver, reflecting the nature of American trade. They were literally treasure ships. Since numerous pirates were targeting the treasures, a fleet of galleons convoyed them. Twice a year, a fleet composed of 30 ships brought the goods from Spain for colonial rulers. The fleet anchored under the cannons of coastal fortresses and unloaded the goods and equipment. Then they loaded sealed gold and silver boxes and returned to Seville under the convoy of armed ships.

The convoy system added to the costs of sailing across the Atlantic since enormous expenses were required to operate the large-scale convoy fleets. Spain sought a large-scale measure to prepare for attacks by English and French privateers to protect the storage of gold and silver. Spain built enormous fortresses in treasure ports, such as Veracruz, Cartagena, Portobello and Havana, to protect villages from sea-borne attacks. Despite a fortified defense, vulnerabilities existed, and pirates targeted them. Pirates took advantage of loose watches and raided while the ship was at anchor in port. These were the tactics that Drake used to attack Cartagena.

The New World that Spain had explored rapidly declined in the 17th and 18th centuries, as exclusive trade was no longer possible. By the early 17th century, the Spanish convoy system began to gradually decline. The influx of enormous amounts of silver into Europe downgraded the quality of merchandise and caused inflation. The number of merchant fleets was reduced to fewer than 10 by the late 17th century. By the 1740s, the treasure fleet system almost disappeared, and separate warships carried goods to Spain. The trade network which had been the envy of the rest of the world, and the prey of pirates, disappeared.

Concept of Modern Pirates and Typology

How might these Age of Discovery pirates be classified in terms of their piratical activities and the regions in which they operated? Generally, pirates may be described as the persons engaged in depredation and looting by force and coercion at sea. As international maritime law was formulated in modern times, the definition of piracy was provided in the UN Convention on the Law of the Sea, widely known as the Constitution of the Sea. However, it is only the legal definition of piracy and was formulated in modern times.

Contemporary pirates can be classified in accordance with the typology of criminal acts. Pirates in modern times may be classified depending on their relationship with states or the regions in which they operate. What is apparent is that regardless of their typology, the nature of piracy – depredation by force and threats to the safety of navigation – remains unchanged.

Modern piracy might be described as a social phenomenon, in which pirates fight against the ruling order of society by forming groups based on their own rules, deviating from established maritime order and practices.

The principal reason that pirates were prevalent in early modern times was that state power did not extend to the sea. Pirates exercised violence in the sea where state power was invalid. At first, pirates exercised violence for states, and later they did so outside of the control of states, and ultimately, they exercised violence against states. As such, in order to understand modern pirates, we need to explore how the relationship between pirates and states has changed.

Privateer

A privateer is a private person or ship that engages in maritime warfare under a commission of war. The commission, also known as a letter of marque or reprisal, empowers the person to carry on all forms of hostility permissible at sea by the usages of war, including attacking foreign vessels during wartime and taking them as prizes. The letter of marque was a certificate written in legal terms. Originally, the letter of marque was granted by a ruler to the merchants who had been looted or lost their ships or goods by enemies, to allow them to engage in revenge or recovery of their losses.

In the 16th century, European states made use of the permission to make it easier to attack enemy ships during wartime. European maritime powers encouraged armed private ships to attack and plunder enemy ships by empowering them to seize enemy ships. This was the empowerment of the private sector to participate in the state's task of warfare. Thus, states could save the costs of creating and maintaining standing troops.

Privateers with a letter of marque were exempted from the indictment of piracy and recognized as war prisoners once they were seized by enemies.

On the other hand, from an economic perspective, privateering was a national project carried out under the strict control of the state. Those who intended to get engaged in privateering would apply for the letter of marque and pay deposits on the conditions imposed by the government. Prior to departure, a privateer, a notary and two witnesses signed the contract, and they checked compliance with the regulations when a privateer returned to port. The captain was required to complete a logbook and report it. The ships and cargos captured by a privateer were transferred to the admiralty court to be assessed their values. A certain portion of income reverted to the state, and the rest was distributed among the shipowner, the captain and crew. For European maritime states, privateering was just like killing two birds with one stone since they could inflict damage to enemies using private ships without spending state finances – all while earning income from privateering.

For privateers, they could have a sense of serving their homelands while making money by attacking enemy ships. Privateers at the time did not attack ships from their own countries. As time passed, however, privateering was abused. Privateers turned into pirates, as they continued to commit acts of looting after war had ended.

Corsair

The pirates operating in the Mediterranean were called corsairs. The most widely known among them were the Barbary pirates. As described in the previous chapter, they operated along the coasts of Algeria, Tunis, Sale, and northern North Africa.

Corsairs were granted permission by Muslim rulers governing these regions to attack the ships from Christian states. Saracen pirates also fall within the category of corsairs. And although they are not as well known, Maltese pirates were also corsairs. The Maltese corsairs were engaged in looting ships from the Knights of St. John, which was created to fight Muslims during the crusades. Regardless of the causes of piracy, corsairs were the pirates for ships sailing across the Mediterranean. European states had sent fleets of warships to fight the corsairs, but these actions were not very effective. At last, in 1816, combat against corsairs by a massive joint fleet made the threat of corsairs disappear.

Buccaneer

Buccaneers were the pirates who had been active in the Caribbean Sea and off the coast of South America in the 17th century. Originally, they were hunters who had lived in the woods and valleys in the Hispaniola Island (modern Haiti and Dominican Republic). Most of them were French who raised cattle and pigs brought by early Spanish settlers. They cooked with outdoor stoves or barbeques, and dried meats. They were described as *boucaner* in French and the term 'buccaneer' was derived from it. They lived a harsh life, like wild beasts. They loved to eat the skull of animals and enjoyed drinking and gambling. They looked like butchers because they put on bloody furs, carrying axes and swords. Buccaneers complied with their own rules, living in groups of six to eight.

The Spanish government had hunters kill wild animals Santo Domingo. This deprived poachers of their living. Under this circumstance, they had no choice but to become pirates and they began to fight against the Spanish government. In the 1620s, they moved from the interior of Hispaniola Island to the northern coast of the island, especially the coast of Tortuga Island. Tortuga Island became a base for attacking Spanish merchant ships and for galleons sailing back to Spain, carrying treasures exploited from Mexico and Peru. Tortuga Island, situated in the northern part of Hispaniola, was a small, turtle-shaped island. It had fertile lands and abundant water, and a good geography for defense against invasions – an ideal hideout for buccaneers.

In 1640, the Tortuga pirates began to call themselves 'Sea Brothers.' The buccaneer organizations were not large, but they evolved into a loose coalition, known as the 'Brethren of the Coast.' They attempted a joint attack on important prey. The most notable example was the attack on Panama in 1671 under the command of Henry Morgan, in which they destroyed and burned Spanish cities.

Golden Age of Pirates

The period between the late 17th century and the early 18th century (1690–1730) was called the 'Golden Age of Pirates,' during which piracy was at its height. Over 40 years, Caribbean and African pirates mainly targeted the merchant ships shuttling between Europe and Africa and the slave ships transporting African slaves to the Caribbean Sea, which brought alcohol and sugar back to Africa.

This was the era that novelists such as Robert Louis Stevenson or J.M Barrie, illustrator Howard Pyle, and Hollywood movies depicted when they portrayed the life of pirates. As England and France signed the Treaties of Utrecht to end the War of Spanish Succession (1701–1714), the West Indies and colonies were booming. England ascended to the dominant position in slave trade and commerce, taking the place of a declining Spain. The booming colonial business of England, France and the Netherlands provided pirates a good opportunity to grab wealth. Spain also operated treasure ships, which were the best attraction for pirates.

Blackbeard

At the time, various different nationalities of pirate ships were anchored in the Virgin Islands. New Providence in the Bahamas was home of English and American pirates. Spanish pirates were based in Cuba, Puerto Rico and Saint Augustin, and Martinique was home to French pirates. In their heyday, the Bahamas were a perfect hideout. The islands, which were barely inhabited, had become a nest for pirates since the 1680s. New Providence, capable of accommodating 500 ships at once, was a natural hideout for them, given that warships could not chase them deep into the ports due to shallow waters. Merchants who had settled alongside the pirates provided supplies needed for pirates and traded the prizes that pirates had looted. Along the sandy beach of New Providence, numerous pubs and brothels were booming. The damage inflicted by pirates to European states' business in the new continent was said to be larger than the damage from warfare.

It is estimated that the number of pirates active in the Atlantic during the golden age of pirates was from 1,000 to 2,000. According to one record, 1,800 to 2,400 English and American pirates were active between 1716 and 1718. That number was reduced to 1,500 to 2,000 between 1719 and 1722, and 1,000 to 1,500 between 1723 and 1725, and ultimately fewer than 200. Law enforcement agencies estimated that there were 4,500 to 5,500 pirates, of which 2,400 pirates were active on the sea.

The British government dispatched governors to combat the New Providence pirates, but their efforts were in vain. English pirates Thomas Barrow and Benjamin Hornigold proclaimed the foundation of a Pirate Republic and set themselves up as its governors. The Pirate Republic attracted many pirates to New Providence Island. They were mostly privateers, escaped slaves and criminals. Since alcohol, women and gambling were readily available in New Providence, pirates based in other regions stopped by whenever they departed for a voyage.

Golden Age pirates have been widely used as the subject of novels, movies and dramas. Most of the images of pirates that we are familiar with today were created through these works. The golden age of pirates ended with the death sentence of 12 pirates, who were under command of Bartholomew Roberts, at the admiralty court. Although piracy continued afterwards, no pirate achieved the fame of those who operated during the Golden Age.

England: Country of Pirates

It was England which overtly supported the pirates that looted Spanish fleets carrying treasures from the new continent.
For England, an island state whose many geographical barri-
ers had helped prevent it from becoming the dominant power
in Europe, piracy helped lay the foundation for building 'the
empire on which sun never sets,' helping it rise to the center of
the Atlantic world.

How England, a small island country, built the largest empire in history was well described by Professor Niall Ferguson at
Harvard in his book *Empire*. By 1655, Spain's dominion stretched
from Madrid to Manila, with American lands under its control –
but during that year, English control was limited to only a few
islands in the Caribbean, plantations in North Africa, and ports
in India. What England envied most was the gold and silver that
Spain had discovered in Mexico and Peru. England searched for
silver in the rivers of Canada, the Guianas, Virginia and Gambia,
but most of its efforts were in vain. As a consequence, the English
resorted to the plunder of the Spanish treasure fleets.

Relations between Spain and England were already poor
because of England's persistent looting. In the meantime, the
Protestant Reformation swept through Europe, further dete-
riorating the relationship between the two countries. In 1517,
the Protestant Reformation was initiated by Martin Luther,
condemning the corruption of the pope and Catholic priests.
Bloody conflicts between Catholics and Protestants erupted
across Europe. In 1543, Henry VIII of England proclaimed the
Act of Supremacy, separating from the Vatican. As a result, the
now-officially Protestant England became rivals with Catholic
states such as Spain and France.

Domestically in Spain, Felipe II, who was said to be more
Catholic than the pope, branded the Protestants as pagans and
burnt them at the stake. He sent troops to the Spanish-controlled
Netherlands and executed over 8,000 Dutch Protestants at the
Inquisition. In 1567, the Inquisition in the Netherlands was

instituted with the name of the Council of Troubles on the orders of Felipe II. It was also known as the 'Council of Blood' since many death sentences were pronounced by the tribunal. Outraged by the harsh Spanish oppression of Protestantism, the Dutch went from battling Spain in a religious war to battling it in a war for independence. Anti-Spanish sentiment was so fierce that some Dutch began to swear that it would be better to sink the nation by making holes on its banks, rather than continue under Spanish rule.

Felipe II sent the 130-ship Spanish Armada to suppress the independence movement in the Netherlands. Elizabeth I of England also sent troops to the Netherlands because she believed that Spain would invade England after the suppression of the Dutch revolt. Subsequently, the relationship of the two countries greatly deteriorated, ultimately leading to war. Elizabeth I ordered Francis Drake, the captain of a privateer, to lead the English fleets to fight the Spanish fleets. The English fleets defeated the Spanish Armada at the Battle of Calais.

When the threat of war with Spain was on the horizon, Elizabeth I made a pivotal decision in the history of sea battles and pirates. It was to grant the commission to English ships to plunder Spanish ships. This resulted in the emergence of privateers. In a 15-year period during her reign, 150 to 200 privateers appeared in England annually. On average, privateers generated earnings of 105,000 to 300,000 pounds for England. Elizabeth overtly supported the privateers, which looted Spanish merchant ships and paid tributes to the crown. The Spanish lamented that nine-tenths of the Atlantic trade was under the control of foreigners, even as the Spanish king was nominally ruling the West Indies. Francis Drake was Spain's foremost enemy. However, he was a national hero for England, generating enormous wealth.

Although it was a nation that had supported piracy, England eventually started to turn against them. After war ended, the nation could not afford to control the privateers who had replenished sailors and disturbed supply lines and the commercial networks of enemies. As the pirates who exercised violence for states saw state support begin to wane, they began to exercise violence against those states. England's piracy days were over. It rose to become a civilized empire, dedicated to protecting the universal maritime order.

Trade Wars between England and the Netherlands

England enthusiastically took to the sea in the late 16th century. It concentrated on coal transport as well as cod and herring fishing. Its dominance over shipping across the Atlantic was possible with the subsequent establishment of trade companies, including the Russia Company in 1553, the Eastland Company in 1578, the Levant Company in 1581, the East India Company in 1600 and the Royal African Company in 1660. These trade companies, having privileges granted by the English court, engaged in the trade of slaves and luxury goods. They earned enormous profits by selling expensively while buying cheaply by taking advantage of price gaps between the market and the production areas located across the world.

In the early 17th century, free-trade advocates spoke out against England's exclusive control of trade. They turned their eyes to the African trade, as they were excluded from the luxury trade, which was highly profitable. Since new trade routes were concentrated on tobaccos and sugars, newly emerging merchants were required to throw enormous labor into the transport of goods. By the time Elizabeth I was about to end the war, the Netherlands was emerging as a new maritime power in the 17th century. The Netherlands, a lowland country, was highly developed in manufacturing, shipping, and financing, and had a good commerce relationship with Spain. Since regaining its independence from Spain, the Netherlands rapidly expanded to Africa, Brazil, Asia and the Caribbean Sea. The Netherlands began to engage in the slave trade and smuggling, following the path of England and France.

The Netherlands, now with a footprint in several continents, began to plunder Spanish ships and attack its colonies and trade bases. Instead of having France and England as its chief antagonists, the Netherlands became Spain's principal enemy. The Dutch, as the main shippers in the early Atlantic trade, were on the top of the international capitalist economy. As such, the Dutch became a most powerful enemy, hampering English attempts to exclusively control maritime trade.

The period between 1640 and 1660 in England was a revolutionary era. In 1640, as King Charles I attempted to raise taxes to finance the English invasion of Scotland, the House of Commons, which mostly consisted of rich merchants and middle-class landlords, voiced opposition. As Charles I dissolved the Parliament, the members of the Parliament seized the Palace of Westminster and stood up against the king. With the failure of negotiations, the standoff between the Parliamentary force and Royalists eventually escalated into armed conflicts, leading to the First English Civil War, which raged throughout England, Scotland and Ireland. A majority faction of the Parliament were from the newly emergent merchant class, who were mostly Puritans.

After the victory of the Parliamentary force in the Puritan Revolution (1645–1646) commanded by Oliver Cromwell, the Parliamentary force executed the king and proclaimed the foundation of a republic, known as the 'Commonwealth of England.' During his five-year tenure, Oliver Cromwell wielded an iron rule as the Lord Protector. In the meantime, the merchants, who were determined to dominate the sea, took many seats of the Parliament in 1651 by virtue of the rising wealth and social status that they gained from trade.

They forged a coalition with Cromwell, who was pursuing a policy of mercantilism to focus the country's efforts on promoting commerce and trade, and passed the Navigation Act in 1651 to reinforce their maritime trade dominance. The Navigation Act solidified the nation's long-held policy that its trade had to be carried by English vessels, which included those of the colonies. The Navigation Act prohibited foreign ships from transporting goods to England and its colonies, and it prevented the colonies from directly trading with the Netherlands, Spain, France and their colonies. Under the act, the goods bound for England should be transported by ships with English sailors aboard, and any foreign ship was prohibited from doing coastal trading in England.

The Navigation Act apparently targeted the Dutch traders who took a large part of European trade and the coastal trade of England. Following the Eighty Years' War (1568–1648), the Netherlands, which regained independence, vigorously took to the sea. As the overseas trade of England deteriorated, and Dutch dominated the trade with English colonies, England saw the need to impose sanctions on the Netherlands. The relevant acts of the Navigation Act were subsequently enacted in 1660, 1663 and 1673. They enumerated the goods that were subject to the exclusive control of England in trade with the new continent, which included sugar, tobacco, indigo, rice, cacao, molasses and ship supplies. Against this backdrop, the Navigation Acts served as the mainstay of English overseas trade over the next 200 years.

The Dutch were strongly opposed to the Navigation Acts. As a consequence, three trade wars between England and the Netherlands broke out in the periods between 1652 and 1654, 1665 and 1667, 1672 and 1674. Victorious in the wars with the Netherlands throughout the 17th century, the Navigation Acts allowed England to reinforce its imperial dominance and control trade. These efforts made the English outstrip the Dutch in overseas trade and prompted the commerce revolution in England. As a result, the gross tonnage of ships in England tripled in the late 17th century. English merchants who intended to reinforce the nation's exclusive status in overseas trade ushered England into the era of a trade war that had persisted over a century in the period between 1651 and 1763.

Slave Trade of England

Following the War of Spanish Succession, England had become the principal country in the slave trade by having the privilege of slave trade ('*asiento*'). Louis XIV of France recognized England's having the *asiento* that had been possessed by Spain, in exchange for the ascension of his grandson Philip to the Spanish Crown. Thus, England was able to earn enormous profits by monopolizing the slave trade across the Atlantic. The *asiento* granted English traders the rights to supply 4,800 slaves annually to Spanish America through the South Sea Company.

Here, we need to take a look at the historical background of England's role in the slave trade. As England expanded to the Caribbean, it occupied Spanish islands and explored the colonies on the east coast of the new continent. England created a new revenue model, which was different from that of early explorers such as Spain and the Netherlands. Spain brought enormous amounts of gold and silver from mines in Spanish America, and the massive influx of gold and silver rapidly increased currencies throughout Europe. Spain, which had few manufacturing bases, imported its industrial goods from other European countries by paying with the gold and silver brought from the new continent.

As a result, other European countries enjoyed the greater benefits from trade with the new continent. The Dutch earned large profits from the spices brought from South Asia. Nevertheless, they were not substantial goods that could affect all of Europe. The latecomer England built production bases of sugar, tobacco and cotton in the Caribbean and the colonies in North America, targeting the European market. Thus, England brought in substantial revenue from selling manufactured goods made by its advanced manufacturing technology

The overseas-based trade of England required a massive labor force, and the slave trade supplied a large amount of cheap labor. As described earlier, they were involved in a triangular trade: English traders sailed to the west coast of Africa carrying the goods from England that had so fascinated the Africans.

They bartered with local slave traders for slaves. Then they sold the slaves to the plantation owners on the new continent, and brought the plantations' sugar and tobacco back home. This was an extremely lucrative business that generated enormous revenues once ships came back safely.

An episode about the slave trade at the time was well described in *Robinson Crusoe* by Daniel Defoe. Crusoe, an Englishman who ran a plantation in Brazil with other owners, attempted to secretly engage in the slave trade to supply their plantation with labor. On the voyage, they had a shipwreck in stormy weather, and Robinson Crusoe was the only survivor. He landed on an uninhabited island and spent 28 years there alone. In the 1600s, the background of the novel, nations needed permission from the Spanish and Portuguese courts before they engaged in the slave trade, as those two countries had exclusive control over the trade.

Otherwise, one might be involved in smuggling slaves from Africa. The novel depicted how these trades were committed in this passage: "We carried trivial goods to trade with Africans onboard ship, such as beads, pieces of glass, shells, small glasses and knives, scissors and axes. As we could buy a bunch of slaves, along with gold dust, grains and ivories in exchange for these goods, we could use them by bringing them to Brazil."

Anti-Piracy Measures by England

The pirates in the West Indies were a barrier to the lucrative slave trade of England. Attacks on English slave ships and merchant ships by the pirates based in Nassau on New Providence Island continued to increase. Pirates targeted slaves ships not for the slaves themselves, but rather to seize vessels that were suitable for long voyages, fully stocked with food and ammunition. In the early 18th century, many of the slave ships held captive were used for pirate ships. The *Whydah* was a case in point. The *Whydah,* used for the slave ship, was captured by the notorious Caribbean pirate captain 'Black Sam' Bellamy in February 1717. It sank in April 1717, loaded with valuable goods, while under the control of the pirates.

For England, the pirates were targeted for removal in order to protect the booming slave trade across the Atlantic. Traders in slave trade ports such as Liverpool, Bristol and London filed a petition requesting that the Parliament enact anti-piracy legislation. In the meantime, they appealed to the Navy to take measures to protect their properties. England, fearing that the prestige of the Great British Empire was hurt, came up with comprehensive anti-piracy measures. The House of Commons passed the Piracy Act in 1698 and deployed three additional warships to the Caribbean Sea. England declared that if they surrendered, pirates were sure to be pardoned. If they did not, they would be suppressed. The governor of the Bahamas was granted full authority to suppress the pirates in New Providence and Harbor Islands.

England also deployed a small fleet to the coast of Africa. The small fleet was engaged in a battle with the pirate ships of Bartholomew Roberts, killing over 100 pirates, seizing hundreds and putting them on trial. The captured pirates were brought to the Cape Coast Castle, which had been the hub of slave trade, and hanged. Their corpses were hung on public display, a practice called 'gibbeting,' to discourage other potential pirates.

By 1726, by virtue of the persistent anti-piracy efforts of maritime powers, led by England, the pirates who were a barrier to the accumulation of capital were completely removed. Aa a result, England, which achieved maritime supremacy in the west coast of Africa, became the largest exporter of slaves – a status it maintained until 1807. Capital from colonial plantations in the Caribbean Sea, combined with merchant capital in major cities, was used to fight the first generation of pirates in the 1670s. Afterwards, the capital of the East India Company fought the pirates in the 1690s. It was the capital of the slave trade which fought the pirates in the early 18th century.

But by 1808, England – which had earned enormous wealth from the slave trade – declared it illegal, and urged other European countries to follow suit. The ban was principally brought about by the massive Anti-Slave Trade Campaign in England, which had claimed that the slave trade was contrary to humanism and universal moral values. Additionally, by this point an alternative to slave labor was available, thanks to steam engines. Europeans immigrated on a grand scale to America aboard steam engine locomotives, and they could afford to meet the labor force demand to some degree.

Denmark had prohibited the slave trade prior to England. However, England's move to ban the trade directly affected the subsequent bans of other countries across the Atlantic in the 19th century. The U.S. (1808), Sweden (1813), the Netherlands (1814), France (1815), Spain (1820) and Brazil (1830) subsequently banned the slave trade, and shortly thereafter, the slave trade itself was repealed. In the period between Europeans' sailing to America across the Atlantic and American slaves' being freed in the wake of American Civil War, the number of African slaves exported to America was up to 20 million.

Chapter 11

Life of Pirates

Who Became a Pirate?

One might wonder why people were motivated to become pirates, especially in light of the heavy punishments of hanging or grueling slave labor that were meted out for the crime. The motives for becoming a pirate were mixed: a combination of individual desire and social structural factors. Among them, the individual desire to enjoy an affluent life and rise out of the misery of the lowest class was the principal motive. Piracy allowed pirates to have money to spend, food to eat, and drink and women to indulge in.

The pirate community, known for the fair allocation of prizes and equal treatment among crew members, was very attractive to merchant ship sailors who suffered from hunger, low wages and hard labor. At worst, a pirate could expect to be hanged. However, this fear was minimal for a hungry, oppressed person who saw piracy as a path to affluence, pleasure and freedom. The immediate and realistic goal of pirates was to live a short but pleasant life. English pirates were mostly from the lowest class in the West or Wales. Of the 52 pirates sentenced to hanging in the west coast of Africa in 1722, more than half were from these regions. Escaped slaves and the biracial offspring of black and white parents, already disfavored in society, were readily ushered into piracy. The pirate group composed of those from Scotland, England, Spain and Portugal, as well as mixed-race people, had dominated the Bahamas region for over 20 years. Most pirates were unmarried and vagabonds without family. Married persons were not accepted because it was assumed that they would be more concerned with supporting their families than being loyal to their shipmates.

Although it was very rare, a few well-educated nobles were among the pirates. Pirate John Hinchey graduated from Edinburgh University. When he was arrested, he appealed on the grounds that he was forced to become a pirate, and ultimately he was freed. The case of Henry Mainwaring was very interesting. He received a law degree from the Oxford University in 1602. After military service, he bought a ship to take to the sea and turned to piracy. Mainwaring engaged in the looting of Spanish ships in the English Channel and off the coast of Spain between 1613 and 1615. He was eventually pardoned, and later he served as the Minister of Navy and a member of the House of Commons and a novelist.

The example of Stede Bonnet, known as the Gentleman Pirate, showed how the wealthy and educated man could have a miserable fate by recklessly engaging in piracy. Bonnet, who became tired of his comfortable life in Barbados, bought a ship and arms, recruited 70 sailors, and then engaged in piracy. He joined the infamous pirate Blackbeard in Nassau as he engaged in piracy along the coasts of Virginia and Carolina. Bonnet, who lacked sailing experience, ceded his ship's command to Blackbeard and stayed as a guest. Later, he was pardoned and received a commission to go privateering against Spanish ships.

However, Bonnet was tempted to resume piracy. So as not to lose his pardon, he went back to piracy under the alias Captain Thomas. He was captured by a naval anti-piracy expedition sent by the governor of South Carolina in October 1718. In trial, the judge referred to him as "a well-educated, polite and respected gentleman." However, his good education and background rather worked against him, and he was sentenced to death. Bonnet wrote to the governor appealing for clemency, but the governor endorsed the judge's decision. Eventually he was hanged in Charles Town in December 1718.

Captain John Silver in *Treasure Island* by Robert Louis Stevens was alluded to as an intelligent person in the conversation of his fellow pirates: "John is not an ordinary man. He was well educated when he was young. He knows how to speak and act in a noble manner, like someone out of a book." Many pirates were from merchant ships, naval ships and privateers. The pirates from merchant ships were mostly those who had volunteered to become pirates when their ship was captured by pirates. Merchant ship sailors, who suffered from rampant disease, poor food, barbaric discipline and low wages, did not hesitate to become a pirate once their ship was held captive. When the captain or quartermaster of the pirate ship asked the captives if they would work under the flag of the King of Hell, many of them stepped forward without hesitation. For the sailors who had nothing to lose, they regarded being a pirate as a better way.

Cooper Mower to Become a Pirate

Becoming a pirate was not necessarily voluntary. After taking a ship, one of the pirates' principal tasks was to recruit skilled men needed for the pirates' vessel. Skilled men were forced to join the pirates one way or another. The most in-demand were carpenters for repair and maintenance, and coopers to manage barrels. The job of carpenter was very important for warships. They worked under the apprenticeship system at shipyards and were qualified shipbuilders. They were responsible for the maintenance and repair of the ship, ranging from the keel to the mast. Carpenters were always busy because the pressure of harsh waves on the ship was very heavy. The carpenters played an essential role in repairing holes and broken gears, and replacing broken parts during or after a battle.

For the pirates who could not repair their ship in the shipyard, the carpenter was even more critical. Tropical downpours and intense heat in the Caribbean caused seams to open and wood to rot. Besides the growth of seaweed and barnacles, the warm water encouraged the teredo worm to attack the ship. Under these circumstances, ships were required to be regularly checked and repaired for the safety of the voyage.

The role of cooper was no less critical than the carpenter, although less essential for the safety of the ship. The cooper was a key person for providing food for the crew. In the 17th and the 18th centuries, most food on ship was stored in barrels. The bottom of a merchant ship or a warship was fully loaded with various sizes of barrels holding beef, biscuit, water, beer and wine. The cooper made and repaired barrels and managed the stored foods in barrels. For this reason, pirates first searched for these skilled craftsmen when they took a ship.

The dramatic account of the pirates' need for skilled craftsmen appeared in an article of the *Boston Gazette* on November 29, 1725. When the ship that a man called Cooper Mower was aboard was approached by a pirate ship, he "shewed more concern than any of us, crying and saying he was sure they would force him because he was a cooper." And just as he suspected, he was forced to join them as soon as pirates took the ship. The methods that the pirates used left him little choice. "One of the pirates stuck Mower many blows on his head with the helve of axe. His head was bruised and bloodied. The same pirate forced Mower to lay his head down on the coaming of the hatch, and lifting the axe over his head swore that if he did not sign their Articles immediately, he would chop off his head. Mower begged hard for his life. After the same pirate carried Mower into the Round House where they continued a short time, Mower coming out told the declarant and other prisoners that he was ruined and undone, for they forced him to sign their Articles."

Pirates and the Irony of Peacetime

In peacetime, a greater number of pirates appeared. Many pirates were granted the privilege of privateering during wartime in the 18th century, but after the war ended, numerous sailors and seamen lost their jobs. Thus, they opted to become pirates as a last resort for their survival. Since England, France and Spain ended the War of the Spanish Succession in 1714, ironically, the number of pirates soared during the next 25 years. The rolls of the Royal Navy of England help explain why: In 1703 the navy had 53,785 sailors – by 1715, that number was reduced to 13,439, with 40,000 sailors losing their jobs.

The unemployed seamen and sailors had no homes and no livelihoods, and if they did find jobs, they made less money in harsher conditions. For the privateers, which were granted the authority to plunder enemy ships during wartime, the letter of marque became void with the end of war. As such, the sailors or privateers had no choice but to become pirates. Against this backdrop, England and France tacitly acknowledged their piracy, and the pirates took advantage of it to expand their activities. Some mutinied in their own merchant ships, stealing the vessel and engaging in piracy.

With the sufficient replenishment of the labor force, the wages of sailors plunged, the quality of food deteriorated and violence aboard ship became prevalent. Some sailors mutinied against harsh working conditions, took a ship and flew a black flag. Especially in the period between 1716 and 1726, crewmen onboard slave ships bound for West Africa mutinied against poor working conditions, shaking the foundation of the slave trade. The ages of pirates at the time ranged from 17 to 50, of which the ages of 20-29 were the vast majority. According to the findings of historian Marcus Rediker, the age distribution was almost equivalent to that of merchant ships. This might demonstrate that piracy was equally attractive to sailors of all ages.

Democratic Pirate Community

The term 'democratic' may not match the image of pirates who committed brutal violence and illegal activities, especially in the oppressive, authoritarian Golden Age in which these pirates lived. Nevertheless, the term 'democratic' may apply, given the way that pirates ran their community. Pirates created a new order. They drew up a pirate code, which was a common discipline for pirates, to maintain order among them. The code was self-imposed, often improvised discipline from the bottom, agreed upon by sailors. The pirate code was tough, but was based in equalitarianism under which the authority of the captain was placed under the control of sailors.

Exploring the motives these people had in choosing a life of piracy helps shed light on why equality was such a highly regarded value in their society. These people desired to escape the oppression and abuses of their ships, live lives free of the oppressive authority of the captain and senior sailors, and be free from harsh labor.

In fact, pirates' labor was much less intense than that of sailors on merchant ships. Much greater numbers of pirates were aboard ship in comparison with merchant ships of the same size. As illustrated previously, for a merchant ship of 200 tons, 13 to 17 sailors were aboard, but about 80 pirates were aboard the same size pirate ship. As a result, the allocation of work and labor intensity was much less.

On pirate ships, the captain was elected by a majority of sailors and only retained his authority by permission of the crew. The captain was granted full authority in chasing prey and plundering, but had to follow the decisions of the majority of pirates for other things. The pirates decided the destination of voyages and the ships or coastal settlements to attack. The formation of a new pirate code or the election of a new captain required approval from all pirates. The captain was not given special treatment such as additional food or special facilities. He was, however, to be expelled for cowardly acts or a refusal to loot. If the captain exercised power beyond his authority, he would even be executed.

The pirates protected their interests by having a quartermaster elected by the rank-and-file pirates. The quartermaster was not only a representative of the pirates, but also a trustee for all. He had authority to impose punishment, like whipping and beating. He was responsible for leading attacks and managing the prizes. A principal policy that could affect the well-being of pirates was decided in the pirate council, which was the body of highest authority in the ship. The decisions made in the council were irreversible.

The equalitarianism was notable in allocating the prizes. The captain and the quartermaster were allocated from one and half shares to two shares of a prize. Senior sailors such as gunner, boatswain, navigator, minister, doctor, and craftsman were given from one share and a quarter to one share and half of a prize. The rest of sailors were given one share. Notably, the gap between the top and the bottom in the allocation of prizes was largely lessened by balancing the wage hierarchy. It was the most equal allocation system across society in the early 18th century. This might be because pirates regarded themselves as sharing the risks together, not merely as wage laborers.

Pirates faithfully complied with the rule that no one deserved more than their proper share. They had to take an oath before the allocation of prizes that they would not take more than their proper shares from the seized ship and would not deceive their fellow pirates upon this point. Once they violated the rule, they were expelled from the pirate community and never allowed to come back. The nine complete and nearly complete sets of pirate codes that have survived were chiefly from Charles Johnson's *A General History of the Pyrates*, first published in 1724, and from the records kept by Admiralty Court proceedings at the trials of pirates. The below, contained in Johnson's book, is the pirate code made by the pirates under command of Bartholomew Robert. By exploring the code, one might take a look at the life of pirates at the time. The accounts in parentheses were added by the author.

1. Every man has a vote in affairs of moment; has equal title to the fresh provisions, or strong liquors, at any time seized, and may use them at pleasure, unless a scarcity (*not an uncommon thing among them*) makes it necessary, for the good of all, to vote a retrenchment.

2. Every man to be called fairly in turn, by list, on board of prizes because, (*over and above their proper share*) they were on these occasions allowed a shift of clothes: but if they defrauded the company to the value of a dollar in plate, jewels, or money, marooning was their punishment. If the robbery was only betwixt one another, they contented themselves with slitting the ears and nose of him that was guilty, and set him on shore, not in an uninhabited place, but somewhere, where he was sure to encounter hardships.

3. No person to game at cards or dice for money.

4. The lights and candles to be put out at eight o'clock at night: if any of the crew, after that hour still remained inclined for drinking, they were to do it on the open deck.

5. To keep their piece, pistols, and cutlass clean and fit for service.

6. No boy or woman to be allowed amongst them. If any man were to be found seducing any of the latter sex, and carried her to sea, disguised, he was to suffer death; (*so that when any fell into their hands, as it chanced in the Onslow, they put a sentinel immediately over her to prevent ill consequences from so dangerous an instrument of division and quarrel; but then here lies the roguery; they contend who shall be sentinel, which happens generally to be one of the greatest bullies, who, to secure the lady's virtue, will let none lie with her but himself.*)

7. To desert the ship or their quarters in battle was punished with death or marooning.

8. No striking one another on board, but every man's quarrels to be ended on shore, at sword and pistol. (*The quartermaster of the ship, when the parties will not come to any reconciliation, accompanies them on shore with what assistance he thinks proper, and turns the disputants back to back at so many paces distance; at the word of command, they turn and fire immediately (or else the piece*)

is knocked out of their hands). If both miss, they come to their cut-lasses, and then he is declared the victor who draws the first blood.)

9. No man to talk of breaking up their way of living, till each had shared one thousand pounds. If in order to this, any man should lose a limb, or become a cripple in their service, he was to have eight hundred dollars out of the public stock, and for lesser hurts proportionately.

10. The captain and quartermaster to receive two shares of a prize: the master, boatswain, and gunner, one share and a half, and other officers one and quarter.

11. The musicians to have rest on the Sabbath Day, but the other six days and nights, none without special favour.

In most pirate codes, the values of democracy, equality and discipline were the most highly regarded, but a particular value was highlighted in some codes – namely, a provision that the sailor who discovered a target for plundering would be rewarded with money, the best guns or arms.

Other provisions in the code warned of punishments: Article 6 of Captain John Phillips' articles, set for his men in 1724, provided: "*That man that shall snap his arms, or smoke tobacco in the hold, without a cap to his pipe, or carry a candle lighted without a lanthorn, shall suffer the same punishment as in the former Article.*" Interestingly, there existed an early form of disability insurance in the pirate community. Pirates were always exposed to the risk of being injured. Injured pirates were paid rewards in accordance to the degree of their wounds. If one lost his right arm in battle, he was paid 600 silver pesos, which was the highest reward; for the left arm, 500 pesos; for the right leg, 500 pesos; for the left leg, 400 pesos; for an eye or finger, 100 pesos.

Discipline aboard a pirate ship

The discipline aboard pirate ship was less arbitrary and barbaric. Although some of the rules were strict, generally some acts that warranted punishment in other maritime sectors were tolerated here. As illustrated in the code of Bartholomew Roberts, some method of managing disputes among pirates was required in order to maintain order and unity in the closed space of a ship where 80 tough men lived together. In the event that a quarrel turned into a fight, a duel was not allowed aboard ship, but must take place on the shore. It was a tactic for maintaining unity among the pirates. The rule of duels was clearly stated so that victory or defeat was apparent, and thus prevented the dispute from escalating into a gang fight.

Those who were intolerable to their shipmates or violated a principal rule were punished with marooning – in other words, being left alone on an uninhabited island, a practice sardonically referred to as 'being appointed the governor of the island.' In the event of defrauding colleagues to take more than one's proper share, desertion or pretending to be sick in battle, or stealing, the probability of punishment by marooning became higher. Indeed, marooning was a much harsher punishment than death.

There is an episode in *Treasure Island* about Ben Gunn marooned on an uninhabited island. Ben Gunn persuaded his colleagues to go to Treasure Island to explore the treasures that Captain Flint had hidden. As the pirates had no success in finding treasures, they turned on Ben Gunn, and finally marooned him. Ben Gunn was given only a gun and an axe when he was abandoned on the island. He had been marooned for three years, living on wild goats, strawberries and oysters, until he was discovered by Jim Hawkins.

The last resort to maintain order aboard ship was execution. The punishment of execution was exercised when pirates had a boy or woman aboard ship, but was mostly used to punish captains who abused their authority.

When a new pirate joined the crew, he was required to take an oath of allegiance and not deceive his colleagues. If a man was willing to leave, in many cases pirates did not force him to stay; as many had undergone the closed and authoritarian world of the merchant ships, they held the freedom to come and go as one pleased in high regard. Opponents to the captain used to leave the ship by drawing up a new pirate code. When a new group was created, the social homogeneity of pirates was secured.

fast Living

Pirates at sea wore trousers and jackets made of coarse fabric. In battle, they protected themselves by putting on clothes coated with pine resin or made of thick fur. However, on the shore, they put on luxurious clothes looted from the ship. Some pirates looked like the London playboys of the day by putting on wigs and makeup. They loved luxurious decorations, and wore jewelry of gold and crosses of pearl. Pirates had their own way of speaking as well, with speech heavily layered with curses, vile language and profanity. Using this language was a signal of their belonging to the group and a way to forge bonds between them.

Pirates loved hot and spicy foods and strong liquors. Drunken merrymaking was their daily life. Drinking strong liquor was routine. They relieved the harsh working conditions aboard ship and the tension of piracy by drinking. Pirates who had always lived with hunger in their previous lives weren't worried about going without food here, where they spent their days eating and drinking. Famous pirate drinks involved cocktails called bombs – one was a blend of rum, water, sugar and beans, while another was a combination of egg, sugar, sherry and beer. Brandy, sherry and wine were also eagerly consumed. Many pirates died of alcoholism.

When pirates were hanged, they blamed drinking for leading them down the wrong path and engaging in heinous acts of piracy. In 1724, before William White was hanged, he regretted: "I was ruined by drinking and was drunk when I embarked on the pirate ship for the first time." John Archer, who was hanged on the same day, shed tears of regret: "Excessive drinking made me commit crimes that were worse than death. Charles Johnson in *A General History of the Pyrates* depicted the life of pirates enjoying fast living. According to his depiction, since pirates had a strong bond with each other, they helped fellow pirates who found themselves penniless. Not everyone was so helpful, though: Although the owners of pubs were generous about providing drinks and foods on credit, they sold out the pirates once debts piled up. A pirate spent 3,000 pesos to see the nude body of a prostitute and was sold out by those debts in three months.

(Methods of Pirate Attack

Pirates generally used a large sailing boat when they attacked targets. But they sometimes used a small boat with no deck. The West Indies pirates used canoes taken from local fishermen, for example. A small canoe could accommodate five to six people and a large canoe 25 people at maximum. Canoes were powered by either oars or sails. Attacks using a small boat without a deck was a tactic preferred by buccaneers in the late 17th century. Henry Morgan, especially, frequently used canoes to attack Spanish coastal settlements. The raid of Portobello was the most dramatic example – Morgan used canoes to land because they were much harder to spot from shore.

On 23 April 1680, pirates rowing in canoes left their mother ship and attacked a Spanish fleet of three ships at anchor. The 68 pirates, aboard five canoes and two larger dugouts, approached and attacked the Spanish fleet. They used muskets to precisely target and kill a number of sailors on deck. Despite being heavily armed and vigilant about possible pirate attacks, the Spanish fleet was helpless against the clever tactics of bold pirates. Only 26 out of 86 aboard the flagship survived, and the ship was seized by the pirates.

Pirates had always an upper hand in terms of selecting targets and attacking, but they were very cautious when planning an attack. Pirates were able to chase the target ship for several hours, speculating about its defensive capabilities and estimating the number of sailors and cannons aboard. In the event that the target ship was an Indian merchant ship – which had strong defenses – pirates changed their route to search for a ship with weaker defenses. If the target ship was identified as attackable, pirates could choose to do a raid or a frontal attack. As illustrated in the case of Saracen pirates, the best way to make a target ship defenseless was to fly a fake flag. This method had been used by warships during wartime. Before wireless communications and Morse Code were invented, the only way to identify the nationality of ships at sea was to fly flags. In the 1700s, national flags were used, and skilled seamen were able to identify the nationality of a ship by the flag that flew on the top mast.

The method of attack used by the pirates who dominated the Caribbean Sea in the 18th century was slightly different. When they approached the target, they rushed toward the ship without hiding their intentions. The typical method of attack was to fly the black flag on the top mast and attack by firing on the target ship. Their weaponry and number of sailors was greater than that of their targets, and the pirates believed in their own infamy. Since there were few sailors aboard merchant ships who had battle experience, the pirate ship's attack was like being attacked by a warship. Furthermore, the sailors could not afford to resist, out of fear that they would be tortured or killed once they were caught. Some pirates escalated the horror by firing lethal sniper shots. Above all, the most powerful and destructive method of pirate attack was a broadside, firing all guns on one side of ship. Pirates rarely used this method so as not to damage their prizes. However, they did not hesitate at all to use a broadside to have a target ship surrender.

Pirate Attack

Pirates did not get onboard the target ship immediately after stopping it. Instead, they usually had the captain come over to the pirate ship in a boat that they provided. This was for holding the captain hostage while they looted the merchant ship. An interesting point is that the sailors obediently surrendered without resistance once they were attacked by pirates. They knew that they could not afford to fight against a pirate ship armed with heavy cannons and 100 sailors aboard. Of the victim ships of pirate attacks in 1719, the largest ship had 12 cannons and 30 sailors aboard. Most other merchant ships were armed with four to six cannons and 14 to 16 sailors. A merchant ship loaded with heavy goods could not easily escape a swiftly moving pirate ship.

Methods of Looting

Pirates refrained from beating sailors once they surrendered without resistance. Indeed, some pirates behaved gently. They treated the captain warmly or, in rare cases, refrained from looting or even paid them money. However, that was extremely exceptional. Typically, pirates heavily punished the captains and senior sailors who abused rank-and-file sailors. Another feature of pirate attacks was that pirates took time in their looting, contrary to contemporary pirates, who loot and run away swiftly.

Pirates were not hasty. They had sufficient reason to loot at their leisure. Most attacks were committed in the distant sea, invisible to the land. Since these events were prior to the invention of wireless communication, there was no way for the victim ship to call for rescue. This was also the case in the event that pirate attacks occurred off a port or shore. For example, in the Caribbean Sea, which stretches 2,000 miles to the east and west and 1,500 miles to the north and south, the patrol in 1715 was conducted by only four warships and two sailing ships. Under this circumstance, pirates were able to loot without worry that a patrol would catch them.

As we are well aware, pirates had a keen interest in treasures, and most pirates joined up to attain them. Interestingly, however, household items were also highly prized. After all, pirates who spent a long time at sea could not survive on treasure alone, no matter how valuable. They needed essential items for life aboard ship – not only food and drinks, but also ropes and sails.

Pirates could not repair their ships at port, unlike merchant ships. They could not call in ship items to vendors and repairmen either. Since they had to repair their ships in the sea or in an uninhabited estuary by themselves, they looted necessary ship items for their use. In 1717, when the pirate ship attacked a small sailing boat *Restoration*, the pirates took all goods aboard ship, including food, masts, pumps, bolts, needles, strings, kettles and frying pans. In October 1723, pirates took 14 boxes of candles, jib, strings, anchors, wire ropes and other woodworking tools when they attacked a ship off Barbados.

Clamor For Revenge

Historian Eric Hobsbawm described the revolt of farmers against oppression and poverty as a clamor for revenge, and piracy was no different. Pirates, mostly from the lowest class, suffered the painful trauma of oppressive social systems or abuse on board merchant ships or warships. For this reason, in many cases, pirates named their ship '*Revenge*.' Such naming was intended primarily to threaten the target ship. However, it was also a result of the internal sense of injustice and the grudge they bore against their entire society. The legendary pirate Blackbeard named his ship *Queen Anne's Revenge*. The infamous captains Stede Bonnet and John Call named their ships *Revenge* and *New York's Revenge,* respectively.

The primary target of this revenge was the captain of a seized merchant ship. Pirates exercised 'justice' in their own manner once they seized a merchant ship. They asked the sailors how the captain had treated them, then they exercised the 'judgement of justice' in their own way for any captain who was believed to have abused the sailors and exercised oppressive authority. The most common punishment was to spray salt over a captain's sores after whipping. In the ship of Bartholomew Roberts, an 'executer of justice' was appointed.

One of these punishments against the captain was known as 'sweating.' This involved poking and prodding the victim with cutlasses, swords and various sharp instruments while he tried to dodge the blows. The victim's only option was to 'run' or 'dance' around the mast, all the time accompanied by the sound of the ship's fiddle. Many of the captains held captive were punished with sweating, by which infamous captains were executed immediately. The acts of revenge were a tit for tat against the tyrannical and arbitrary authority that the captain had wielded.

Nevertheless, punishments against the captains were not necessarily imposed indiscriminately. The captain known to have never abused sailors was greeted cordially by pirates. The example of Captain William Snelgrave, captured and freed by pirates, may illustrate the case. He was captured by a group of pirates along the coast of West Africa in 1719. He was originally attacked by the quartermaster for failing to surrender. He was beaten and shot in the arm, but his men cried out "For God's sake, don't kill our captain, for we were never with a better man."

The quartermaster stopped the beating and interviewed the sailors over the captain's abuses. No one spoke ill of him. Eventually, Snelgrave was spared. The pirate captain apologized for his men's violent acts, saying that their acts were to revenge sordid merchants and cruel captains. Recognizing that Snelgrave was respected by his men, the captain returned the ship to him and offered to buy the goods aboard ship. The pirates intended to demonstrate to merchants that good luck would befall a good captain. The offer was decided unanimously among the pirates, but Snelgrave hesitated to accept the offer in fear that he would be suspected of collusion with pirates. The pirates accepted his refusal, believing that it was better to let any man live in his own way.

Pirates cried out that vagabonds and poor men like themselves never received the benefit of law and justice, and that just punishments were never exacted against merchants or captains. So, they took matters into their own hands.

Pirates' Flag: Jolly Roger

Pirates had their own flags, known as '*Jolly Roger*,' which is the traditional 18th century name for the flags flown to identify a pirate ship about to attack. The design most commonly identified as the *Jolly Roger* today is the skull and crossbones symbol on a black background, which was used during the 1710s by a number of pirate captains, including Black Sam Bellamy, Edward England, and John Taylor. The symbol went on to become the

Jolly Roger

most commonly used pirate flag during the 1720s. This symbol has since become emblazoned in the popular imagination as the primary image of piracy, appearing in all novels and movies that depict the pirate life.

The skull and crossbones was only part of various pirate symbols. In the golden era of piracy during the early 18th century, there were a variety of popular symbols in use, including bloody hearts, burning cannons, sandglasses, spears, swords and skulls. Red or bloody symbol flags were commonly used by the middle of the 18th century. The common feature of these flags, regardless of the symbol they used, was that they were able to strike terror into the sailors aboard the target ship. The flags should arouse a sense of horror and the promise of a threat that they would not survive unless they obediently surrendered. The pirate flags depicted a triad of interlocking symbols, according to historian Marcus Rediker – 'death, violence and limited time.'

The origin of these flags has been the subject of some controversy. The skull and crossbones, widely known as the 'dead man's head,' had been the symbol of death since the Middle Ages. The symbol was commonly used by churches or on gravestones in cathedrals. Sailors used the symbol to record the death of sailors in the logbook. In a certain period between 1700 and 1720, the symbol, along with the image of a sandglass or arms, had been perceived by pirates as the most intimidating image to use. Pirates used simple red and black flags to convey different meanings as well. A red flag meant no mercy, while the *Jolly Roger* meant mercy could be granted. During the golden era of piracy, captains had their own flags. Bartholomew Roberts used a flag depicting himself stepping on two skulls representing Barbados and Martinique. As the authorities of Barbados and Martinique intended to capture him, he used this design to express his resentment and dominance over them. The pirate captain Calico Jack used the symbol of the dead man's head on the crossed swords.

There are arguments over the origin of the term '*Jolly Roger.*' One argument is that it stems from a mispronunciation of the French words 'Jolie Rogue' which means 'pretty red color.'. Another argument is that it was derived from the Tamil pirate captain Ali Raja, who operated in the Indian Ocean. The most appealing argument is that it originated from the nickname of the devil, *Old Roger*. The description of *Old Roger* is found in the judicial record of the trial of a captain and sailors held in Boston in 1702: "After three months, pirates sailed flying the *Old Roger*, leaving the coast of Brazil. The *Old Roger* was designed with the symbol in which one hand held a sandglass and the other hand held an arrow stuck into a bloody heart."

Most pirate flags used a white symbol on a black background, but black flags were persistently used as well. In 1718, when the fleet commanded by Blackbeard raided a merchant ship in the Gulf of Honduras, two pirate ships were flying the flag of the dead man's head, and the other three ships were flying red flags.

Bases of Pirates

What was used for pirate land bases in the Age of Discovery? Although pirates spent a great deal of time in search of prey at sea, they needed a land base for rest, ship maintenance and to deal out prizes. Pirates preferred places beyond the reach of national authority, or islands with natural protections from invasion. Although remote islands might be expected to be an ideal base, pirates could not remain isolated from the outside world; they had to live with other people so as to draw support from them.

Furthermore, land bases should be located close to the shipping routes of merchant ships that carried valuable goods. Thus, pirates typically aimed to build their bases in the Caribbean Sea and the Indian Ocean. Pirates travelled all around the world and built bases off the principal shipping routes while remaining far away from the reach of national authority. They preferred uninhabited islands and shallow seas, which made it difficult for warships to give chase.

The Bahamas, which had been out of the control of the British government, had been attractive to pirates since 1716, and hundreds of them settled in. As national authority did not reach their base, pirates regarded the Bahamas as their meeting place – their own islands. The islands were a kind of free zone for pirates, where their acts were not controlled at all. As the complaints of colonial settlers surged, George I of England ordered Woodes Rogers to lead the expedition to combat the Bahamas pirates. His expedition was successful, and as a result, the pirates were expelled from the Bahamas and dispersed to uninhabited small islands off the Carolinas, in the Caribbean Sea and off the coast of Africa.

Madagascar Island in the Indian Ocean, where pirates began to settle in 1691, was used as a place to stay as well as store prizes. Merchant ships bound for or departing from India called in the ports of Madagascar for supply and rest. Saint Mary's Island off the northwest coast was a cesspool of privateers and buccaneers. The island was easy to defend and was a known base for 17 pirate ships and 1,500 pirates until 1700. By 1696, another pirate base was built at the northern end of the island. As Madagascar became a favored location for pirates, it brought a great deal of terror and disruption for the countries engaged in trade with India. Pirates primarily preyed upon merchant ships sailing through the Indian Ocean. The most notable incident here occurred in 1695, when infamous pirate captain Henry Every seized the enormous treasure ship *Ganj-i-Sawai,* which carried the princess of the Mughal Empire.

As Madagascar was booming as a pirate hotspot, merchants flowed in to facilitate the trade of prizes and the supply of food and other necessities. They provided pirates with foods, drink and ship items, and brokered the transaction of prizes such as gold, silver, silk and slaves between the merchants in Boston and New York and the pirates. As the attacks of Madagascar pirates had become a frequent occurrence by 1705, the Parliament of England came up with the measures to reduce the risk of piracy. An escort service was provided for the ships sailing around Madagascar, and the naval fleets composed of warships patrolled this hotspot of piracy. As a result, attacks in this region began to decrease. Many pirates moved to other regions or settled on islands as farmers. Some pirates joined the Angria pirates based off the west coast of India. In 1711, only 60 to 70 pirates remained in Madagascar.

Port Royal in Jamaica was the busiest trade hub in the West Indies. The prosperous village centered around the fortress that the English had built, and pirates were rampant therein. Port Royal was originally a fortress that England had built to protect itself from attacks after it occupied Spanish-controlled Jamaica in 1655. Over four years, 200 houses, stores and storage buildings were densely packed around the fortress. Port Royal, named with the restoration of Charles II, prospered as a center to trade goods exploited from English and American colonies.

Port Royal was one of the major slave trading ports in the West Indies. Between 1671 and 1679, approximately 12,000 African slaves were brought through Port Royal. By 1680, a total of 2,850 people lived there. By the end of the 17th century,

Port Royal became a hotspot for privateers, who attacked the Spanish islands and merchant ships. Jamaica was the ideal spot for launching such attacks. The rulers of the island encouraged pirates to use Port Royal and protected them.

The infamous pirate Henry Morgan, himself based in Port Royal, attacked Portobello, Maracaibo and Panama. Merchants flocked to the port to enrich themselves by dealing in prizes looted from Spanish merchant ships and villages. As such, Port Royal became the most affluent as well as evil city across the Americas. The extravagance of pirates in Port Royal was legendary. They lavished an enormous amount of money and gold on pubs and brothels. A priest who had visited there spoke: "Port Royal was the Sodom of the New World. The inhabitants were pirates, murderers, prostitutes and the most corrupt people in the world."

In June 1692, an enormous earthquake hit Port Royal. The northern section, densely packed with storehouses, was swallowed by the sea, and a tsunami hit the city. Most houses were destroyed and many parts of the city were submerged into the sea. More than 2,000 people died and the survivors moved to Kingston across the port. Many people believed that the suffering was a divine punishment.

With the end of the War of the Spanish Succession in 1714, pirates gathered in New Providence, creating a new pirate heaven. Nassau was the busiest port for pirates who operated in the Caribbean and the Americas. For privateers who turned pirates after the war, Nassau was a natural hideout. Since its waters were shallow, large warships could not risk entering. It was close to the shipping routes, and its adequate winds enabled pirates to quickly access the hunting ground. Water and food were sufficient, and there was a high hill from which to post lookouts. The buccaneers expelled from Port Royal moved to and settled in New Providence in the 1680s.

Traders and merchants, as always, followed the pirates. The island economy increasingly prospered through trade with them. Nassau became the free marketplace where smuggled goods, slaves and drink were abundant. The pirates based in Nassau included most of the infamous pirates such as Benjamin Hornigold, Charles Vane, Henry Jennings, Calico Jack Rackham, Edward Teach (known as Blackbeard) and Samuel Bellamy.

Word of what was happening in New Providence made its way to London, and the British government decided to target the pirate haven. Captain Woods Rogers was appointed as the new governor of the Bahamas and three warships were deployed. Many pirates fled or quit piracy in response, but some strongly resisted. The governor appointed the pirate Hornigold as a pirate hunter and he engaged in anti-pirate operations that yielded many prisoners. The pirates held captive in December 1718 were hanged on a large scale. As public order was restored, the era of New Providence as a pirate haven ended. Today, Nassau, capital city of the Bahamas, uses its pirate history as a tourist attraction. Even now, piracy plays a vital role in the city's economy.

Homosexuality

During the Age of Discovery, homosexuality was a crime punishable by death or a thousand lashes of the whip. This may demonstrate that homosexuality was considered very problematic aboard ships. In early modern times, homosexual behavior was not allowed for any reason. It is believed that homosexuality was strictly prohibited out of a concern that it might disrupt discipline and cause conflicts among the sailors.

Despite a strict ban in merchant ships, homosexuality was not covered in the Bartholomew Code. This might imply that homosexuality was not a problem in the pirate ship or otherwise it was tacitly acknowledged. Given that relationships among sailors in pirate ships was much freer than in merchant ships, homosexuality could be permitted. This, however, is no more than guesswork. This could create a different image from the general idea of pirates who indulged in drinking and whoring after a successful raid. Indeed, judicial records found in the Admiralty Court demonstrate several cases of homosexuality, especially in the case of captains or senior sailors punished for sexual acts with rank-and-file sailors.

This might be a clue that there were same-sex relationships aboard ship, but it is hard to tell whether ships had higher-than-average rates of same-sex relationships. Meanwhile, in the early 19th century, homosexuality was widespread among Chinese pirates operating in the South China Sea. Some were initiated into the pirate group by being raped, and captains indulged in sexual acts with their men. At any rate, despite the common modern-day image of pirates' lustful heterosexual behavior, same-sex behavior existed and demonstrates another aspect of pirate life.

Chapter 12

END OF THE GOLDEN AGE OF PIRATES AND PRIVATEERS IN AMERICA

The Brutal Torture and Violence of Pirates

Although pirates were often forced into piracy to escape from violent working conditions, abuse and cruelty aboard lawful ships, they were no more than outlaws at sea who committed all kinds of atrocities. Pirates who made the sea into the realm of horror were regarded as sub-human beings. They were called 'cruel sea monsters,' 'blood hungry monsters,' 'merciless monsters,' 'sea wolves' or 'dogs of hell' – terms which highlighted their cruelty. These nicknames were derived from the brutal violence, slaughter and torture that they committed while they attacked and looted ships.

They exercised brutality to discover hidden treasures and to exact revenge. But beyond that, captives were often tortured simply for pirates' amusement. This fact makes it easier to understand why the term 'monster' was so often used to describe them. Pirates located hidden treasures by threatening captives with all kinds of methods.

Walking the plank was a commonly used method to horrify captives. Captives were bound so that they could not swim or tread water and forced to walk off a wooden plank or beam extended over the side of a ship. Pirates fired at the foot of captive to weaken him before forcing him into the sea. Pirates were amused to see it. One of the most commonly used tortures at the end of the 17th century was to pull the legs and arms of a captive with a rope while beating him with sticks or other instruments. They burnt captives alive by lighting a fuse inserted between their fingers. Pirates used a method to twist the head of a captive using a thin string until their eyes bulged out of their sockets. When pirates occupied a village, they committed cruelties against villagers, both men and women. In particular, women captives were the target of sexual attack and torture. A woman captive was once roasted naked when she refused to reveal the location of her money.

There were infamous pirates who terrified seamen with brutal tortures. The French pirate Francois l'Olonnais was notorious for cruel tortures practiced on captives. He was a natural sadist who amused himself with torture and was obsessed with the desire to see blood. When he attacked a small port in Cuba, he seized warships and killed all the captives except a sailor. If a captive did not answer the pirate's questions quickly, he slashed the captive all over his body and then licked the blood off the knife. He cut out the heart of one captive and forced another captive to eat it. Another form of torture was to cut the ears, noses, arms and hands of a captive, then rub the wounds with honey, and tie him to a tree to let bugs bite into the injuries.

French buccaneer Daniel Montbars, better known as Montbars the Exterminator, devised a most creative and cruel torture method. He liked to slit open a victim's belly just enough to reach in and pull out one end of the man's bowels. This he nailed to a tree or wall, whatever was close at hand, then he beat the man with a burning log so he twitched and jerked in agony, unwinding his own bowels in the process. The Dutch pirate Locke was also infamous for atrocities. If someone ran into an occupied village, he would slash their arms and legs. If anyone tried to intervene, that person would receive the same treatment. He burnt captives alive after tying them to a wooden stick.

The pirate captain Vane harshly beat sailors after seizing their ship. He tied their hands and legs to the mast and then put a burning match into their eyes and a pistol into their mouths. There were acts of perversion and violence practiced to simply alleviate boredom among the pirates. Edward Low, also a sadist, discovered a passenger had hung a bag of his gold outside a ship's window to hide it from the pirates. He cut the lips off the passenger and burnt them in front of him. Subsequently, he murdered all 32 crew members.

Pirate Trials

Out of various art works featuring pirates, the paintings illustrating a pirate hanged in front of many onlookers perhaps best symbolizes their miserable fates. They illustrate the image of pirates making their last statements before being executed – whether by being hanged or hanging on a gibbet like Captain Kidd. There are a number of paintings of Howard Pyle depicting hanging of pirates. Pirates were the common enemy of states because they disturbed international trade. These acts were regarded as treason. When pirates were found guilty, they were mostly hanged. When less serious involvement in piracy or similar offenses were discovered, pirates were occasionally punished with labor or imprisonment, but these incidents were rare compared with hanging.

Cases where pirates were found innocent or had their executions suspended were extremely rare. Pirate trials proceeded expeditiously, usually within a day or two, even though 20 to 30 pirates were put on trial at a time. Expeditious trials were the norm in part because busy judges wanted to finish trials early. Other than that, trials were swift because the pirates could put up no serious defense. They were not well educated and had no means to protect themselves. They merely claimed that they had been drunk while committing piracy or their ships were forcefully seized or they were forced to sign the pirate code or otherwise forced to engage in piracy.

How the British government handled piracy was well illustrated in an indictment handed over to juries by the Admiralty Court Judge Nicolas Trot at a trial held in Charleston, South Carolina in 1718. "The sea, which was accorded by God to human beings for use, is subject to rule and ownership, like land. Under international law, pirates are not authorized to change the ownership. Pirates are the common enemy of mankind and beasts as well as predators for whom faith or allegiance cannot be achieved. Other than the lesson learned from their death, any goodness or benefit cannot be expected from pirates." Such view of pirates by the British government generated a vicious cycle of terrorism. As the British government announced rewards for capturing pirates, pirates responded that they would pay unlimited rewards to those who captured government officials.

In 1720, one of six pirates who were about to be hanged cried, "a curse with the governor, a chaos with the colony," while drinking wine. The rest of his colleagues agreed. Outraged, Governor Woods executed them by chaining four pirates together to make them more terrified. Distrust and disdain of the authority of government did not change even when George I granted a pardon to pirates. Some pirates refused to convert to a good life even though they were granted a pardon. Some of them ignored it, while the most provocative pirates tore up the royal letter of pardon.

Hanging

In London, the execution of pirates was carried out in a place called the 'Execution Dock.' It was located in the River Thames near the shoreline at Wapping. Today in Wapping, East London, there is a pub called 'Captain Kidd' named after pirate William Kidd in the 17th century, who was executed at the nearby Execution Dock. On the signboard, the face of captain Kidd is painted and an imitation scaffold is set up at the entrance. You can look over the Execution Dock from there.

The Execution Dock was the place where all the infamous pirates in the 18th century were executed. The scaffold for hanging was set up beyond the low-tide mark. The bodies of pirates remained untouched and were submerged during high tide. After three changes in low and high tide, the bodies could be claimed. It is interesting to note the reason for submerging corpses in water. Since the commander of the Navy was responsible for the punishment of all crimes committed at sea, from the high seas to the low-tide mark, it symbolized that the execution of pirates was carried out within his jurisdiction.

An execution at the dock usually meant that crowds lined the river's banks or chartered boats moored in the Thames to get a better view of the hanging. The pirates who had been sentenced to death were usually brought to the Execution Dock from the Marshalsea Prison. The condemned were paraded across the London Bridge and past the Tower of London. The procession was led by the High Court Marshal on horseback. He carried a silver oar that represented the authority of the admiralty. Prisoners were transported in a cart to Wapping. With them was a chaplain who encouraged them to confess their sins. The condemned prisoners were allowed to drink a quart of ale at a public house on the way to the gallows. When they arrived at the river, the prisoners were allowed to talk to the crowds. Some spoke of repentance, but most of them were still confrontational. Its last executions were in 1830.

Marcus Rediker vividly portrayed the scene of an execution in his book *Villains of All Nations*: "In the early afternoon of July 12, 1726, William Fly ascended Boston's gallows to be hanged for piracy. His body was nimble in manner, like a sailor going aloft; his rope-roughened hands carried a nosegay of flowers; his weather-beaten face had a smiling aspect. He showed no guilt, no shame, and no contrition. Once he stood on the gallows, he threw the hanging rope over the beam and made it fast and carefully inspected the noose that would go around his neck. He soon turned to the hangman in disappointment and reproached him for not understanding his trade. Fly offered to teach him how to tie a proper noose. He, with his own hands, rectified matters, to render all things more convenient and effectual. Then informed the hangman and the crowd that he was not afraid to die and he did nothing wrong."

When attending minister Cotton Mather asked for the last words of pirates in order to provide an example and a warning to those who were assembled to watch the execution, three pirates warned all to obey their parents and superiors and not to curse, drink, whore or profane the Lord's day. They acknowledged the justice of the proceedings against them and thanked the ministers for their assistance. Fly, however, did not ask for forgiveness, did not praise the authorities, and did not affirm the values of Christianity, but he did issue a warning. He proclaimed his final and fondest wish: that all masters of vessels might take warning by the fate of the captain that he had murdered and to pay sailors their wages when due and to treat them better; that their barbarity to them made so many turn pirates. Fly thus used his last breath to protest the conditions of work at sea, what he called "bad usage."

A gallows was a simple frame where a horizontal crossbeam was tied to two upright poles and the rope noose was attached to the crossbeam. Pirates ascended the ladder with assistance from a hangman and a noose went around their necks. When a law enforcement officer made the signal, the hangman released the prisoners. In the case that the pirate was not killed immediately, friends or relatives of the pirate pulled his legs so as to make the process go more quickly and relieve his pain. Occasionally the noose was broken and the almost-dead pirate was hanged again.

The bodies of pirates at the Execution Dock were not immediately laid down following death. Customarily, these corpses were left hanging until at least three tides had washed over their heads. This practice stopped at the end of the 18th century. Ultimately the bodies were either buried at sea or used for autopsy and hung in chains. The autopsy of corpses had been acknowledged since Henry VIII and became a custom throughout the 18th century. On the part of the most notorious offenders, the admiralty would order that their bodies be tarred and hung in chains on the River Thames, as a warning to all seafarers of the fate awaiting those who turned to piracy. The infamous Captain Kidd, for example, who had been convicted of piracy and murder, was taken from the Newgate Prison and executed at the dock in 1701. During his execution, the rope was broken and Kidd was hanged on the second attempt. His remains were gibbeted at Tilbury by the Thames River for three years.

Hanging

Much larger number of pirates were executed in other regions of the Atlantic Ocean. Small islands off the Port Royal of Jamaica were infamous for the execution of pirates. On the East Coast of the U.S., the executions of pirates were largely carried out in Charleston, South Carolina; Williamsburg, Virginia; and New Port, Rhode Island. But the highest number of North American pirates executed took place in Boston, Massachusetts. Between 1716 and 1726, more than 400 pirates were executed, averaging 40 annually. At its peak in 1723, 82 pirates were executed.

The trial of the pirates commanded by Bartholomew Roberts was the largest pirate trial ever in history. The infamous pirate captain Bartholomew Roberts, also known as Black Bart, was killed in battle in February 1722 with the British warship *Swallow,* led by Captain Chaloner Ogle, and his men were captured. The trial was held on March 28, 1722 in Cape Coast in the west coast of Africa. The pirates were convicted of two charges: they disturbed the trade of the king by burning ships and goods sailing along the coast of Africa; and they attacked the king's warship *Swallow.*

The 20 sailors aboard Roberts' ship *Ranger* strongly claimed that they were forced to be engaged in the battle and did not fire any cannon and that they were forced to assist the pirates under the threat of death. The court adjudged 'a merciful ruling' on account of the lack of evidence. Despite the same appeal of the 80 pirates who had been under the direct command of Roberts, most of them were found guilty and condemned to hanging. Out of 165 pirates who were put on a trial, 74 were found innocent and 54 were sentenced to death, of whom 52 were hanged and two reprieved. Another 20 were allowed to sign indentures with the Royal African Company. Seventeen men were sent to the Marshalsea prison in London for trial, where some were acquitted and released.

The condemned pirates were executed over several days in two weeks. Large crowds watched the executions. The 18 bodies were hung as a warning to the public. Indeed, the largest pirate trial and mass execution brought the golden age of pirates to a close.

The Golden Age of Pirates Ends

The golden age of pirates ended on account of several factors. It ended, in part, thanks to the pirates' own successes. As piracy peaked, a consensus among the colonial government in the new continent, trading states and navies was reached that the problem of piracy should be addressed immediately and that tougher measures should be taken.

In the early golden age of pirates, some governors of islands in the Atlantic Ocean and the Caribbean Sea regarded pirates' prizes as a very lucrative source of income. Once the War of Spanish Succession ended, the ensuing economic boom changed this circumstance. Since European and American markets opened, trade had tripled in less than 15 years. However, as pirates disturbed the economic growth of American colonies and cut off their incomes, local authorities were no longer willing to tolerate them. With growing demand for anti-piracy legislation and maritime security on both sides of the Atlantic, tougher measures against piracy were employed.

England heavily punished those engaged in trade with pirates under the Piracy Act of 1721, such as merchants who assisted pirates in selling their prizes. Captured pirates were also subject to harsh punishment. Many gallows were set up at docks to execute pirates and those who transacted with them. Hundreds of pirates were hanged and their bodies were hung at ports across the world as a warning to potential pirates. The infamous pirates who were executed at the time included Black Beard, Captain Kidd, Stede Bonnet and John Rackham.

The convoy system and patrols in the hotspots of piracy helped reduce the threat. English merchant ships sailing across the Atlantic Ocean were convoyed by naval ships for several years. Spanish merchant ships sailing across the Indian Ocean used also a convoy system that the Spanish treasure fleets organized. As a result, piracy became difficult, and piracy attacks were significantly reduced. By 1731, pirates disappeared in the seas across the world except in the Far East. During this period, some pirates opted to start a new life or retire, but this was very exceptional. Most of them were killed in battles or hanged at gallows.

With the end of the age of pirates, the heads of the hydra were cut off. However, its roots were not completely removed. Pirates were under the surface, awaiting a favorable change of circumstances. Although the golden age of pirates in the Caribbean Sea and the Atlantic Ocean ended, the pirates were succeeded by privateers in the American continent and ultimately contemporary pirates.

Golden Age of Privateers in America

The end of the golden age did not at all mean the complete disappearance of pirates. It was merely a temporary decline because of state power. The privateers who the state granted the right to seize enemy ships, violently if necessary, enjoyed a golden era in America. As illustrated in the previous chapter, European countries employed privateers as part of their navy in wartime. The letter of marque granted privateers the right to loot ships and property of enemy states. Acts of piracy by privateers in wartime were justified as legal acts, and the government levied a tax and premium on privateers. Privateers generated a fairly good income for the government, but the problem was that it was hard to control them. They often engaged in illegal plundering and exploitation.

In the 16th century when England, France, Spain, Portugal and the Netherlands were engaged in wars, a large number of privateers from various states were active in the West Indies and raided enemy merchant ships. The privateers who had lost their jobs following peace treaties among European states turned pirate and continued to be engaged in looting and plundering. Francis Drake opened the era of privateering during the rule of Elizabeth I, and a century later, French privateers enjoyed a heyday in the wake of the Dutch War of Independence.

Even though the golden era of pirates during the 17th and 18th centuries became a chapter of past history, privateering never ended. As the war between English and Spanish colonies, known as the War of Jenkin's Ear, broke out, the age of North American privateers emerged. George II of England authorized the governors of American colonies to issue a letter of marque. During the war between England and Spain, France participated in the war by taking side with Spain. As a consequence, the ship from France and its colonies were subject to attack from English and American privateers.

The American Congress passed the Instruction to the Commanders of Private Ships or Vessels of War to manage and control privateers. Since then, a large number of privateers emerged in America and sailors rushed to become privateers because they were attracted by higher wages. Some cities of the American colonies served as privateer bases. Spain and France also issued a letter of marque to plunder the ships of England and its colonies. The French colony Louisbourg, which served as a base of French privateers, became a hub for looting English vessels.

In 1748, the Eight Years' War ended with the Treaty of Aix-La Chapelle. During the war, 10 percent of English ships were victimized by French privateers. In 1754, England and France competed against each other in India and North America, resulting in the emergence of a great number of privateers. In the period between 1758 and 1760, England took French bases in Louisbourg, Martinique and Dominique, but the Atlantic bases were out of reach.

American Independence and Prosperity of Privateers

England won the war against France in 1763. However, this brought about resistance from its American colonies and sparked a desire for independence from colonial rule. The self-declared independent territories began to build up a naval force to protect their trading routes. Out of the 13 colonies represented in the Continental Congress, 11 created navies, but they were not capable of standing up to the English navy. Thus, the leaders of American colonies opted to resist by attacking English merchant ships, instead of directly fighting the English Navy with their weak naval forces. As a result, English merchants pressed the British government to surrender to American insurgents in order to protect their interests.

On November 1, 1775, the Supreme Court of Massachusetts for the first time approved privateering and the Admiralty Court held trial on captured ships. When the Continental Congress first permitted privateering, it allowed privateers to seize the warships and cargo transport ships of the enemy, but civilian ships were off limits. However, states expanded the scope of seizure to all English ships when they enacted legislation on privateering. This aroused heated controversy. Critics argued that privateers took seamen, navy reserves and civilian ship engineers. In accordance with the Continental Congress and colony governments, warships were allowed to take two-third of prizes, and armed civilian ships were allowed all of the prize.

Regarding the discipline of privateers, it was generally loose. Captains often embezzled the sailors' share of prizes, and some captains took the shares of sailors while trials for allocation were underway. Privateers were completely focused on plunder, and had no involvement in cargo transport or other commercial activities. The colonial government, although cognizant of the abuses of privateers, turned a blind eye to them because the incomes that they generated were enormous. Instead, the Continental Congress created strict regulations to prohibit the reckless issuance of the letter of marque. The captains of privateers had to pay taxes depending on their ship size, and those who were abusive or became involved in murder and torture were subject to a heavy punishment. The prizes plundered from English merchant ships provided colonial Americans with various cargo. Privateers played a role in protecting coastal areas during the American Revolutionary War by scattering English troops.

As the damage to English fishing vessels and merchant ships shuttling between the mainland and the colony grew, the British navy commander stationed in America suggested that the navy should convoy the merchant ships. Thereafter, the British Navy created a convoy unit and convoyed merchant ships gathered in Portsmouth or Dublin to sail across the Atlantic. However, the ships left behind became the prey of privateers. It was known that 3,000 English ships and cargo became victims of privateers and were taken to American ports during this period. Numerous English merchant ships were missing or captured. As the war continued, the number of privateers soared. Privateering was also allowed for foreign ships. The letter of marque was issued excessively by colonial governments during wartime. In particular, Massachusetts issued one-third of all privateering certificates. With a large number of issuance of privateering certificates, the scale of prizes increased enormously.

American privateers shifted the fire of war to England. In 1778, England and France formally declared war. During the war, English merchant ships were left insecure in voyage. French privateers who gained the letter of marque from the American embassy in France made a great deal of income by plundering English merchant ships.

Dunkirk, a pirate hotspot northeast of France, enjoyed prosperity as a base of privateers during the American Revolutionary War. The main stage of American privateers was the Caribbean Sea. American privateers, who knew the waters of the West Indies very well, inflicted enormous damage on English trade. England attempted to recover the damages and exact revenge on American and French privateers by issuing a letter of marque. It is hard to know exactly how privateers affected the American Revolutionary War, but it is obvious that they put strain on English naval forces because England had to deploy convoy units to the Caribbean to protect its merchant ships. In this sense, it can be said that privateers made a contribution to the American victory in the war.

Privateers after the American Revolutionary War

The peace following the American Revolutionary War was broken by the war between England and France. French ports were hemmed in by the ships of the enemy, and French naval power was too weak to stand up against England. While England concentrated on the Caribbean, French privateers were waiting for an opportunity to plunder English ships. France promised to open the Caribbean for American merchants, and America in return promised to assist France in case it was attacked by England in this region. England seized American ships carrying French cargo, and France in retaliation issued a letter of marque in a large quantity.

In April 1793, the French ambassador to America issued letters of marque to American ships, and American privateers used them to seize English ships. However, this was opposed by U.S bureaucrats on the grounds that it violated U.S. neutrality, and ultimately the U.S. prohibited French privateers' calling in its ports. Along with this, France was further outraged when America, which had declared neutrality, singed the Jay Treaty with England to relieve the animosity incurred by the American Revolutionary War. French outrage resulted in the capture of 316 American ships by the French Navy over 11 months.

As the plundering of French privateers increased, America recreated its navy in July 1798 to protect its merchant ships. The first priority of the American navy was to combat French privateers in American waters. Thus, America waged a war against France, known as the Pirate War or Quasi-War, to combat French privateers. As a result of the war, French privateers were driven out of the Caribbean and the sea became a main combat field of America from then on. French privateers were no longer a threat to America. French privateers operated in South American waters where American merchant ships did not operate. As a consequence, they suffered an enormous loss.

In Europe, the Napoleonic Wars (1803-1815) which were driven by Napoleon's desire to conquer Europe, broke out. Against France's continental containment, England implemented a sea containment strategy and stopped trade between neutral countries and the European continent. England contained all ports of France and forced ships from neutral states to call in English ports to pay tariffs.

As a consequence, the U.S., which remained neutral, suffered enormous losses. The U.S. completely stopped its overseas trade by passing the Embargo Act to relieve public outrage and to recover economic losses. However, this act, as well as a series of policy measures, did not work as intended. As diplomatic efforts failed, the U.S. declared war against England on June 6, 1812. It was the beginning of War of 1812 (1812-1814). With the declaration of war, the U.S. Congress permitted privateering, and traders began to arm their ships. Since the war was primarily one involving naval battles, it allowed privateers to prosper once again.

The shipowners – who had good memories of successful privateering during the American Revolutionary War – operated 150 privateers within less than two months. Privateer ships at the early stage of the war were small in size as well as poorly armed, so they relied on the tactic of getting aboard ship rather than firing cannons in engagements. As the war continued, the shipowners of privateers built specialized ships whose keels were on the upper side, capable of carrying more than 150 sailors and battling English frigates. In contrast, the English navy was not able to protect its merchant ships because it was engaged in war with France.

Baltimore was the hub of American privateers on the coast of the Atlantic. Seasoned by its experiences in the Revolutionary War, the shipyard in Baltimore built speedy and easily maneuverable privateers. Among them was the large privateer the *American* of 350 tons, equipped with 20 cannons and capable of carrying 120 sailors. The *American* plundered 40 English ships during the war and earned $600,000 in prize money. In 1814, there were more than 500 privateers in American ports. England was not able to deal with American privateers, which plagued its merchant ships until Napoleon surrendered in that year. As England contained the bays of Chesapeake and Delaware and ports in Carolina, American maritime trade greatly shrank and the activities of privateers eventually ended.

The shipowners, who were unable to do any privateering business, called for Congress to end the war and at last a peace treaty was signed in 1815. During three years of war, 1,300 English ships were subject to the plunder of American privateers. This was the last wave in the history of privateers in America, except when Confederate forces used them during the American Civil War.

As a result, state-sponsored piracy virtually ended. Officially, it completely vanished by the Paris Declaration Respecting Maritime Law of 16 April 1856, which abolished privateering. It is true that American privateers made a great contribution to the American Revolutionary War, but it is apparent that their activities were not inspired by patriotism. Likewise in previous European privateering, American privateering was about the pursuit of wealth.

The Meaning of Pirates in the Age of the Atlantic

The acts of piracy prevalent in the Age of Discovery were maritime crimes committed on a massive scale. These acts were a form of resistance in which low-class sailors challenged the existing social order and authority, as well as state authority. Piracy was the way of life that numerous sailors opted for voluntarily. Furthermore, they were a subversive alternative to the order of merchant ships, naval ships, and privateers. Against the oppressive order aboard law-abiding ships, which included exploitation and violence, pirates pursued their own social order which was autonomous and democratic and desired to establish a democratic community in which those values were implemented. It was a resistance against the Atlantic culture in which feudal exploitations prevailed.

Individually, pirates were only common people who were driven over the edge in a harsh environment. They were humans who had a natural desire to live freely and abundantly out of hunger and violence. Even though pirates were outlaws who exercised brutal violence themselves, they were monsters created by the oppressive maritime order – bastards delivered by the regime of the Atlantic.

Chapter 13

ASIA, ENCLOSED IN THE SEA

Asia Enclosed in the Sea

What were Asian states like when European states were navigating around the world? Asian states like China, Japan and Korea, which were enclosed in Sino-centrism (中華主義) and Confucianism (儒教), were focused on being completely continental states, and were largely blind to the power and potential of using the sea. When Europeans were prevailing in maritime trade by sailing around the world, Asians completely banned sea-going. Asian economies fell into closed and self-sufficient economies, as a consequence of enforcing a 'Forbidden to the Sea' (海禁) policy and restricting overseas trade.

China, in particular, indulged in the idea of Sino-centrism, regarding itself as the center of the world and its neighbors as barbarians since ancient times. China was obsessed with the idea that 'The territory is enormous and goods are sufficient enough' (地大物博). China was complacent in its belief that there was no need to trade with the outside world, since China could be self-sufficient without trading with other states for goods. In this context, China was implementing a strong closed-door policy. As a result, China fell behind a major global trend and ultimately underwent a shameful colonial history.

During the Ming (明) dynasty, where Confucianism dominated society as a ruling ideology, the sea was no longer a space for trade and exchange. The sea was a security vulnerability, as well as an area where coastal residents could secretly communicate with enemies. Because the Confucian view was that 'agriculture is the foundation of nations,' maritime affairs were regarded as very low and ignoble. Maritime trade was actively undertaken during the Song (宋) and Yuan (元) dynasties. However, it declined following the foundation of the Ming dynasty by Chu Yuanchang (朱元璋) in 1368, which advocated exclusive Chinese nationalism.

In 1371, shortly after the foundation of the Ming dynasty, Chu Yuanchang proclaimed a Ban on Sea-Going (海禁). It was an extremely strict ban, saying "any piece of a wooden board is forbidden to fall into the sea." As a consequence, the overseas trade that had been booming during the Song and Yuan dynasties was completely prohibited, and private trade was replaced by the tributary trade. After Zheng He (鄭和)'s expeditions ended, enormous fleets were left unrepaired and the building of ships for going to distant waters was prohibited. The imperial decree that "all ships with more than two masts should be demolished" was proclaimed.

When Europe took to the oceans, Asia was busy isolating itself from the outside world, turning its eyes away from the sea. Asia increasingly became a continental power, and as such the sea became a barrier that interrupted international relations. As the booming overseas trade diminished, shipbuilding and navigation skills declined. The capability and means for sea-going had totally disappeared. Literally, Asia ended up 'being enclosed in the sea.' This was a watershed moment that set Asia on a path to being colonized by European maritime powers.

Why did China, a former maritime power that had taken to the sea much earlier than Europe, proclaim a ban on ocean navigation? Among a number of reasons, primarily it was because pirates were rampant at the end of the Yuan and the early Ming dynasties. Rebel groups based in the coastal areas of Zhejiang and Fujian plagued the newly born dynasty, in connection with Japanese pirates who were prevalent along the coasts of the Korean Peninsula and southeast China.

The founder of the Ming intended to prevent the rebel groups from growing into a serious force while being linked to low class people in the coastal areas. Along with the Ban on Sea-Going, the founder of the Ming prohibited overseas as well as private trade and strengthened the tributary system as a mode of international relations. He regarded agriculture highly and suppressed commerce and industry to prevent the pursuit of individual wealth – a pursuit that he believed would harm society – and by doing so he intended to maintain the traditional Sino-centric hegemonic order. However, the strategy of isolation and the abandonment of ocean-going resulted in a far worse outcome: seven major invasions from European maritime powers, and ultimately China's subjugation as a colony.

The Chosun Dynasty Ban on Sea-Going

Chosun (朝鮮, 1392–1910), the dynasty which ruled the Korean Peninsula for 500 years and had served China, had a similar ban on sea-going. In fact, it enforced a much stricter policy that suppressed maritime force. There had not been a significant maritime force on the Korean Peninsula since Jang Bogo (張保皐), an admiral at the end of Silla dynasty (新羅, BC 53-AD 935), had dominated trade in the southern Yellow Sea, established the *Chunghae Jin* naval base and established the maritime order throughout Northeast Asia. However, the overseas trade with merchants from China and Japan as well as Arabia was very active throughout the Korea dynasty (高麗, 918–1392). In the southern coastal areas of the Korean Peninsula, trade with Japan was booming.

One key factor that turned the Chosun away from the sea was the implementation of the Empty Island (空島) policy and the Ban on Sea-Going. The Empty Island policy decrees that islands be left uninhabited – no one was allowed to live there. For the rulers of Chosun, thousands of islands on the southwest coast were viewed as very vulnerable. The driving force that led to the Empty Island policy was Japanese pirates, who were prevalent at the end of the Korea dynasty.

The Empty Island policy, which began in 1403, was mitigated in the wake of Japanese invasions of the Chosun (1592–1598) for a while and ultimately abolished in 1882. Unlike in the Korea dynasty, in which the policy was confined to some islands, the Chosun expanded it to include the southern part of the Korean Peninsula. As a result, all but a few large islands were left uninhabited.

The Confucian Chosun was loyal to the idea of 'agriculture first,' represented by the principle: "Focus on the loftier jobs, ignore the lowly jobs." (棄末而反本) The Chosun banned trade with foreign countries while discouraging jobs that were considered "low" such as commerce and industry, instead encouraging the "principal" work of agriculture. The ruling class of Chosun believed that the Ban on Sea-Going would discourage commerce and prevent the fast flow of people and goods, and thus enhance the stability of an agriculture-centric society and help strengthen government control.

Under these circumstances, engaging in private trade by using large ships was treated like a treasonous act, which would harm the stability of society. On the part of the Chosun, which tied up with Confucianism, the sea was not a space of opportunity that could generate wealth by fishery and overseas trade – it was merely a place where rebellious people and lowly seamen were engaged in lowly jobs. While European maritime powers created a 'sea of imperialism,' the ruling class of the Chosun was devoted to the anti-maritime Confucian ideology.

Envoys to China took a land route, which took several months, instead of traveling only a few days by sea. It was the only channel by which the Chosun could know about the outside world. For the Chosun, which had been closed and continentally oriented, the sea was merely an outer area as well as a dangerous space. Against this backdrop, the abolition of the Ban on Sea-Going was one of the major goals that reformists for independence and modernization pursued at the end of the 19th century. Ok-Kyoon Kim, the main player of the political coup in 1882, wrote in his book: "those who were discussing urgent national affairs should employ competent people, save finances and discourage luxury, and abolish the Ban on Sea-Going policy."

The Sea of Colonization

In China, the problem of the Ban on Sea-Going had been raised much earlier than it had been for the Chosun. As the demand for the Open Sea (開洋論) grew stronger, the Ming opened Guangzhou in 1509 to merchants from tributary states. In 1576, the Ming permitted private trade, the first since its enforcement of the ban 200 years ago. However, it was not completely free trading. The port for trade with Southeast Asia was limited only to Changchou, and merchant ships were limited to making 50 voyages. With the mitigation of the Ban on Sea-Going, trade routes that had been either closed or hidden were quickly re-covered. Accordingly, permission to conduct overseas trade was extended to 100 ships in 1577 and 137 ships in 1597.

However, limited permission did not change the funda-mental results of the Ban on Sea-Going. Even though the Ban on Sea-Going, the suppression of commerce, and the tributary trade had brought stability internally, these policies also caused China to lose its power in the sea – allowing European mari-time powers to dominate. Shrinking in maritime activities re-sulted in the fall of China. European maritime powers threat-ened China with fleets armed with cannons. Ultimately, China and the Chosun were exploited by enemies that sailed across the sea. They paid a harsh price for turning their backs on the ocean, creating a 'sea of colonization' for themselves.

Maritime Exchange in East Asia

In fact, East Asia did not stay away from the sea in the begin-ning. In ancient East Asia, sea exchanges were more active than in any other place. Secure land routes were used for exchanges among regions and states, but sea routes were also active. China and the Islamic world developed an advanced culture and economy between the 8ᵗʰ and 10ᵗʰ centuries. The two civilizations did not remain isolated, but communicated with each other by the sea. This brought synergy in the development of civilization. The two worlds affected other parts of the globe by spreading their civilizations.

This was made possible because these two worlds, across the Indian and Pacific Oceans, were connected with a maritime Silk Road. The two worlds were able to transport goods more cheaply, and could understand each other better through repeated exchanges. Trade through the maritime Silk Road was driven by Arabs. Arab merchant ships departed from Port Siraf or the Hormuz Island in April, when monsoon began, and called in at ports in Sohar or Muscart in Oman first. They supplied themselves water, food and live cows for the voyage across the Indian Ocean. After a month of travel, they arrived in a port in southwest India. After resupply, they set sail for Malacca, which served as the middle point for maritime trade between the West and the East. They arrived in the Gulf of Siam via Singapore. In 10 or 20 days, they stopped over small islands and resupplied with water and food. In another month, they arrived in their final destination in China, Guangzhou (廣州), called Canton.

Between the 10ᵗʰ century and early 11ᵗʰ century, merchant ships from the Song Dynasty called in at ports of Japan. In the early 12ᵗʰ century, as the compass was widely available and the building of large ships was possible, Chinese merchants advanced to East Indonesia and further South India. In the 11ᵗʰ century, exchange between China and Japan was very active, to the extent that there was a Chinese town in Hakata of Kyushu. Since the middle of the 11ᵗʰ century, merchants from Hakata had sent merchant ships to Korea. In the early age of the Southern Song (南宋) dynasty in the 12ᵗʰ century, trade was very active and extended to China. The Song's initial position was to disallow maritime trade with Japanese merchants, but the relationship between the two countries became very close after the Southern Song was founded. As a result, the exchange of people and goods was very active and Japanese merchant ships were engaged in the free private trade in the estuary of the Yangtze River, centered in Mingzhou (明州).

During the Yuan dynasty, powerful feudal lords called "Daimyos" (大名), along with the merchants under their control, actively undertook overseas trade in Japan. The Yuan officially banned private trade, and thus Japanese merchant ships called in Fuzhen, instead of the official trade port. The Ming dynasty was devoted to rebuilding the economy after it collapsed at the end of the Yuan dynasty. Even though the Ming very strictly enforced the Ban on Sea-Going, smuggling was booming along the coastal areas in Zhejiang, Fuzhen and Guangdong. Growth in the handicraft industry and an increase in navigational skills lead to smuggling by large ships. It was contrary to the Ban on Sea-Going, enforced since the early Ming dynasty. Since the ban strictly prohibited people living in coastal areas from taking to the sea, the private trade prospered with through piracy.

On the Korean Peninsula, trade with Arabs had been undertaken through the land-route Silk Road prior to the Unified Silla Kingdom (676–935). During the 8th century, maritime trade became active through Arabs who resided in the Arab community in the coastal region of China. The Silla community, built in the Shandong Peninsula and Jiangsu, served as a trade hub. The merchants from Silla were engaged in transit trade, in which they sold the goods from Arab traders to northern China, Silla and Japan.

Since maritime trade routes connecting China, Korea and Japan were under the complete control of Jang Bogo, the trade between Silla and the Arabs had been indirect. Following the death of Jang Bogo, the Arabs directly engaged in trade with Silla by the sea. Apparently, maritime trade routes in Asia had been open since ancient times, and the maritime trade was booming when heated controversies over the Copernican theory and the Ptolemaic theory were underway in the West.

Zheng He's Expeditions

The rule of the third emperor of the Ming dynasty, Yongle (永樂帝), brought China's greatest period of ocean navigation. This was the work of Admiral Zheng He (鄭和), who completed great maritime expeditions from 1405–1433 – during the Ban on Sea-Going. One might be curious as to how enormous expeditions were possible at the early era of the Ming dynasty, during which the strict ban was enforced. In fact, China had been the most powerful maritime state during the 450 years before the implementation of the Ban on Sea-Going. Larger ships from China were able to carry 500 people, and navigators sailed using a hydrographical chart and a compass.

During the Song dynasty, trade with Japan and Southeast Asia in coastal regions boomed. The Song, which highly regarded exchange with foreign countries, expanded their exchanges to include Central Asia, India and eastern Africa as well as Japan and East Asian countries. Even though the Chinese economy declined and overseas trade shrank when the Song fell to the Mongols, the Yuan dynasty shortly thereafter recognized the importance of shipping, trade and traffic by the sea.

Oriental goods loaded in Guangzhou and Fuzhou, such as ceramics, peppers and spices, arrived in the coastal regions of the Mediterranean, like Alexandria, via the Gulf of Persia and the Red Sea. These oriental goods were collected by traders from Venice and Genoa and sold to Western Europe through the Gibraltar Strait in the Iberian Peninsula. As illustrated in active oversea trades in the Ming and Yuan dynasties, China had the highest capability of maritime expansion, despite the Ban on Sea-Going. This was demonstrated by Zheng He's seven maritime expeditions.

Zheng He was a Muslim with colored eyes, captured in Yunnan in 1381 in the transitional period from the Yuan to the Ming. As a eunuch, he had served the Emperor Yongle since he was a prince. He made a great contribution to the success of Yongle' coup against his younger brother Chienwen (建文帝).

When Yongle took emperorship, Zheng He became his closest aid. Following his emperorship, Emperor Yongle made the unprecedented move of appointing eunuchs to important positions, and sent three fleets commanded by them to proclaim his emperorship across Southeast Asia from Java to southern India. Yongle, who had been more strategic than any other emperor in Chinese history, intended to be recognized by foreign rulers. As such, he commanded Zheng He to take expeditionary voyages.

The Magnificence of Zheng He's Fleets

Zheng He's expeditionary fleets were so magnificent, they were unprecedented in world history. His fleets were composed of 60 larger ships, known as 'treasure ships' (寶船), which stretched 138 or 150 meters in length and 60 meters in width, and 200 smaller ships. The number of crewmen who participated in each expeditionary voyage was up to 27,000. Those figures create a strong contrast to the fleet Vasco da Gama used to explore the trade route to India: Three ships, the largest of which was 120 tons and 27 meters in length, while the other two were 100 tons and 50 tons, respectively. 'Treasure ships,' which were literally carrying treasure, were the mainstay of fleets. The treasure ships carried the emperor's presents for the rulers of the regions where the fleets visited and the tributes that the rulers paid to the emperor. Each treasure ship was structured with 16 compartments, so even though two of them were flooded, it did not sink. Parts of some compartments, which were designed to hold water, were used as an aquarium to raise fish or an entrance for divers.

Zheng He's first voyage departed on 11 July 1405 from Suzhou and visited more than 30 regions and countries, including Brunei, Java, Thailand and Southeast Asia, India, the

Horn of Africa, and Arabia, dispensing and receiving goods along the way. During the voyage, he deployed a special unit to Aden, Mecca and Mogadishu in Kenya. For the last expedition, which used his largest fleet, the total navigational distance was up to 20,000 kilometers. The fleets navigated at an unbelievably fast speed at the time, sailing 5,000 kilometers from Hormuz to Malacca in less than 44 days. Zheng He died in 1433 during his last voyage. His body, wrapped in white fabric, was thrown into the sea amid the sound of prayers.

The Purposes of Great Expeditions

One might wonder what led the early Ming dynasty, which began to enforce the Ban on Sea-Going, to attempt these costly and resource-draining voyages. Of various arguments on the topic, one theory posits that the voyages were motivated by the events of Emperor Yongle's coup. The emperor occupied Nanjing, the capital, three years after starting the bloody conflict against his nephew Chienwen. However, the whereabouts of his nephew was not known. Since his body was not discovered, there was speculation that he might have been burnt to death or gone into exile overseas. There was a rumor around that the supposedly exiled Chienwen pursued his reinstatement, and Zheng He's expeditions were meant to discover Chienwen's whereabouts.

This argument, however, collapses when one considers that Yongle's emperorship was already stable, and the scale of the expeditions was extremely large and costly. Another argument claims the purpose was to create a Sino-centric order built on a tributary system. Emperor Yongle was a strong ruler who had invaded Mongol territory beyond the Great Wall. Another purpose was to protect the safety of trade routes and to promote trade by combating the pirates that ran rampant in the waters off Malacca. Just as it is today, the waters off the Malacca Strait were a hub of maritime traffic and commerce, as well as a hotspot for piracy. Indeed, Zheng He's fleets sank 10 pirate ships in the second expedition. The fleets captured the head of the pirates and brought him to China to execute; thousands of other pirates were killed on the spot. However, it is hard to accept that anti-piracy operations were a single purpose of these expeditions. There seems to be no need to undertake seven expeditions at tremendous cost over 30 years, advancing even as far as Kenya, merely for the purpose of fighting pirates.

It seems that Zheng He's expeditions sought to achieve a combination of the purposes above. Perhaps the most convincing argument is that the main purpose of these expeditions was to spread the dignity of the emperor to Southeast Asian countries and to create a Sino-centric order by subjugating them under the tributary system. The dream of Emperor Yongle was to build a maritime imperial state that would dominate oceans, a feat that Kublai Khan had never achieved. This was claimed on the ground that Zheng He's fleets were deeply involved in civil wars or political affairs in Malacca, Java and Ceylon, and he brought those who resisted them to execute in China. Such an argument was supported by the fifth emperor Xuande(章帝)'s decree delivered to the seventh expedition fleets, stating that "all things are going smoothly, but countries away across the sea do not know about it. Thus, Admiral Zheng He was specially dispatched to teach them respect and obedience."

After Xuande died in 1435, China allowed its maritime powers to diminish as it quit sea-going and turned into a land-focused state. In the face of a growing threat from barbarians in the northern territory and the rebellions of farmers, the Ming could not afford to continue expensive expeditions. As a result, the strict Ban on Sea-Going was enforced. Treasure ships were dismantled to be used for fuel, and crewmen were re-deployed to become construction workers and general soldiers. The records of the expeditions were completely destroyed.

However, this was only the superficial reason for discontinuing the voyages. The true motivation behind it was that

Confucian bureaucrats saw these expeditions as incompatible with the ideology of the Confucian Ming dynasty. China, which had taken to oceans more than 80 years before the European maritime powers, began to lose its dominance and eventually handed over their maritime Silk Road – stretching from India to China – to those European countries.

Great Voyages of Zheng He's Fleets

Due to the lack of historical records, it is hard to figure out the exact number of Zheng He's fleets. There is an argument that the full scale of the fleet, which included newly built and repaired ships, was 2,020 vessels throughout the seven expeditions. Emperor Yongle ordered Zheng He to build 1,681 ships, other than warships and merchant ships. These consisted of traditional Chinese junk ships. Under the emperor's ambitious plan, there had been a significant progress in shipbuilding technology. By virtue of advanced shipbuilding technology and the use of good timber, Zheng He built robust ships which were capable of navigating through harsh oceans.

The preparation for enormous and long voyages required a great deal of time. In addition, shipbuilding and navigational skills were prerequisite for the success of voyages. Yongle inspired the development of navigational skills. Following the imperial order to make precise hydrographical charts, Zheng He and his admirals collected data on currents, islands, mountains, straits and the position of stars, and they updated existing hydrographical charts with their newly collected data. Two years prior to the departure of the first expedition, they were directed to visit countries in the distant westward sea and to employ skillful navigators. For voyages in distant waters, they needed to have local navigators who were well aware of regional seas.

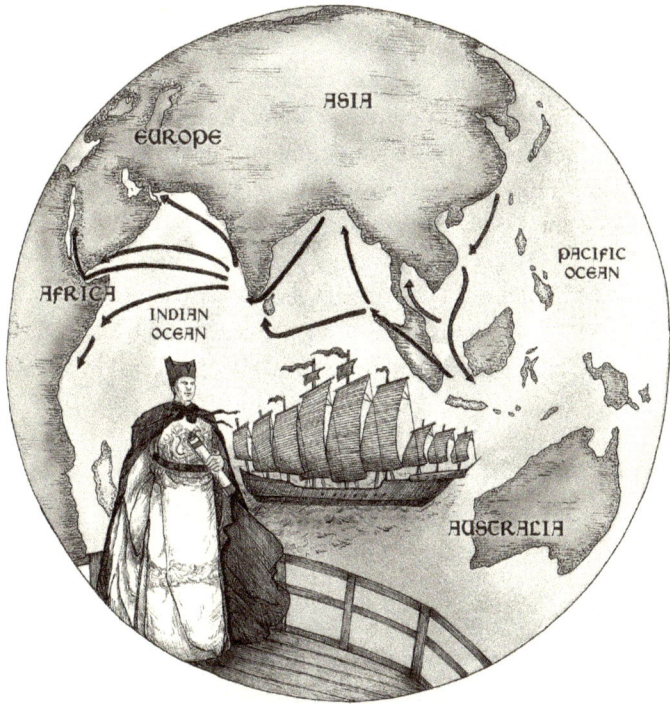

Voyages of Zheng He

The Chinese had employed Arab navigators and astronomers since ancient times, particularly during the Yuan dynasty. It seemed natural to hire Muslim navigators from Arabia, which was highly advanced in navigation and astronomy. These two cultures had engaged in trade through maritime routes in Southeast Asia and the Indian Ocean over hundreds of years. As a result, some Chinese people settled in Cairo as a minority and Arabs settled in the Arab community in Chuanchou in Fujian (福建).

Zheng He's fleets carried the emperor's presents for foreign rulers. The emperor gave precious presents such as silk, ceramics, books or other impressive items to demonstrate his majesty and to establish a tributary relationship. Among the presents were women. Allegedly, more than 100 women were presented to the foreign rulers to serve as maids or mistresses.

In the early Ming dynasty when Zheng He's expeditions were undertaken, China was much stronger and more highly advanced than Europe in every aspect of maritime capabilities, including the number of ships, shipbuilding, cargo transport, navigational capability, ability to travel long distances, and maintenance and repair capability. At the time, Venice had the strongest fleets in Europe. The fleets of Venice consisted of 300 speedy and light galleys. The larger ships among them were capable of carrying 50 tons of cargo and were suitable for the mild summer climate of the Mediterranean. By contrast, the treasure ships of Zheng He's fleets were much larger and capable of navigating oceans for several weeks in stormy weather.

The treasure ships were able to reach Malacca and the Hormuz Strait within fewer than five and 12 weeks, respectively, with thousands of tons of cargo aboard. The treasure ships had special rooms for ambassadors returning to India, the Gulf of Persia and Africa. There were more than 180 doctors deployed under the command of an admiral and every ship had one doctor per 150 crewmen. Crewmen had sufficient oranges, coconuts, cabbage, radish and bamboo shoots for two months to prevent scurvy. When vegetables were out of stock, they had green bean sprouts raised aboard ship. They ate unpolished rice.

They carried a great amount of water at any given time and distilled salty water into fresh water using sea lion fat. Rulers of states, astronomers and interpreters of various languages, including Hindi, Swahili, Arabic and Romance languages, were aboard ships. Mistresses were aboard treasure ships as well. They were the prostitutes who had worked at barrelhouses on board ship in Guangdong. These fleets were also heavily armed with bombards, splinter throwers, cannons, fire arrows and even excrement cannons. With these formidable armaments, they could easily combat pirates and subjugate the rulers who refused to surrender.

One might be curious as to how they were able to navigate such long distances. Zheng He's fleets sailed on long voyages from China to India and Africa using the monsoon. The monsoon, which blows in the Indian Ocean and Southeast Asia, is the term for seasonal winds created by the temperature differences between the huge Himalayan heights and the sea. In summer the Asian continent becomes warmer than the ocean, absorbing moisture and wind from the ocean. In April, as the westward winds from the Indian Ocean begin to blow, the southwestward monsoon begins. In May, the southwestward monsoon reaches the Indo-China Peninsula and peaks in July, during which time the wind speed is up to 30 knots in the South China Sea. The northeastward monsoon begins at the end of December.

The seamen shuttling between China, India and Africa sailed along the monsoon's course and came back home using the next monsoon. They waited at secure ports for the winds to reverse the direction. By the time ships from India riding the southwestward monsoon were arriving at the Malacca Strait, Chinese junk ships were yet to depart from China. By the time the Chinese junk ships arrived at the Malacca Strait, the Indian ships had left.

Under this circumstance, ports along the coast of the Indian Ocean were required to store goods and cargo until the direction of the monsoon changed. Chinese and Arab traders built ports in the coastal region of the Indian Ocean for transit trade to call in and store cargo. Malacca rose to become a transit trade hub, taking advantage of its prime geographical location. Actually, Malacca was like a colony of China. Chinese traders transported valuable goods like white ceramics and silks to Malacca, India and Cairo, while Arab and Chinese traders met in Calicut to exchange their goods.

Had Zheng He Discovered America?

Gavin Menzies, a retired British navy officer who has been devoted to the navigational history of China, has claimed astonishing theories that run quite contrary to widely accepted history. Based on his findings, he argued that Zheng He's fleets sailed around the Cape of Good Hope 30 years earlier than Bartolomeu Dias did in 1488 and discovered America earlier than Columbus did in 1492.

His arguments are based on old world maps that he has discovered. He claims that Columbus and Magellan might have been aware of America and the Magellan Strait when they set sail. Menzies claims that the Cape of Good Hope and the Magellan Strait were precisely marked on the map that Prince Pedro of Portugal, older brother of Prince Henry, delivered to Prince Henry in 1428. The map was brought from Venice. In 1492, Columbus acquired the map, which was regarded as highly confidential and preserved in a Portuguese government's safe.

Menzies argues that evidence has also been found in the remains of shipwreck in the Caribbean Sea, along with the old maps and hydrographical charts. Additionally, he puts forward a unique argument regarding the location of Zheng He's death. On 11 November 1432, when the fleets were south of Sri Lanka, Zheng He ordered Commander Hong Bao to sail toward Calicut. Hong Bao arrived at Calicut on 25 March and heard news that Zheng He died while sailing for China on 9 April. According to Menzies' theory, Zheng He left for Africa and North America after he issued orders to Hong Bao and died at Asheville, North Carolina in the U.S.

Ryu Kang, a map historian and practicing lawyer in China, puts forward a similar argument. He acquired a copy of the world map published in the 16th year of Yongle's emperorship. The map, which contained all the continents and oceans on the earth, included America and the Australian continent as well as the South and North Poles. Like Menzies, he argues that the Chinese discovered America a century earlier than Columbus. By the 15th century, when the Chinese world map was published, world maps in Europe published by Martin Waldseemüller (1507), Karl Martell (1489) and Virga (1489) were available. He claimes that this implies that Eurpeans, including Columbus and Magellan, were well aware of world geography. He states that the world maps were not made by Europeans, but were copied from Chinese world maps.

Even though the arguments raised by Menzies and Ryu Kang fully build on the Chinese perspective, and the reliablity of the historical materials is questionable, it is true that they have some convicing evidence. Their arquments may sound odd from a European perspective. However, it is possible that their arguments have merit, given China's advanced shipbuilding, navigation and expedition capabilities, as well as the scale of the expediton fleets at the time when Zheng He was active. If they are proved to be true, the maritime history of the world would futher expand and deepen beyond the Europe-centric perspective.

Zheng He and China's Maritime Rising

The accomplishments of Zheng He have been highlighted as China rises to become a global power. China's renewed desire to become a maritime power and the strategy of Maritime Rising (海洋屈起), literally meaning 'Rising from the Sea,' led to a move to shed light on the glory of Zheng He and the promotion of his accomplishments. In 2005, China was devoted to inspiring 'Maritime China,' with a wide array of events to commemorate the 600th anniversary of Zheng He's expeditions. The intention of China to become a maritime power was also illustrated in the opening ceremony of the 2008 Beijing Olympics, which portrayed Zheng He's expeditions and the spread of China's civilization across the world.

The Chinese view Zheng He's expeditions as a symbol of Chinese influence on globalization, as well as a way to promote the image of China as a peaceful global state. Chinese historians claim that China's maritime expansions were peaceful in comparison with Europeans' conquests. They highlight that Chinese maritime expansions were inclusive of other cultures, without violent rule and exploitation, while Europeans were extremely violent, brutal and suppressive of other religions and cultures. They stress that the purpose of Zheng He's expeditions was only to spread the majesty of the emperor across the world, not to invade or exploit. However, while Zheng He's expeditions were in part motivated by a desire for exchange and trade, the relationships with foreign countries that he had visited were not fully peaceful.

Between 1840 and 1948, China was invaded by European powers 479 times. Eighty-four of those were large-scale invasions. During this period, 470,000 foreign troops aboard 1,860 ships attacked the country. The most shocking loss was the defeat of the North Sea Fleet (北洋艦隊), one of the four modernized Chinese naval forces in the late Qing (清) dynasty. In the sea off the west coast of the Korean Peninsula, in the morning of 25 July 1894, the North Sea Fleet under the control of Li Hongzhang (李鴻章), the Minister of Beiyang Commerce (北洋通商大臣) as well as one of the most trusted vassals of Empress Dowager Cixi (西太后), was completely defeated by the surprise attack of the Japanese naval fleet. In two months, the warships of China and Japan were engaged in a sea battle in the Yellow Sea. As a consequence, four out of 14 Chinese warships were sunk, whereas no Japanese warships were damaged. The North Sea Fleet, with 18 warships, was created in 1881 by reformists who attempted to modernize China by following the path of the West. The North Sea Fleet appeared superior to the Japanese fleet. However, crewmen were ill-trained and parts and equipment purchased from various European countries were not exchangeable with each other. Empress Dowager Cixi had spent the nation's naval defense budget on her 60th birthday party and renovations on her palace.

When the Chinese Navy was created in 1950, Mao Zedong (毛澤東) stated that imperial invasions had been through the sea, and thus, they should have a powerful navy to oppose such attacks. Recognizing this historical context, Chinese leaders today are devoted to protecting the country's maritime rights by building up naval power. 'Maritime Rising' signifies China's pursuit of maritime power and the assertive maritime policy it is using for that purpose. Chinese leaders believe that the core of hegemonic competition lies in the sea, and thus are committed to secure maritime rights with an assertive maritime policy. Remembering how China had been trampled by European maritime powers in the past, Chinese leaders have shifted their military strategy priorities from the land to the sea.

Many military strategists believe that a series of recent aggressive actions of China in the East and South China Seas and the Indian Ocean is directly related to Chinese efforts to develop its maritime strength over the last 40 years. China has devoted itself to promoting its maritime industry as well. In defining itself as a maritime power as well as a land power, China recognizes the strategic importance of maritime industry for national defense and the protection of its sovereignty and resources. The Chinese government has adopted a foundational philosophy for maritime industry development, but it remains confidential.

A third generation of Chinese leadership was determined that "the sea should be recognized in accordance with our strategic goal and national awareness of the sea should be enhanced." In this context, they defined sea-going as the 'development of blue territory.' In the 18th National People's Congress held in November 2012, President Hu Jintao highlighted the goal of a maritime power as part of the vision of China in the upcoming decade. He stressed that "China needs to enhance the capability to develop maritime resources and build a powerful maritime state by protecting maritime interests."

As part of this goal, a number of maritime enforcement organizations were incorporated into a single organization. In 2013, China created the State Oceanic Administration under the Ministry of Land and Resources to incorporate maritime enforcement affairs that had previously been carried out by various organizations into a single organization. Previously, the Marine Surveillance (海監), Ministry of Land and Resources was responsible for maritime resources management, maritime sovereignty protection, search and rescue; and the Bureau of Fisheries (漁政局), Ministry of Agriculture was dedicated to the supervision and management of fisheries; the Border Control (边检),

Ministry of Public Security was for law enforcement offshore; the Maritime Customs Services (海關) of Chinese Customs was for anti-smuggling efforts. In addition, China created the China Coast Guard (中國海警) under the State Oceanic Administration in 2013. In 2018, the China Coast Guard was transferred to the Central Military Commission and placed under control of the paramilitary People's Armed Police (武警). Such moves bring about deep interest as well as concern from China's neighbors.

Having learned from its historic experiences, Chinese leaders today have expanded its perspective from a land-centric view to include the ocean. Zheng He's belief that "in order for a state to be wealthy, one must not to stay away from the sea. Wealth as well as risk come from the water" is reviving as a belief among Chinese leadership today.

Chapter 14

PIRATES IN ASIAN SEAS

Pirates in Ancient China

China had been a maritime power since ancient times. Because it had been active on the sea before many other regions, its encounters with pirates predate that of many other regions as well. The first pirate who appeared in Chinese history was Zhang Bairo in the era of the Eastern Han (東漢, 25–220 A.D.). The record tells that Zhang ravaged nine coastal areas and killed local officials in July 109, with a pirate group composed of 3,000. The Eastern Han government sent a special force to combat the pirates. Zhang pretended to surrender, but regrouped and attacked local governments in collaboration with bandits, and set prisoners free. The pirate group led by Zhang was so extensive that the organization referred to itself as a state. The Eastern Han government engaged in combating the pirate group. Zhang fled to the sea and was killed when he failed to attack the local government.

There are some records about pirates operating in the late Eastern Han and the Three Kingdoms (220–280 A.D.) – the tripartite division of China between the states of Wei (魏), Shu (蜀) and Wu (吳). In 206, Cao Cao (曹操), chancellor of Wei, made an expedition to the eastern region and suppressed a pirate group. After the pirate group based in the Shandong Peninsula was defeated, they fled to islands. At the end of the Eastern Han, there had been frequent sea-based rebellions that went beyond mere piracy. The rebels were similar to Japanese pirate groups in the later era in that they used the ocean as a home base to avoid the suppression of government attacks on the land.

The first incident involving pirates during the Tang (唐) Dynasty (618–907 A.D.) was that King Mu of Balhae (渤海, 698–926) had Zhang Munhwi attack Dengzhou with pirates in 732 during the Balhae-Tang War. In response, Emperor Xuanzong of Tang sent a punitive force and suppressed the pirates. The pirate group, led by Zhang Munhwi, was actively engaged in piracy in the Bohai Bay. At the time, a pirate group was operating on the southeast coast of China. They attacked the coastal area of Zhejiang. During the Tang Dynasty, there had been rampant human trafficking, where the victims were largely the people from the Silla Kingdom on the Korean Peninsula. In 821, a local governor sent a letter asking for the central government to prohibit the trafficking of Silla people by pirates. He argued in the letter that since the Silla people paid taxes to the Tang, they should be treated the same as the Chinese – and, he pointed out, the Chinese coastal people were also in danger of kidnapping by pirates.

This was similar to Admiral Jang Bogo's report to the King of Silla, made when he returned from Tang. Jang Bogo was a powerful maritime figure who effectively controlled the Yellow Sea and dominated the trade between Silla, Heian Japan, and Tang China for decades. This may indicate that piratical activities at the time extended to the Korean Peninsula beyond the coast of China. During the Tang dynasty, the maritime trade that was centered in Guangzhou prospered, along with western trade through the Silk Road. Prosperity in maritime trade led pirates to rage in this region as well. Arab merchant ships sailing for Tang with valuable goods aboard were good prey for pirates.

During the Song Dynasty (宋, A.D. 960–1279), following the Five Dynasties and Ten Kingdoms period, the maritime trade of China greatly prospered. As a result, along with the expansion of maritime trade in the South China Sea, maritime trade in East Asia, including in the Korean Peninsula and Japan, boomed as well. As river transport also developed, piracy in the river increased. For the Song Dynasty, committed to addressing the unrest brought about in the Five Dynasties period, it was essential to control and conciliate pirates to maintain stability in the coastal regions. The Song suppressed the pirates operating off-shore of Jiangsu and Dengzhou several times. As illustrated ear-lier, Dengzhou was the region where pirates had been rampant since ancient times. Since Shandong and Jiangsu were a trade hub at the time, they became a hotspot of piracy.

The political order in this period greatly changed with the fall of the Northern Song (北宋) and the foundation of the Southern Song (南宋) based in Hangzhou (杭州). Maritime trade greatly expanded in the Southern Song Dynasty due to threats posed from the northern territory. The prominent feature of piracy in this era was that it centered in the regions of Zhejiang and Fujian, likely because those regions had become political and economic hubs.

The Shandong Peninsula had been the main region where merchant ships called in until the Northern Song Dynasty, but the circumstance had greatly changed. Chenzhou of Fujian, which had rapidly grown during the Southern Song dynasty, was a stopover for merchant ships and the largest beneficiary of such trade circumstances. It appears natural that pirates were attracted to this region to target merchant ships carrying valu-able goods. The Southern Song, beyond merely combatting pi-rates, employed them as military resources. In 1135, when a pi-rate group surrendered, they were assigned to the navy. On the part of the politically unstable Southern Song, such gestures were a conciliatory measure for locals as well as an opportuni-ty to build up the military.

Political Pirates in China

The prominent feature of Chinese pirate groups that had op-erated off the shores of China and Southeast Asia was that they were 'political pirates,' who were closely linked to particular political groups in the transitional period of dynasties, and they shared a destiny with those political groups. Chinese rulers did not make use of them as a means of exploring trade and overseas colonies. However, the political chaos in the transitional period of dynasties provided these pirates with an opportunity to rampage. These pirate groups reached the South China Sea as the threat of Japanese pirates was alleviated by the 16th century.

Piracy committed by political pirates in Far East Asia was eventually terminated by European powers. Europeans had been responsible for the safety of trade routes since China's defeat in the Opium Wars in the 19th century. Piracy committed by the political pirate groups in China and Southeast Asia for over a thousand years was doomed by Europeans who employed far-reaching anti-piracy measures in the South China Sea and Indonesian waters. In the sections below, the infamous political pirates who dominated the South China Sea and China at the height of piracy in Far East Asia are highlighted.

Zheng Zhilong (鄭芝龍) and His Son Zheng Chengong (鄭成功)

In the 16th century, a pirate empire built by Zheng Zhilong emerged. Zheng Zhilong, a Chinese merchant, pirate and military leader in the late Ming Dynasty, built enormous wealth and went to Macao to trade with Europeans. He joined the pirate group in 1624 and engaged in looting Chinese and Dutch merchant ships. Taking advantage of a power vacuum in the central government, he expanded his power and ruled most of the coastal areas of Fujian and the islands of Twain by the 1630s. As the Ming underwent political chaos in its late years, it appointed him a government position responsible for combating pirates. By virtue of his contribution, he was appointed to defend Fujian in 1629, as 'Admiral of the Coastal Seas.' With legal power in his hands, Zheng Zhilong had no barrier to prevent his plans.

By exclusively controlling the maritime trade of this region, he protected trade by using junk ships, which were built for war. Meanwhile, he continued to be engaged in his main job – that is, piracy – and thus expanded his activities from the estuary of the Yangtze River to Hainan Island, plundering the ships sailing the region. Traders were required to pay money to the captains he employed in order to guarantee their safe passage. If they refused, they were subject to attack.

As the power of Zheng Zhilong grew, the emperor could not help appointing him to a higher position to combat pirates in 1641. In the transitional period from the Ming to the Qing, he made a risky attempt in between the falling and emerging dynasties. When Nanjing was felled by the Manchu in 1644, Zheng enthroned a new emperor. He served as commander-in-chief of the imperial forces and was ordered to defend the newly established capital in Fuzhou. He made use of the emperor as a political hostage to the fullest extent but eventually surrendered to the Qing, believing he would be shown mercy. Upon his surrender, however, he was placed under house arrest and executed in Beijing in 1661.

After Zheng Zhilong's death, Zheng Chenggong, better known as Koxinga, fully succeeded to his father's 'pirate empire.' When the castle of Fujian fell to Manchu forces, the young leader, at the age of 22, led his fleet to Taiwan. He regarded the Manchu who had killed his father as an irreconcilable enemy and became a leader of Ming loyalists. His junk ship fleets attacked the ships of the Qing and effectively contained the estuary of the Yangtze River – thus blocking Nanjing from maritime trade between Chinese and Europeans.

In 1650, the Zheng force occupied Xiamen by attacking from the land and the sea. Over a decade, he fully dominated a coastal region ranging from the Yangtze to the delta of the Mekong River. However, Zheng Chenggong returned to Taiwan after his coalition with the anti-Qing force was defeated. Witnessing how Europeans were expanding their territory, an outraged Zheng drove the Dutch from Taiwan and established a dynasty which ruled the island as the Kingdom of Tungning from 1661 to 1683.

The Qing contained coastal regions and imposed an embargo to suppress the Zheng forces. Subsequently, the embargo was imposed on the coastal regions of Fujian, Guangdong and Zhejiang, and villages and settlements were completely destroyed. In 1662, when Zheng Chenggong died of malaria at the age of 37, the Zheng regime was taken over by his son Zheng Jing. In 1683, following the death of Zheng Jing, Taiwan was placed under the complete rule of the Qing. To this day, the pirate Zheng Chenggong is respected as a national hero in Taiwan.

Zheng Yi (鄭一)

Zheng Yi was a powerful Chinese pirate who operated from Guangdong and throughout the South China Sea in the late 1700s. He was born in Vietnam in 1765, the son of a Chinese pirate. The Tay Son Dynasty (1778–1862) in the late 18th century employed Chinese pirates on a grand scale. The pirates were deployed to the navy of the dynasty and engaged in sea battles. Zheng Yi was the most famous among them.

In 1795, Zheng Yi and his colleagues organized a pirate group and engaged in piracy on the frontier of China and Vietnam. Eventually, he had eight pirate groups under his control. After he was defeated in battle in 1801, he moved to Guangdong. Over four years, he incorporated the pirates operating in coastal areas into a single massive coalition. The pirate coalition consisted of six fleets, and each fleet had its own color. Each fleet was assigned an area of activity and given autonomy; they did not fight each other.

He maintained loose control over the coalition of pirates and commanded the Red Flag Fleet, one of the most powerful pirate fleets in all of China. By 1804, the coalition had grown into a formidable force. He kept raiding coastal fortresses and looting merchant ships. He contained the Portuguese colonial city of Macao on the grounds that Europeans refused to pay him for safe passage. The British Navy, responsible for offshore patrol, was incapable of combating the fast-growing pirate coalition.

The fleets of the coalition started out with 200 ships. By 1807, massive fleets were composed of 600 junk ships and 30,000 troops under the direct command of Zheng Yi. Zheng Yi's organization, with more than 150,000 personnel, became the largest in history. Zheng Yi died in Vietnam on 16 November 1807. Allegedly, he died in a typhoon or in an accident, falling overboard.

Zheng Yi Sao (鄭一嫂) and Cheung Po (張保)

Shortly after Zheng Yi's death, the command of the pirate coalition was succeeded by his wife Zheng Yi Sao. Zheng Yi Sao, who had been a Cantonese brothel madam or prostitute known as Shi Xianggu, married Zheng Yi in 1801. She skillfully took control over the coalition. She quickly acted to solidify the partnership with her stepson Cheung Po, taking him as a lover. Their first success came when they were able to secure the loyalty of Zheng's relatives. She appointed Cheung Po the commander of the Red Flag Fleet.

Previously in 1798, Zheng Yi had kidnapped Cheung Po, a 15-year-old son of a Tankan fisherman, and pressed him into piracy. Cheung Po's natural talent helped him adapt well to the pirate life, and he rose swiftly through the ranks. As he built a reputation among his fellow pirates, he was adopted by the Zheng couple as their step-son, making him Zheng's legal heir. Shortly after Zheng Yi's death, they married. Afterwards, Zheng Yi Sao acted as commander-in-chief of the pirate coalition. Cheung Po was merely an aide to her as vice commander.

The couple commanded the pirate coalition with strict regulations, stricter even than the pirate codes of the West Indies in the 1720s. Those who disobeyed orders or stole prizes or public funds were subject to execution. Those who abandoned their posts were subject to having their ears cut off. Those who hid or withheld prizes were punished with whipping. Those who repeatedly committed misdemeanors were also subject to execution. The same punishments were applied to women. The rape of women captives was punished with execution. If love affairs with women captives were discovered, men were executed and women were thrown overboard with a weight on their legs.

The pirate coalition led by Zheng Yi Shao and Cheung Po defeated all Qing's anti-piracy forces. In January 1808, the Qing Navy was defeated in a large-scale sea battle off the coast of Guangdong. As a consequence, the Qing Navy fled when encountering the pirates afterward. They ultimately quit doing sea patrols. The pirate coalition was so powerful that a pirate ship could defeat four Qing warships. The pirates began to threaten the cities of Guangdong Province. When their supplies were blocked in the sea, they landed on shores and attacked coastal settlements. By the end of 1808, all the Qing's anti-piracy forces were defeated. The pirates committed brutal revenge against villagers who resisted them. When Cheung Po attacked an island in 1809, 1,000 islanders were slaughtered and 20 women were kidnapped.

The scale of the pirate coalition led by Zheng Yi Sao and Cheung Po was larger than that of the European pirates who had operated in the West Indies during the Age of Discovery. In 1809, at the height of the coalition, it was stronger than the navies of a number of countries combined. The pirate coalition had 200 ships for ocean-going, armed with 20 to 30 cannons and 400 crewmen aboard. It had 600 to 800 ships for offshore, equipped with 12 to 25 cannons and 200 crewmen aboard. They also had dozens of junk ships for river sailing, with 20 to 30 pirates aboard. These junk ships, with approximately 20 oars, were used to plunder inland towns and the farmland of landlords who were delinquent in paying protection money.

The heyday of the pirate coalition ended in 1810. The Qing had to call for assistance from Portuguese and English fleets, even though such a move harmed the dynasty's dignity and pride. England accepted Qing's offer to protect tributes from Thailand, and sent a privateer armed with 20 cannons. Portugal provided six warships for six months. The Qing government built up its navy and enforced the Ban on Sea-Going to prevent the maritime activities of pirates. The Qing government stepped up its anti-piracy operations as it offered the pirates a chance to surrender in exchange for a pardon.

Because of the Qing's anti-piracy efforts and the more strict Ban on Sea-Going, Zheng Yi Sao and Cheung Po decided to accept the offer of pardon. They handed over their ships and arms to the Qing Navy. They negotiated the terms of surrender, under which the surrendered pirates would be employed by the Qing Navy if they wanted. Cheung Po was offered the rank of captain and to lead a fleet of 20 junk ships. At last, the negotiations reached an agreement on 20 April 1810. Under the agreement, a total of 17,318 pirates officially surrendered, and 226 pirate ships were handed over. However, not all pirates were exempt from punishment. Sixty pirates were expelled for two years and 151 were exiled for good. Another 126 pirates were executed.

Zheng Yi Sao and Cheung Po settled in Guangdong. Later Cheung Po was promoted to colonel and died in 1822 at the age of 36. After his death, Zheng Yi Sao opened a gambling house with abundant funds in Guangdong. She died in 1844 at the age of 69. The end of the infamous Chinese pirate was quite peaceful. Zheng Yi Sao was very shrewd and charismatic.

For this reason, some argue that she was the greatest pirate in history. Some argue against that, but it is beyond dispute that she successfully led a massive pirate group – she reacted intelligently to new circumstances and was fully committed to implementing her decisions.

Japanese Pirates: Wakou (倭寇)

Japanese pirates, better known as the Wakou, were groups of outlaws who wore their hair in topknots (*chonmage*, **ちょんまげ**), wore traditional white undergarments (*fundoshi,* **ふんどし**), carried long swords as they looted, kidnapped, burned homes and settlements, and murdered along the coasts.

The Wakou significantly affected the history of East Asia while operating in in the regions ranging from China, Japan and Korea to Southeast Asia. In particular, the ceaseless invasions of Japanese pirates during the Age of the Three Kingdoms (三國時代, B.C. 57–A.D. 668) significantly influenced the history of the Korean Peninsula. In the late Korea (高麗) Dynasty, their persistent attacks caused chaos in the government and a decline in a national power. Ultimately, it led to the fall of the Korea Dynasty and the foundation of the Chosun (朝鮮) Dynasty by General Lee Sung Kye, who won popular support by taking a strong stand against the Wakou. As illustrated previously, the Chosun feared the connection between islanders and Japanese pirates, and so enforced the Ban on Sea-Going. This, inevitably, affected the Chosun destiny.

Japanese Pirates

In China, Wakou attacks on coastal regions brought about the decline of the Yuan (元) by destabilizing the central government's local control. The rebels in the late Yuan were linked to the Wakou. Even after the rebels were suppressed by the founder of the Ming (明), Chu Yuanchang, they continued to plunder coastal regions in connection with the Wakou. As examined earlier, the Ming's Ban on Sea-Going was a protectionary measure against piracy committed by the Wakou in the late Yuan and the rebels connected to the pirates. Given its influence on Chinese history, it would not be improper to say that the Wakou played a role in the fate of modern China.

The Wakou were also a group of people who were involved in exchange and trade in the sea beyond the wall of nation and peoples. The perspective of Wakou differs between China, Japan and Korea. Whereas China and Korea regard themselves as victims of the Wakou and thus are negative towards them, Japan appears to be of the view that the Wakou were part of Japanese maritime activities and expansions overseas. It is understood in such context that the term 'Wakou' is not used in Japanese literature, while it appears in the ancient literature of China and Korea.

Then how are the Wakou different from other pirates? In Chinese, 'Wakou' (倭寇) means 'Japanese bandits.' It is similarly defined in a dictionary as "Japanese pirates who were engaged in looting off the shores of East Asia." Despite such a description, it is not easy to define them in simple words. This is because the term 'pirate' in East Asia was more nuanced than it is today.

Unlike the modern conception of the term 'pirate,' the word carried a number of different connotations in ancient times. On one side, they were villains threatening peace in the sea; on the other, they were protectors of maritime peace and maritime traders. In order to articulate this view, we need to shed light on maritime trade in ancient East Asia. Only public, government-managed trade was allowed, and private trade and commerce were strictly prohibited. Such a system was officially established in the Ming Dynasty, but had existed in the previous era as well. On the part of the government, those who refused to follow policies were regarded as pirates and were treated as such. In fact, it was hard to discern pirates from merchants, given that the authority of the central government was unable to reach the sea, and it was hard to know what was going on off shore. Since merchants were armed to protect their cargo, it was difficult for the government to guess whether their intentions were to defend their trade or to attack others.

In China, the Wakou were widely called 'Haigou' (海寇) or 'sea pirates.' In the early Ming, when the Ban on Sea-Going was enforced, those who operated in the sea were regarded as Haigou. As offshore pirates were connected to the Wakou, it became harder to tell them apart, and both 'Wakou' and 'Haigou' carried the same meaning.

Regarding the origin of the Wakou, there are a number of different theories, including the origin of Silla and the coastal region of the East China Sea. The most convincing theory is the origin of western seamen. According to this theory, the founders of the Wakou were Japanese and their ancestors were western seamen. The western seamen were some of the people who engaged in both fishing and farming on the coasts, centered in the estuary of Yangtze, in the era of Five Kingdoms (907–960). They moved to Japan and settled in the coastal areas of Kitakyushu.

Activities of the Wakou

The Wakou group operated for approximately 200 years, between the 14th and 16th centuries. This was a period of great political, social and economic change in East Asia, and the Wakou evolved accordingly. Tanaka Takeo, a prominent researcher of the Wakou in Japan, makes a distinction between the Wakou who operated in the 14th and 15th centuries and those who lived in the 16th century.

Takeo, along with a majority of Japanese researchers, are of the view that the Wakou in the earlier period were largely Japanese, but the latter Wakou were mostly Chinese – with Japanese pirates making up only 10 percent to 20 percent of their number. Many Japanese scholars argue the theory of the 'Korean Wakou' – that actually the Wakou who operated on the Korean Peninsula were mostly Koreans, while Japanese were few in number. According to this theory, the Wakou operating in the Chinese continent had close ties with the Wakou on the Korean Peninsula. Occasionally those on the Korean Peninsula moved to operate on the Chinese continent. This theory is supported by the argument that the prevalence of Wakou in the Korea dynasty, prevalent since 1350, overlapped with Wakou activities in China, which started in 1350 or 1358.

The Wakou in the first period were people who started out as coastal settlers, islanders, warriors and seamen but turned pirate after civil wars and bad weather created food shortages. They engaged in piracy in the Liaotung and Shandong Peninsulas. Their main goal was to steal food and capture coastal settlers. On the contrary, the majority of the Wakou in the 16th century were Chinese, and they operated in Zhejiang, Fujian and Guangdong. As they were blocked from maritime trade due to the strict enforcement of the Ban on Sea-Going, they engaged in private, illegal trade with Chinese, Japanese and merchants from other regions. The government, in response, named them the Wakou and suppressed their activities. While the Wakou in the first period concentrated on stealing food and capturing prisoners, the Wakou in the second half were largely engaged in private trade.

With the greater emphasis on trade of the later Wakou in both Japan and China, their brutal attacks were relatively ignored. However, the later Wakou were large in scale and more violent and destructive. The scale of Wakou was up to hundreds of ships and thousands of people during the rule of Emperor Jiajing (嘉靖帝, 1521–1567) during the Ming dynasty. Their activities stretched from Liaotung to Guangdong. The Wakou prizes were important goods for exchange on the market in Japan, and were critical goods to trade with merchants from Japan, Southeast Asia and the West.

At the height of the Wakou, the silver trade between Japan and China was active. Japan, a silver exporter, was unable to get necessary goods through formal trade. Chinese Wakou leaders were closely linked to Daimyos (大名) – the most powerful feudal rulers from the 10th century to the middle 19th century in Japan – in the Sengoku period (戦国時代 or Age of Warring States; 1467-1568). The Wakou provided Chinese-sourced war supplies to Japan. The most preferred prize of the Wakou in the 14th and 15th centuries was humans. In the 16th century, humans were valuable commodities. There was a labor shortage throughout the Nanbokucho period (南北朝時代 or South and North courts period; 1336-1392) in Japan. Under this circumstance, captives were sold as slaves or used as local guides, rowers and warriors.

The majority of historians accept that the Wakou probably engaged in piracy because of the harsh living conditions in their native homes. Most of the Wakou were from the western islands of Japan, including Tsushima Island, which was an isolated and impoverished location. In addition, the rule of the central government of Japan at the time was unable to reach the sea due to civil wars in the Nanbokucho period. The Wakou, with advanced navigational skills, sailed across the sea and reached the Korean Peninsula or the Chinese continent, taking advantage of the chaotic period.

As the Wakou became unable to do normal trade with China and Korea, they engaged in piracy to survive. Such a view is argued mostly by Chinese scholars who regard the Wakou in the 14th and 15th centuries as a stricken people.

The Korean Peninsula and the Wakou

The Wakou had a huge impact on the history of the Korean Peninsula over a long period, particularly its coastal regions. Their first appearance was in the time of the Three Kingdoms (Goguryeo, Bakje and Silla: B.C. 57–A.D. 668) and Unified Silla (668–935). The inscription on the monument of King Gwanggaeto the Great (廣開土大王) of Goguryeo (高句麗), built in 404, states that "the Wakou ran away after defeat and many Wakou were killed." This was the first time the word 'Wakou' appears in the written record.

King Munmu, who united the Three Kingdoms into a unified Silla during his reign (661–681), built the Buddhist temple of Gameunsa to protect the land from pirates. The king also requested that he be buried in an underwater tomb in the sea, east of the temple, called 'Daewangam' (大王巖). He said, "In this way, 'Munmu of Silla' will become a great dragon and protect the country." These actions demonstrate the depth of Silla's fears about pirate attacks, and illustrate the high priority of the Wakou issue in the national agenda. Clearly, the Korean Peninsula greatly suffered from Wakou attacks all the way back to the early Age of Three Kingdoms.

However, the Wakou in this period were not the same group as in the Korea Dynasty (918–1392). According to this theory, the Wakou in the inscription on the monument of King Gwanggaeto the Great were the Japanese force that Baekje (百濟), in conflict with Goguryeo, had employed for military purposes. It is not obvious whether Wakou invasions of Silla were for political purposes or merely for looting.

However, given the close relationship between Baekje and the Wakou at the time, these invasions were more likely to be for political purposes. In this context, some argue that Wakou invasions in the Three Kingdom period should be distinguished from those in the later Korea and Chosun dynasties, which concentrated on looting and kidnapping. They further argue that the Wakou in the Three Kingdoms should be excluded from the scope of Wakou on the Korean Peninsula. In the Korea Dynasty, the Wakou first appeared in literatures in 1223. During the 40-year period afterward, they invaded up to 11 times. They looted southern coastal areas and then quickly retreated. Even though the Wakou at the time threatened the living of coastal settlers and plundered government ships carrying grain paid as taxes, they were not serious enough to pose a threat to the safety of the state. However, circumstances were quite different between 1350–1391, a 40-year period which ended in the collapse of the Korea dynasty. The Wakou in this period were much more serious in terms of scale, invading and looting a greater area and employing different methods as well. The fleets ranged from 20 to 500 ships, and they invaded up to 591 times during those four decades.

This period was the heyday of the Wakou. The methods of looting were quite different from the past. Quick retreats were no more; instead, they lingered, setting fire to government offices and, very frequently, capturing locals. The frequent attacks of Wakou brought about poverty and a diaspora of coastal settlers. Meanwhile, their legendary status grew: In some cases, lower-class people disguised themselves as Wakou by adopting their costume and hairstyle.

The scope of Wakou activities extended even to Vladivostok in Russia and China beyond the Korean Peninsula. The Wakou issue escalated into a diplomatic issue between Korea and China, as China called for Korea to suppress the Wakou. As a result, the Korean government feared that Chinese fleets would overwhelm its coastal regions if they went on the offensive against the Wakou in Tsushima, or that Chinese troops would come over the peninsula to make a direct attack.

Wakou attacks on shipments of grain that were meant to be paid as taxes meant that the Korean government occasionally could not afford to pay officials. As a consequence, the government moved coastal storages inland, and taxes were temporarily shipped overland. The Wakou in the later Korea Dynasty inflicted enormous damage to the entire country, to the extent that the survival of the state was at stake.

The Wakou at the time were not merely engaged in piracy – they were competent enough to fight against military forces. In 1377, the Wakou lured military forces out by attacking the region next to the capital city of Kaesung and attempting to invade the capital city. The Korean government, with its very existence at stake, planned to move the capital city landward.

The Annals of King Taejo, founder of the Chonsun Dynasty, portrayed the brutal pillaging of the Wakou: "In August 1380, 500 ships of Wakou anchored in Jinpo and attacked three southern provinces and slaughtered locals and set fire to coastal towns. The slaughtered and captured were countless. Dead bodies covered mountains and fields, and after the Wakou transported grain to their ships, the grain left on the road piled up to 30 centimeters high. The dead bodies of captives were piled up like a mountain and made a pool of blood. Capturing 2- or 3-year-old girls alive, they cut off their heads and cut and cleaned their abdomens and performed a ritual with rice and drink, and as a consequence, the three coastal provinces became empty. Not since the Wakou began their attacks had anything like this ever happened."

In the Chosun Dynasty (1392–1910), there had been a total of 165 attacks during the 160 years between the founding year of 1392 and the southern province attack in 1555. Compared with the late Korea Dynasty, the scale as well as the number of Wakou attacks greatly diminished. The provinces were attacked in the order of Kyngsang, Kangwon and Chungcheng, which covered almost the entire territory of the Chosun. The Wakou in the Chosun were somewhat similar to the massive scale of Wakou attacks in the late Korea Dynasty, but the scale of attacks gradually became lesser.

Chapter 15

CONTEMPORARY PIRACY

Emergence of Contemporary Piracy

Piracy is undoubtedly the oldest threat to safe navigation and seafaring. As illustrated in previous chapters, the origin of piracy goes back to ancient times, and corresponds with the history of shipping. Varying with regions and times, piracy had been prevalent across the oceans throughout the history of the world.

Piracy was believed to have disappeared in the early 19th century across the oceans, as a result of enormous counter-piracy efforts. In the absence of piracy threats, the oceans remained stable and secure during the past century. Pirates, meanwhile, became a popular subject of novels, dramas, movies and other literary works, in which pirates and their life were described as romantic and adventurous. This has helped people have a misconception of pirates, who were outlaws and committed heinous atrocities at sea. However, piracy has never been eradicated throughout the history of the mankind. It would be right to argue that piracy over that period had merely been latent due to strong anti-piracy measures. Unfortunately, this proved to be merely a short-lived respite. In the 1970s, less than a century after piracy's supposed demise, a steady rise in the number of attacks ushered in the present phenomenon of modern-day piracy.

Contemporary piracy, taking advantage of advanced information technologies and weapons, appears in many different forms. The loss of life and damage to property, as well as costs incurred by piracy to the shipping industry at the global level, are tremendous. Piracy has emerged as the gravest threat to the safety of navigation and seaborne trade, becoming an urgent global security issue that the international community needs to address together. The phenomenon of contemporary piracy has not appeared out of nowhere. This is the result of an interaction between a wide range of international and regional factors and stakeholders. The factors that have contributed to the emergence of contemporary piracy may be identified as follows.

First, a booming shipping trade, in tandem with the expansion of seaborne trade in the era of globalization, has served as a primary factor. As it was in the Age of Discovery, valuable cargoes, particularly of energy resources, are a tempting target for pirates. Second, the collapse of maritime supremacy in the post-Cold War era brought about a power vacuum in the oceans, and this has resulted in the weakening of policing and deterrence of piracy. Third, the unstable political situations in some coastal states have helped contribute to the problem. Many piracy attacks are committed by rebels in those countries to finance their activities. Furthermore, those coastal states lack resources for law enforcement and the capability to prevent and suppress piracy. Lastly, geographical conditions suited for piracy, and a long-held tradition of piracy for livelihoods, are also important contributing factors.

The problem of contemporary piracy extends beyond a particular region or a single coastal state – it is a common concern of the international community, as often described as *hostis humani generis* (enemy of mankind). This chapter explores various aspects of acts of piracy and unravel the nature and reality of the global piracy issue from a multi-faceted perspective. Examining aspects of piracy in international law, it provides an overview of the global trend of piracy attacks and global counter-piracy efforts at the international and governmental as well as industry level.

How is piracy defined in international law?

The definition of piracy varies with the perspectives and interests of those concerned. The most challenging problem with defining the term 'piracy' might be that there exists a considerable degree of disparity between the legal definition of piracy and its general usage in journalism or elsewhere. The common usage of the word 'piracy' by the public, which is supposedly derived from the historical context, refers to any unlawful acts of violence at sea or in coastal areas against ships, crews and locals, irrespective of the elements that constitute the legal term. Outside piracy, there are different forms of violence at sea, such as armed robbery, terrorism and other unlawful acts. This occasionally brings about confusion in the distinction between the definition of piracy and other acts of violence at sea.

In legal terms, the definition of piracy in international law is very restrictive, covering certain aspects of unlawful acts at sea. Thus, what constitutes an act of piracy in international law has remained controversial. For this reason, it is crucial to identify the legal elements of acts of piracy in international law, and to separate them from other acts of maritime violence in terms of law enforcement and criminal jurisdiction.

Piracy is defined under the United Nations Convention on the Law of the Sea (UNCLOS) as "any illegal acts of violence, detention or depredation committed for private ends by the crew or passengers of a private ship against another ship or persons or property on board it, on the high sea or outside jurisdiction of any state." "Any act of voluntary participation in the operation of a ship intended to be used for such purposes, and any act of inciting or intentionally facilitating such acts are also piracy."

Despite being a universally accepted legal term, however, a number of problems with the definition of piracy are identified. The problems become more apparent when the definition is applied to the trend of piracy attacks worldwide in recent years. First, the criterion of 'private ends' appears to be inapplicable to an increasing number of piracy attacks in South Asia and West Africa supposedly committed by terrorist groups fighting for political ends or religious beliefs. Second, the two ship-rule requires that at least two ships must be involved in a piracy attack. This requires that a piracy attack should be committed by a ship against another ship. However, the *modus operandi* of piratical acts in Southeast Asia, in which in many cases locals and a small group of people are aboard rubber dinghies and canoes, is unable to meet the requirement. Under this criterion, the growing piratical incidents in West Africa, concentrated in the Gulf of Guinea, in which pirates attack oil and gas tankers and offshore oil rigs for oil theft, are not qualified as piracy defined in the UNCLOS.

Third, the criteria of 'on the high seas' and 'outside the jurisdiction of any state' make the suitability of piracy very restrictive. Given that the majority of unlawful acts at sea take place inshore or offshore, either in the territorial sea or in port, the criteria do not correspond with what is happening, particularly in Southeast Asia.

The criterion that the place of the crime is restricted to the high seas is ill-suited for Southeast Asia, where states are situated adjacent or opposite in an archipelagic geography. The underlying tenet of the criterion is understood to declare that the unlawful acts of violence committed within states' jurisdictions can be enforced by coastal states. However, in many cases, unlawful acts of violence at sea – even within a state's jurisdiction, such as off the coast of Somalia – are transnational and beyond a state's capability.

Typology of Contemporary Piracy

For contemporary piracy, a number of international organizations involved in maritime affairs have developed their own criteria to classify various types of piracy attacks to serve their activities. By taking account of the classifications of piracy by various international organizations, a number of different categories of piracy attacks, based on *modus operandi*, geographic location, violence level, and faciliatory factors, etc. are put forward.

Petty Theft

The goal of this type of attack is to quickly steal movable items on ships, which appear to be valuable and profitable, while ships are in their berths or at anchor. For the most part, the intention of theft is to steal cash and valuables from the safe, or to steal IT equipment, personal effects and ship stores. This type of attack is the most typical in South Asia, particularly in Indonesia.

Robbers take advantage of relatively relaxed security of many small ports in the region. The typical method is that robbers approach near the bow or stern and attempt to board, usually with grappling hooks. The robbers are usually not armed and flee when they are noticed, and thus this type of crime is generally considered to be less violent. Robbers are mostly locals and generally operate in a small group. This type of robbery has been a way of earning a livelihood in the coastal areas of Southeast Asia. Cases of theft of cash or personal effects have generally less significant impacts compared to armed robberies.

Armed Robbery: Maritime Mugging

This type of attack occurs when pirates armed with weapons board the ship and steal ship stores, equipment and the crew's personal effects. Attacks are committed against ships while at anchor/berth or underway. This type of attack is a common form of piracy in Southeast Asia. The purpose of these 'shoot and scoot' pirate attacks is to rob cash and valuables from the safe, the crew, and ship stores, rather than commit more serious acts such as hijacking entire ships and their cargoes.

Attacks committed against ships that are underway usually take place within a short distance from the territory of coastal states, especially in the Malacca Strait where ships sail at low speeds due to narrow sea lanes and underwater features. The typical method of these attacks is that first the target ship is approached by one or more small craft that varies from primitive, homemade vessels to modern high-speed motorboats.

The ship underway is boarded alongside or near the stern, depending on the freeboard and ease of access. In general, ships with low freeboard that sail at a relatively low speed are prime targets for piracy attacks. Pirates, heavily armed with various weapons, including knives, machetes, pistols and automatic weapons, board during the night when ships slow down while they go through the narrow sea lanes off the coast.

This type of pirate attack involves threatening, assault, serious injury, and even kidnapping and killing of the crew. A large number of pirates, who belong to organized syndicates, are engaged in an attack, and the level of violence is much higher than with petty theft, in which the perpetrator flees upon being noticed. This type of pirate incident is considered more significant because it involves large vessels as well as a high probability for use of force.

Phantom Ship: Hijacking of Vessels and Conversion

The phantom ship indicates that an entire ship has been hijacked by pirates, and it has been re-born as a 'phantom' ship. The typical *modus operandi* is that cargo on board a ship is seized, and the crews is killed and thrown overboard or, if they are lucky, set adrift in boats. Then, the ship is renamed, repainted, re-crewed, registered over several times, and made available in international maritime trade.

The phantom ship is given a temporary certificate through the ship registration office in an Asian port. The ship is then fraudulently reregistered – typically under the nationality of Honduras, Belize, Panama or Liberia – and issued with false documents to enable them to board a fresh payload. The new shipper loads his cargo onto the pirate vessel and receives his bill of lading. The ship, instead of heading for the port named on the bill of lading, sails to a different port, unloads the cargo to a conspirator or an unsuspecting buyer, then sheds its temporary registration for another. Phantom ships are often used for smuggling and other unlawful acts at sea.

The phantom ship may illustrate the transnational nature of piracy, given that these piracy attacks are pre-meditated, well-organized and committed by crime syndicates across borders, involving a large number of operatives at each stage. The crime syndicates are well-resourced and carefully laid-out international criminal networks, and the operatives are highly trained, heavily armed and fully prepared to use firearms.

Phantom ship piracy attacks, which had been prevalent until the early 2000s in Southeast Asia, were a grave concern in the region and among the shipping community. Southeast Asia accounted for the vast majority of phantom ships worldwide, recording 48 incidents out of a total of 53 incidents between 1996 and 2013. Phantom ship piracy culminated in 2003 and began to sharply decline since 2005. This type of attack has not been reported in Southeast Asia in recent years. A case of a phantom ship incident that occurred in Southeast Asian waters is presented here as an example: On 27 September 1998, a Panama-registered cargo ship owned by a Japanese citizen, the *Ten Yu Ho* disappeared three hours after departing from Kuala Tanjong, Indonesia. The ship, loaded with a cargo of 3,000 tons of aluminum ingots, was bound for Incheon, Korea. Three months after the ship disappeared, it was found in Zhangjiagang in Jiangsu Province, China, repainted, re-crewed, and renamed the *SANE-1*. The renamed ship was identified as the *Ten Yu Ho* by confirmation of the engine number. Fourteen crewmen (twelve Chinese and two Koreans) and cargo still remain missing.

Hijacking, Hostage-Taking and Ransom-Seeking

The typical method is to hijack a vessel while it is underway and bring it to the pirates' base. There, the pirates will hold the crew hostage for a period of time and negotiate a ransom payment with a shipowner in exchange for the release of the crew and ship. This has been most prevalent off the Somali coast and the Gulf of Aden over the last decade. Piracy attacks in the region, which are perceived as the symbol of contemporary piracy, are at the most significant level in all aspects, such as scale of attack, level of sophistication, degree of violence, damage inflicted, and impact on the international community.

Unlike traditional piracy attacks, the crews are held hostage for a relatively extended period of time and released after a ransom is paid. The use of violence against crews is not common, although pirates carry weapons. This happens because piracy is motivated by the prospect of large monetary gains from ransom payments. This type of attack is usually committed by a relatively large number of pirates under the command of a well-organized criminal network – for instance, one that is connected to rebel groups in Somalia.

These piracy attacks have become a business model involving a complex web of interactions between numerous stakeholders, including financers, instigators and the pirates themselves. The missions of stakeholders are well coordinated and each participant has a role to play, including planning, recruitment, funding, information-gathering, commission of the attack, hostage management and negotiation for ransom, using advanced information technologies and equipment. These piracy attacks are committed against ships that are underway far from offshore or on the high seas by using a mother ship and one or two skiffs, which are small and fast-moving.

Hijacking, Hostage-Taking and Cargo Theft

Unlike Somali pirates seeking a ransom payment, West African pirates, concentrated in the Gulf of Guinea, are engaged in hijacking, hostage-taking and cargo theft. Unlike off the coast of Somalia, which has been in a state of anarchy over the last decade, the piracy-prone region in West Africa is under the rule of developed central governments and is subject to in-port policing. Under these stable circumstances, pirates lack the capacity to capture ships and hold them for a ransom for an extended period of time. Thus, they have developed a combined model of armed robbery, kidnapping for ransom and cargo theft, of which the concentration is on cargo theft.

The prominent feature of such piracy is oil theft. Vessels carrying refined oil products are targeted and attacked specifically for the value of the oil cargo that they carry. When the vessel is hijacked, the crew is often forced to navigate the vessel to an unknown location where the cargo can be lightered to another vessel or to a storage facility on land. The refined oil product then finds its way onto the black market. Eventually, the oil product makes its way back into the clean, mainstream supply and is sold domestically or in the global marketplace.

Aspects of Contemporary Piracy Attacks

Contemporary piracy is a complex and global phenomenon, despite regional variations, and these features may change over time and over space. This section explores and compares the various aspects of contemporary piracy attacks worldwide, including the frequency of piracy occurrences, regional concentrations, contributing factors, *modus operandi* and damage inflicted.

Overview of Piracy Attacks in Recent Years

The occurrences of piracy attacks have an irregular trend, varying with geographical location and time. In terms of a global trend of piracy occurrences, piracy attacks had been constantly on the rise since the mid-1990s and peaked in the period of 2000–2004, averaging 350–450 incidents annually. Over the last decade (2008–2017), a total of 3,010 incidents worldwide were reported to the International Maritime Bureau (IMB), of which Asia and Africa account for 1,325 and 1,455 incidents, respectively. The figures show that piracy attacks are concentrated on the two continents, each accounting for 44 percent and 48 percent of global piracy attacks.

After a peak in 2010 with 445 incidents, piracy attacks world-wide have dramatically declined. Over the five years since 2013, average annual piracy attacks have numbered 225 incidents, which is a significant drop from the past decade. Of particular note is that in 2016, record low occurrences, with 180 incidents overall, were reported. It remains to be seen whether a global trend of piracy reduction will continue or not.

Nonetheless, it may indicate a positive sign that piracy attacks are curbed in piracy-prone regions such as the Somali coast and the Malacca Strait. The statistics of piracy occurrences are based on the data reported to the IMB, which employs a broad piracy definition encompassing the acts of piracy under the UNCLOS and armed robbery together. However, the actual occurrences of piracy are believed to be higher than the statistics of the IMB, given non-reporting or under-reporting. Under-reporting is due to concerns over increases in insurance premiums, disruption of shipping schedules during an investigation, and fears that the ship company and shipmaster will gain a reputation for incompetence.

Features of Piracy Attacks by Region

Piracy is a global phenomenon, reported in the seas of 62 countries in four out of five continents. Of those countries, it is highly concentrated in a number of countries, including Indonesia, Yemen, Malaysia, Somalia, Nigeria, Oman, Bangladesh and India.

Southeast Asia

Southeast Asia has been a traditionally piracy-prone region since ancient times. The vast majority of piracy attacks in Asian waters are concentrated in Southeast Asian seas. In the period from the early 1990s to the mid-2000s, two thirds of piracy attacks worldwide were concentrated in the waters of Asia.

In particular, the Malacca Strait, which is one of the busiest shipping lanes in the world (with an annual traffic volume of over 50,000 ships), as well as a strategic choke point for the global seaborne trade, has been the most vulnerable in the region. But since the mid-2000s, piracy attacks in Southeast Asia have been dramatically reduced. This change was driven by the littoral states of the Malacca Strait, such as Singapore, Malaysia and Indonesia, along with other regional and user states. The stable piracy situation in Southeast has changed since 2010, however, with the waters off Indonesia reemerging as a hotspot of piracy. In 2015, 201 piracy attacks in Southeast Asia were reported, accounting for 82 percent of a total 246 incidents worldwide. The gravity of the piracy issue in this region may be illustrated by the 2016 figures of piracy occurrences: Four incidents (out of a total of seven) ship hijackings and 34 (out of a total of 34) crew kidnapping occurred in that region.

The features of piracy attacks in Asian waters in recent years are identified as follows. First, armed robbery and kidnapping of the crew onboard ships that are underway have been constantly on the rise, while traditional petty theft remains dominant. This may indicate that piracy attacks in that region are becoming increasingly violent. Second, the growing *modus operandi* is that a group of pirates, composed of a maximum of 17 people, armed with rifles and knives on board a fast-moving boat, hijack fishing boats or tug boats that have a low freeboard, and kidnap the crew for a ransom. A notable trend is that kidnapping of general cargo ships and crude oil carriers, attributed to the Philippines militant group the *Abu Sayyaf*, have been significantly increasing. Third, the Sulu-Celebes Seas off the Philippines have newly emerged as a piracy-prone spot. As recently as in October 2016, the ten gunmen of the *Abu Sayyaf* boarded a 11,391-ton Korean cargo ship off Tawi-Tawi Island and kidnapped the Korean master and a Filipino crew and abandoned ship.

The rise in piracy attacks in Southeast Asia can be attributed to some contributing factors: (i) permissive environment toward piracy as a source of livelihood for locals; (ii) archipelagic geography dotted with small islands; (iii) channel for funding militant groups; (iv) lack of law-enforcement capability of littoral states; (iv) bad economic and unstable political situation and relaxed counter-piracy efforts

East Africa

The region of the Somali coast and the Gulf of Aden have been hotspots of piracy over the last decade. The shipping industry and the international community have greatly suffered from tremendous damages inflicted by piracy attacks in that region. A distinctive feature of piracy has been a hijack-for-ransom business model, which depends for its success on a supporting infrastructure on land and which attaches a high economic value to hostages.

The number of piracy attacks in that region continued to rise until 2010, with 111 incidents in 2008 (of a total of 293), 197 (of a total of 410) in 2009, 192 in 2010 (out of 445), which accounted for one-third of piracy attacks worldwide. Unlike in other regions, where piracy attacks tend to occur in coastal waters or nearby trade lanes, Somali pirates have widened their geographical presence and are moving farther away from the coast and territorial waters into the Indian Ocean, the Red Sea, the Gulf of Oman, the Mozambique Channel, the Maldives and Indian territorial waters. Thus the list of countries directly affected by piracy has become extensive, including the Comoros, Djibouti, India, Iran, Kenya, Madagascar, Mozambique, Oman, Qatar, Seychelles, Tanzania, Arab Emirates and Yemen.

The piracy problem in that region has dominated other regions in the scale, scope, severity and damage of the attacks. Several pirate groups have operated in Somali waters, according to a study of the UN and independent sources. Reports suggest that there may be seven to 10 distinct gangs or 'pirate action groups' financed by so-called 'instigators' who organize the funding and delegate operations to group leaders.

Poverty, lack of employment, environmental hardship, pitifully low incomes, reduction of pastoralist and maritime resources due to drought and illegal fishing and a volatile security and political situation are attributed to Somali piracy. In some cases, it is believed that Somali businessmen and international support networks provide pirate groups with financing and supplies in return for shares of ransom payments that are also distributed among pirates themselves.

Somali pirate groups have developed highly sophisticated operational capabilities. The typical Somali pirate team is equipped a variety of small arms, including AK-47 rifles and rocket-propelled grenade (PRC) launchers. Many pirate teams use fishing skiffs powered with large outboard motors to give chase to larger but slower-moving tankers, cargo ships, yachts, cruise ships, barges and tug boats. Local Somali fishermen are often forced to support pirate activities in some cases, while in other cases, coastal Somalis lend their fishing boats, equipment and navigational expertise to teams of would-be pirates from inland communities.

Since 2011, piracy attacks in that region have been dramatically curbed, with only a small number of attacks being reported. For instance, there were no reported attacks in 2015. Various counter-piracy measures implemented by the international community and the shipping industry are credited with the dramatic reduction. Among those, combined naval patrols and escorts and the employment of armed guards onboard ships in the high-risk areas off the Somali coast and the Gulf of Aden are the most salient and successful, deterring piracy attempts and greatly reducing the success rate of piracy attacks as well.

Despite the significant drop in piracy attacks since 2012, piracy is expected to remain a major concern in East Asian waters. This is because Somali pirates may not have totally given up on piracy as a source of revenue – they may be changing their strategy by increasingly targeting ships at anchorage.

Somali Pirates

West Africa

Of particular concern is the recent escalation of piracy attacks in the Gulf of Guinea, which has newly emerged as a hotspot of piracy in West Africa. The littoral states in the Gulf include Benin, Cameroon, Gabon, Ghana, Guinea and Nigeria. Piracy in that region is highly concentrated in Nigeria, which accounted for 92 percent (33) out of 36 incidents in 2017.

Of growing concern is that piracy attacks committed by militant groups, such as *Boko Haram* and *the Movement for the Emancipation of the Niger Delta*, are increasing. The militant groups commit piracy to finance their activities and their *modus operandi* tends to be more violent than any other region. A distinctive feature of piracy attacks in that region is that pirates are increasingly targeting oil production infrastructure and tankers carrying oil, usually in territorial waters. Pirate networks appear to be generally well informed about the operations of the oil industry and to have access to important information, including the names of ships, intended voyage courses, the value of the cargo, whether or not armed guards are aboard, and the extent of the insurance coverage. Given the gravity of the piracy situation, the region was designated by the insurance industry as a 'war risk zone' for shipping, with Benin, Nigeria and Togo waters being identified as 'high risk' areas – that is to say, in the same risk category as Somalia.

Costs of Piracy

The global costs of piracy, including the cost of piracy off eastern Africa, remain uncertain. Studies of global piracy costs tend to primarily focus on calculating first-order costs such as the cost of ransoms, security deterrence equipment and naval forces deployment. The secondary costs of piracy, including the effects on foreign investment in the affected and neighboring regions, or on commodity prices, remain uncovered due to difficulties in estimating the scope of the effects and related costs.

The costs associated with piracy vary with research organizations or institutions, with divergent estimates and conclusions. The RAND Institute and the IMB, for example, have estimated piracy costs to range between $1billion to $16 billion per year.

The One Earth Future (OEF) Foundation, as part of its Oceans Beyond Piracy (OBP) Project, estimates that the total cost of Somali piracy was at $7 billion to $12 billion in 2010, $6.6 billion to $6.9billion in 2011, and $5.7 billion to $6.1 billion in 2012. While over 80 percent of these costs were estimated to be borne by the shipping industry, 20 percent were estimated to be borne by governments. Averaging out all related expenses, the cost per incident was valued at $82.7 million in 2012, a total 189 percent increase from the $28.6 million estimated for 2011. In 2013, the World Bank has estimated the global economic cost of piracy off the coast of Somalia at $18 billion, with a margin of error of roughly $6 billion.

International Counter-Piracy Efforts and Policy Reponses

The Global Level

With growing concern over the piracy problem across the oceans, the international community has struggled to combat piracy, undertaking a wide range of anti-piracy measures and policies. The international efforts to respond to the threat of piracy have taken on a multi-faceted approach. International counter-piracy efforts are driven by the UN and the IMO, in collaboration with principal state stakeholders, including coastal states of regions with high piracy rates, the U.S., and other major trade states.

UN Security Council

The UN Security Council has issued a series of resolutions since 2008 to facilitate an international response to Somali piracy. Among those, Resolution 1816 (June 2008), which was issued first in this regard, authorized relevant states to exercise the right of pursuit into the territorial waters of Somalia for a period of six months. It states that states acting in cooperation with the Somali government are granted to "enter the territorial waters of Somalia for the purpose of repressing acts of piracy and armed robbery at sea" and to "use, within the territorial waters of Somalia, in a manner consistent with action permitted on the high seas with respect to piracy under relevant international law, all means to repress acts of piracy and armed robbery." This measure, by which the period was extended to one year and has been renewed on a yearly basis, has been a principal international cooperative mechanism in fighting pirates.

Resolution 1838 (October 2008) calls on states with military capabilities to "take part actively in the fight against piracy on the high seas off the coast of Somalia, in particular by deploying naval vessels and military aircraft." The UN Security Council has also adopted resolutions to facilitate the prosecution of the Somali pirates. Resolution 1897 (December 2009) encouraged states to conclude special agreements or arrangements that would allow governments to embark law enforcement officials ('shipriders') to facilitate the investigation, and allowed for prosecution of persons detained as a result of anti-piracy operations. Resolution 1918 (April 2010) calls on states to "criminalize piracy under their domestic law and favorably consider the prosecution of suspected, and imprisonment of the convicted, pirates apprehended off Somalia." Resolution 1976 (April 2011) considers the establishment of Somali courts to try suspected pirates both in Somalia and in the region.

CGPCS

Based on UN Security Resolution 1851 (December 2008), which encourages states to establish an international cooperation mechanism to act as a common point of contact on all aspects of combating piracy at sea off Somalia, the Contact Group on Piracy off the Coast of Somalia (CGPCS) was created in 2009. The CGPCS, composed of approximately 60 member governments, 20 international organizations, and shipping associations, has four working groups.

The CGPCS is tasked with: (i) improving operational and informational support to counter-piracy operations; (ii) establishing a counter-piracy coordination mechanism; (iii) strengthening judicial frameworks for arrest, prosecution and detention of pirates; (iv) strengthening commercial shipping self-awareness and other capabilities; (v) pursuing improved diplomatic and public information efforts; and (vi) tracking financial flows related to piracy. The CGPCS has established a trust fund, contributed to by member governments, international organizations, non-governmental organizations and shipping associations to support the activities of states combating piracy off Somalia.

IMO

The International Maritime Organization (IMO) has had a program to combat piracy off Somalia and has successfully engaged on a multilateral basis in other regions to improve anti-piracy cooperation. To assist in the implementation of international instruments to fight piracy, the IMO has promulgated a number of circulars on guidance to ship owners, ship operators and crews on preventing and suppressing piracy, and recommendations to governments for preventing and suppressing piracy. It has adopted the Code of Practice for the Investigation of Crimes of Piracy and Armed Robbery Against Ships. The IMO has also held seminars and regional training programs to assist states in developing the appropriate national framework for combating piracy.

As part of those efforts, an IMO-sponsored international meeting in Djibouti in 2009 adopted a code of conduct concerning the repression of piracy in the western Indian Ocean and the Gulf of Aden. In accordance with the code, three regional facilities were established to support information-sharing: (i) the Maritime Coordination Center in Mombasa, Kenya; (ii) the Sub-Regional Coordination Center in Dar es Salaam, Tanzania; (iii) and a new regional maritime information center in Sana'a, Yemen. The parties also agreed to the establishment of a regional training center in Djibouti. In addition, based on collected data and experience by the military, the IMO has developed detailed guidance and recommendations, commonly known as best management practices for governments and commercial vessels in seeking to prevent, deter and respond to pirate attacks.

The Regional Level

· Southeast Asia

ReCAAP

In order to combat piracy in the Malacca Strait and other Asian waters, the littoral states and other Asian countries formed a multilateral cooperative framework, known as the Regional Cooperation Agreement on Combating Piracy and Armed Robbery against Ships in Asia (ReCAAP). The agreement provides: (i) general obligations of member countries for the prevention and suppression of piracy and armed robbery, and arrest of perpetrators and seizures of pirate ships or aircraft; (ii) rescue of victims of piracy attacks; (iii) establishment of an Information Sharing Center (ISC); (iv) cooperation in the arrest and extradition of pirates; and (v) mutual legal assistance and cooperation in capacity-building.

The ReCAAP, initiated by Japan in 2001, was concluded on 11 November 2004, and came into force on 4 September 2006. As of 2018, the contracting parties include 20 countries, including five extra-regional countries such as Denmark, the Netherlands, Norway, the U.K and the U.S. The ISC, based in Singapore and composed of one representative from each member state, plays a pivotal role in piracy reporting and response coordination among the participating countries.

Operation MALSINDO

The littoral states of the Malacca Strait, including Indonesia, Malaysia and Singapore, have conducted a trilateral patrol, called Operation MALSINDO, a year-round, coordinated naval patrol launched on 20 July 2004. The three littoral states agreed to patrol their respective waters in the 900-km strait with 17 ships and to coordinate their moves through a 24-hour communications link. The arrangement addresses the legal challenge in the narrow strait that the right of hot pursuit is restricted to beyond the territorial sea of the vessel's state or of a third state by allowing warships into one another's waters when pursuing pirates.

Eyes in the Sky

In September 2005, the three littoral states launched coordinated aerial surveillance, named the Eyes in the Sky (EIS) initiative, pursuant to which each country patrols twice per week along the Malacca and Singapore straits and each flight carries a maritime patrol team made up of military personnel from each participating state. To improve the effectiveness of the naval and air patrols, terms of reference and standard operating procedures were agreed on in April 2006, and the combined efforts were renamed the Malacca Straits Patrols (MSP).

The MSP has three elements: (i) the Malacca Straits Surface Patrols (MSSP); (ii) EIS; and (iii) the Intelligence Exchange Group (IEG). The IEG developed the Malacca Straits Patrols Information System (MSP-IS) to improve coordination and situational awareness at sea among the three countries. In September 2008, the MSP was given a boost with the participation of Thailand in both the MSSP and the EIS. Thailand's area of operation is the northern approaches to the Malacca Strait in the Andaman Sea.

· **€ast Africa**

The European Union (EU), the African Union, the League of Arab States and the North Atlantic Treaty Organization (NATO) are actively engaged in combating piracy off the coast of Somalia and the Gulf of Aden. Naval ship patrols are viewed as the most effective deterrent to piracy attacks, as demonstrated in the significant drop in piracy incidents in recent years in this region. Over 40 countries are engaged in counter-piracy operations in East Africa, either in a national capacity or through joint forces. Naval operations to combat piracy in the region include: Operation Ocean Shield by NATO; Operation Atlanta by EU; and Combined Task Force 151 led by the U.S.

Operation Ocean Shield
NATO first deployed a maritime group in 2008 to conduct an anti-piracy operation off the coast of Somalia, with its principal aim the protection of World Food Program (WFP) assistance shipments in the region. In August 2009, NATO replaced the operation with a new anti-piracy mission, called 'Operation

Ocean Shield.' While participating in capacity-building efforts with regional countries, three to five naval ships on a daily basis patrolled the high-risk areas, and these efforts have made a great contribution to suppressing piracy in the region. As piracy attacks off the coast of Somalia greatly diminished, NATO decided to terminate the mandate for Operation Ocean Shield in December 2016.

Operation Atlanta

In December 2008, the EU launched EU NAVFOR 'Operation Atlanta,' its first naval operation under the framework of the European Security and Defense Policy. Operation Atlanta, involving approximately 1,200 personnel, four to six ships and two to three aircraft, has been tasked with providing protection for World Food Programme vessels and merchant vessels in the south of the Red Sea, the Gulf of Aden and the Indian Ocean. For this purpose, it is authorized to employ the necessary measures, including the use of force, to deter, prevent and intervene in order to bring an end to acts of piracy and armed robbery. In May 2012, the aircraft of EU NAVFOR for the first time attacked a land base of pirates in Harardhere, Somalia. In November 2016, the EU extended the mandate for EU NAVFOR to December 2018.

CTF 151

Combined Task Force (CTF) 151 is one of three task forces operated by Combined Maritime Forces (CMF), which is a multi-national naval partnership composed of 31 member states. CMF is commanded by the U.S. Naval Forces Central Command, which covers the Arabian Gulf, the Red Sea, the Gulf of Oman and parts of the Indian Ocean. CTF 151, established in January 2009 and replacing CTF 150, is tasked with counter-piracy missions in these regions under the authority of UN Security Council's resolutions. CTF 151 is a multinational force commanded in rotation by participating countries on an approximately three-to-six-month basis.

The force flow in CTF 151 is constantly changing, as ships and aircraft from a variety of countries assign vessels, aircraft and personnel to the task force. CTF, in conjunction with other counter-piracy operations from NATO and the EU, carries out counter-piracy missions, including patrols and escorts of merchant vessels transiting the Internationally Recommended Corridor in the Gulf of Aden. CTF 151 has played an essential role in combating piracy off Somalia and the Gulf of Aden.

· West Africa

Of various counter-piracy efforts in West Africa, the establishment of a sub-regional Integrated Coast Guard Network (ICGN) has been underway. In the absence of a sub-regional agreement on the right of hot-pursuit across national maritime boundaries, sub-regional countries lack an effective means to pursue and interdict pirates and armed robbers. Against this backdrop, the Maritime Organization for West and Central Africa (MOWCA), with the support of the IMO, developed a Memorandum of Understanding on the Establishment of a Sub-regional ICGN in West and Central Africa, which was adopted in Senegal in July 2008.

The planned ICGN would enable sub-regional countries to collectively respond to unlawful acts at sea, addressing legal challenges in combating pirates. The planned ICGN divides the sub-region into four Coastguard Zones, in which not more than five coastal member states are in a coastguard zone in order to ensure more effective zone coordination. As of 2017, it has been signed by 15 of its 20 coastal member states.

In June 2013, 25 West and Central African countries adopted the Yaounde´ Code of Conduct, developed with technical support from the IMO. The primary objective is to manage and considerably reduce the adverse impacts of piracy, armed robbery against ships and other illicit maritime activities.

The Shipping Industry

The private sector and shipping industry have struggled to cope with the threat of piracy in various ways. With a growing piracy threat off the coast of Somalia, some vessels opted to circumnavigate south of the Cape of Good Hope, rather than risk piracy attacks in the Gulf of Aden while transiting the Suez Canal. Ships are recommended to operate at speeds above 15 knots when transiting high-risk areas. The shipping industry has developed a spate of counter-piracy measures and best practices and employed a variety of security equipment to prevent and abort pirates' attacks.

· Security Equipment

- Radar and GPS: A ship's radar is used to track nearby ships for contact avoidance. Global positioning systems (GPS) allow the shipowner to monitor their ships and to be notified when the ship is in danger.
- Alarms: Sounding the ship's alarms/whistles serves to inform the ship's crew that a piracy attack has commenced and demonstrates to any potential attackers that the ship is aware of the attack and is reacting to it.
- Sonic weapons: A sonic weapon, which blasts earsplitting noise, is used to ward off the attackers. The sonic device was developed by the U.S. Navy in the wake of the terrorist attack on the USS *Cole* in Yemen in 2000 as a way to keep operations of small boats from approaching warships.

- Electric fences: Electric fences are installed onboard ships as an anti-piracy defense mechanism. Attackers are shocked with a non-lethal electric shock of 9,000 volts.
- Razor wires: Known as barbed tapes, razor wires are installed to prevent attackers from boarding a ship by using barbs with piercing effects.
- Water cannons and fire hoses: Water cannons are designed to deliver water in a vertical sweeping arc, thus protecting the greater part of the hull. The water from high-pressure fire hoses is used to repel small boats and boarding pirates. The U.S. Navy has used high-pressure fire hoses to deter unauthorized boarders in port and at sea.
- Citadels: A citadel refers to a room where the crew of the ship can hide in case there is a pirate attack on the ship or when the pirates are aboard the ship. The use of citadels has proven to be a successful mechanism for avoiding capture in several cases. However, there are several aspects that need to be noted about using a citadel as anti-piracy method. The citadel requires having not just food and water supplies but also effective communication channels to be able to communicate with the outside world, along with a proper system of ventilation and a first aid kit. The room can be fitted with CCTV cameras and should have controls for switching off both main and auxiliary engines. The citadel needs to be properly planned and constructed, given that it is a last attempt of crews to escape from the pirates.

· Carriage and use of firearms

In response to the growing violence of pirate attacks, some assert that crews need to be armed for self-protection. However, the shipping community and the international community are opposed to the argument, largely due to a concern that it may lead to an escalation of violence and incur tremendous costs as well.

Recognizing such concerns, the IMO advises that the carriage and use of firearms by crews for protection of personnel or ship is strongly discouraged. It is also concerned that the carriage of arms on board may encourage attackers to carry firearms, thereby escalating an already dangerous situation, and that any firearms on board may themselves become an attractive target for an attacker. Another concern is that the use of firearms requires special training and proficiency, and thus the risk of accidents with the use of firearms by undertrained crews would be great.

In this connection, a worrisome scenario is that if crews equipped with firearms are unable to repel pirate attacks, this may lead to serious casualties in retaliation, such as kidnapping and killing. There is also fear that an exchange of fire between the crews on board a ship carrying chemicals, oil or other flammable substances with pirates who are themselves heavily armed with automatic rifles and rocket propelled grenade (PRC) launchers could inflict disastrous casualties. By all accounts, the carriage and use of firearms by crews as a way of self-protection against piracy attacks is discouraged in the shipping community.

· Privately Contracted Armed Security Personnel

With the increased threat to shipping, ship owners employ privately contracted armed security personnel (PCASP) to protect their vessels, cargo and crews against piracy attacks. The employment of PCASP appears to be quite effective in preventing and suppressing pirate attacks, given that Somali pirates tend to avoid attempts to attack a ship when PCASP is verified on board.

In the absence of applicable international regulations to govern the employment of PCASP on board ships, the positions and policies of states vary significantly. Some coastal states that are highly affected by piracy, including Oman, Djibouti, Durban and Sri Lanka, allow ship owners to employ PCASP on board ships. It is believed that the increased presence of PCASP has contributed to a significant drop in Somali piracy. There are reportedly over 140 companies providing armed protection to vessels, employing a minimum of 2,700 armed guards. The proportion of ships employing PCASP has sharply increased in recent years, rising from 20 percent in 2011 to 50 percent in 2012.

PCASPs on guard

While not endorsing the use of armed guards, the IMO, which recognizes the growing number of private maritime security companies (PMSC) and PCASP, as well as the need for international standards to govern them, has issued a number of recommendations in the form of Maritime Safety Committee (MSC) circulations. In terms of the use of force, the IMO advises that force should be used only after PCASP takes all necessary steps to avoid it. If force is used, it is advised that it should not exceed what is strictly necessary and reasonable under the circumstances. Although the employment of PCASP on board ships serves as an effective counter-piracy measure, it gives rise to legal challenges in practice in terms of accountability and human rights violations. A legal problem may concern who has to be held accountable about possible incidents where PCASP wrongly identifies innocent fishermen as pirates and kills the fishermen. These types of situations may give rise to complicated legal matters of accountability, human right violations, and criminal jurisdiction as well as sovereign rights between flag state and victim state.

Closing Remarks

Contemporary piracy, called the 'scourge of the 21st century,' has had far-reaching and extensively negative effects on the shipping industry and seaborne trade, and furthermore the safety and security of the sea. By virtue of international anti-piracy efforts, overall the incidents of piracy have been in decline since the mid-2010s. Of particular note is that the situations off the coast of Somalia and the Gulf of Aden appear to be under control, as demonstrated by a sharp decline in piracy occurrences in recent years in that region. The reduction is attributable to persistent and concerted counter-piracy efforts at the global, regional and shipping-industry level. However, it is too early to state that the piracy problem in that region is under control, based solely on the figures of recent piracy incidents. Rather, it remains to be seen whether such trends can be sustained or not, given that the underlying causes of piracy in that region, such as the attractive rewards of piracy, a poverty-stricken economy, a chaotic political situation and a lack of counter-piracy capacity from states in the area, have remained unsettled. As such, it is likely that piracy in that region would resurge if stakeholders retreat from the commitment of counter-piracy efforts or allow any chance for pirates to revive their efforts.

Contrary to the significant reduction in piracy attacks at the global level, Southeast Asia and West Africa have undergone an upsurge in recent years. In particular, piracy in Southeast Asia has seen an increase in incidents and a marked rise in the violence and sophistication of pirate activity. The typical Asian piracy, that is, cargo theft while ships are in ports, has tended to shift to hijacking and ransom demands. West Africa, especially in the Gulf of Guinea, has emerged as a piracy-prone region, with growing pirate efforts to hijack oil tankers and seize cargo aboard, or attack oil rigs to steal oil and equipment.

Lastly, some suggestions have been put forward to address the piracy issue. First, the activities of the stakeholders involved in various counter-piracy measures need to be further coordinated and organized in a concerted manner. Piracy is a complicated and multi-faceted problem that involves a wide range of factors. The problem cannot be addressed by only the efforts of governments. As such, governments, the shipping community, and other related civilian sectors need to share burdens in combating piracy together. Second, the international community needs to be more concerned with piracy problems in Southeast Asia and West Africa. At the global level, the UN and international organizations need to be more concerned with and enhance support for regional counter-piracy efforts. Third, the international community needs to formulate regulations to govern the increasing employment of armed security guards aboard ships. Fourth, the establishment of a regional integrated coast guard in South Asia needs to be considered for joint patrols, escorts and law enforcement in high-risk areas of piracy if the regional situation gets worse.

The author

Suk Kyoon Kim studied public affairs at Hanyang University, Seoul, Korea and went on to receive MPAs at Seoul National University and Indiana University and a Ph. D in Public Administration at Hanyang University. His dissertation is about the Asian piracy problem, helping him earn a title of 'Dr. Pirate.' In addition to teaching international maritime law at Inha University, he has been an adjunct professor at the Hanyang University Graduate School of Public Policy. He is serving as professor at Myungji College. He served as a Korean Augmentation to the U.S. Army in Korea, director general of the Security and Safety Bureau, commander, director general of the Planning and Coordination Bureau, deputy commissioner and commissioner general of the Korea Coast Guard. He also has written numerous books and articles on maritime security and law.

The publisher

He who stops getting better stops being good.

This is the motto of novum publishing, and our focus is on finding new manuscripts, publishing them and offering long-term support to the authors.
Our publishing house was founded in 1997, and since then it has become THE expert for new authors and has won numerous awards.

Our editorial team will peruse each manuscript within a few weeks free of charge and without obligation.

You will find more information about
novum publishing and our books on the internet:

www.novumpublishing.com